How to build a LAMP project

Home Automation / Home Security

By

Steve McClure

This book provides instructional information for you:

- To install LAMP (Linux, Apache (Web Server), MySQL and PHP)
- To backup/restore your Linux hard drive
- To automatically execute your application at system startup
- To apply Java Script to your own Web page
- To apply MySQL to your own Web page
- To apply PHP to your own Web page
- To write a complete Home Control / Security application:
    - That communicates over serial ports to external devices
    - That uses the MySQL database
    - That sends email messages with webcam images
    - That speaks alarm and status messages
    - That computes sunrise / sunset times for each day of the year

Oh! And there's one added bonus. With this system you do not require any monthly monitoring fee. Since the Home Control / Security application simply sends you an email when it detects an intruder, you can immediately go home or call a friend or neighbor to check on the house. No need to fork out money each month for some 'service' charge.

They say that knowledge is power. That may be true, but to sit at home using your iPAD or iPHONE (or some other Tablet, or even a web page on one of your computers) and to bring up your Home Control web page and click on a button to turn on a light or to initiate a sequence of events for evening television viewing, well, that is really neat.

And this book presents all this information to you in an easy to read form.

How to build a LAMP project

Home Automation / Home Security

Copyright © 2015 by Steve McClure
All rights reserved.

ISBN-13:	978-1515215943
ISBN-10:	1515215946

Printed in the United States of America

First Edition   July, 2015   Text Version 1-5

Dedication

This book is dedicated to all those who enjoy
building their own computers and
want to control their living environment.

Intended Audience

For the hobbyist who wants to know
how to build a stand-alone computer system
that will provide home automation and security.

Table of Contents

Project Overview

A LAMP project is one that utilizes the features of Linux, Apache (web server), MySQL and PHP, (hence the LAMP acronym).

This project will be implemented using the following tools:

1. PHP Dynamic Web Page Interface Controls
2. MySQL Database
3. Java Script
4. The Apache Web Server
5. The Linux Operating System
6. The C Programming Language

The Home Automation application is interfaced to Infrared Sensors and X10 lamp control devices in order to provide an automated lighting system for the home.

The Home Security feature utilizes the Infrared Sensors to detect movement within the home environment and to warn the user regarding unauthorized access to the property.

It should also be noted that the code examples are in the C programming language. This code could easily be written in C++ but the decision to keep it in C was to allow for understanding by a wider audience.

<u>Note</u>: The code example provided in this book is provided "as is" with no indication as to suitability of purpose.

The Home Control / Security system is best discussed by means of the various web pages that have been developed. Each page presents a picture of your home below which is identified the navigation screen name.

Note: The user may change the provided home image to one of their own.

These screens are as follows:

1. Security
2. Master
3. Lounge
4. Kitchen
5. Family
6. Steve
7. State
8. Events

These screen names are displayed and the user may transition to the relevant screen by simply pressing the relevant button name. The idea was to have these web pages be displayed on an iPAD such that the user could then use the system to control the house lighting and security system.

There is one additional screen (the Systems screen) which we will discuss layer.

The next line on the web page is a text description that informs the user as to the use of the displayed screen. Below that is the user interface. In the case of the Security screen it is a plan layout of the home and location of family members. For other screens it may be a number of push buttons that can either control house lights (or other devices), or can select a specific operating mode (a sequence to switch off various lights for watching television).

The web pages are stored in the Apache HomeControl/php directory.

For example: 192.168.1.176/HomeControl/php/security.php

The Security Web Page

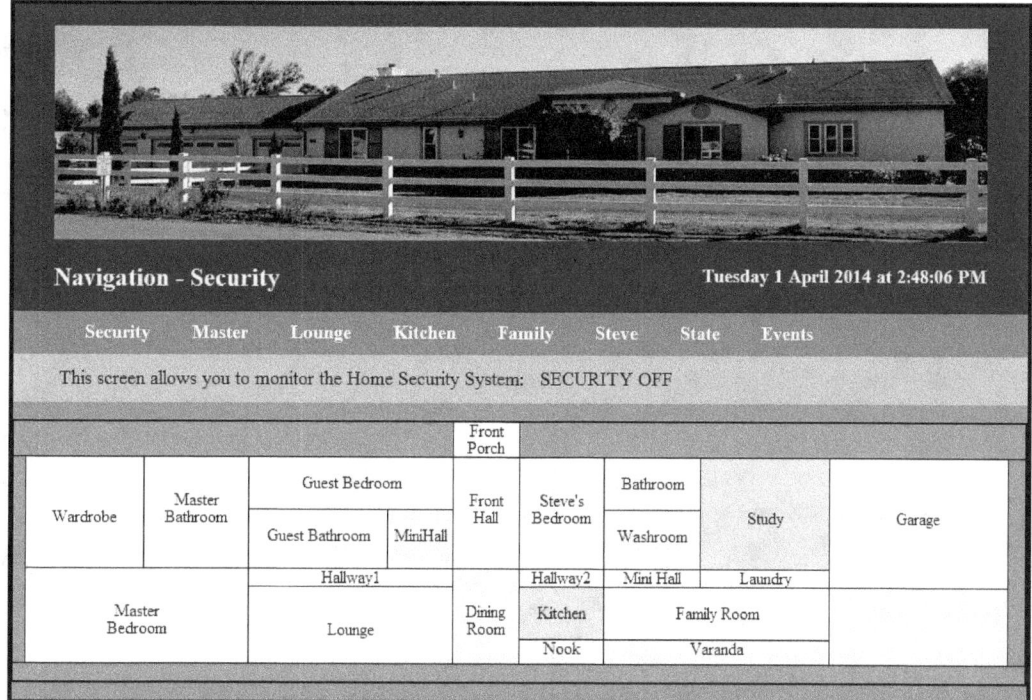

192.168.1.176/HomeControl/php/security.php

This screen permits the operator to navigate their way to the other screens.

The text description identifies the current status of the security system.

The rest of the screen provides a plan layout of the home and provides identification of the various family members (in the above screen there is someone in the kitchen and I am presently in the study). The house perimeter border will be displayed in red if the house security is on otherwise it will be displayed in green. The home sensors are IR (Infra-Red) devices that transmit an RF signal to a base received. This signal identifies a specific code (Home, Unit) and the information is then translated to a colored block on the house plan. During normal operation this information will be used to automatically turn house lights on and off at night, whereas during security mode it will be used to control an alarm.

Note: The user may modify the plan layout to suit their own home.

The Master Bedroom Web Page

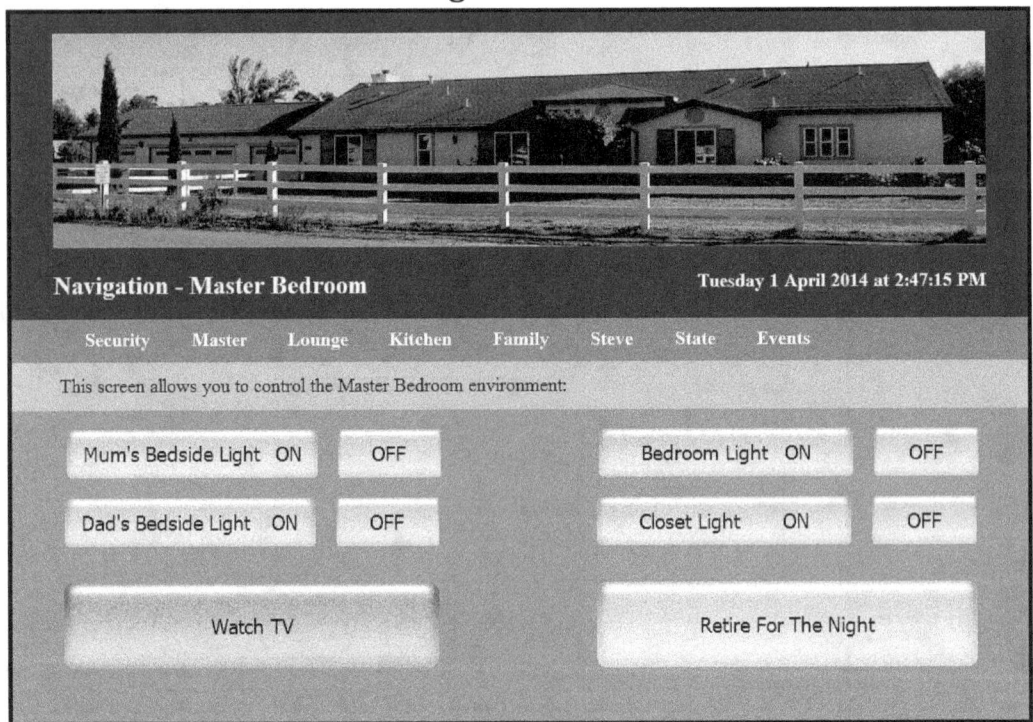

The Master Bedroom screen allows the user to control the lighting environment. Currently four light devices can be switched on or off. These are the two bed side lamps (each can be individually controlled), as can the main bedroom light and the closet light. It should be noted that the X10 controller that is used has the capability of also adjusting the brightness of these lamps. This may be implemented as a future task, however, the current software provides the serial access to the X10 controller. The software 'just' needs to be modified to bring in the light adjustment feature.

The [Watch TV] button, when pressed will switch off the two bedside lamps when it is desired to watch television. The closet light will also be turned off. When watching TV the room lights give the correct viewing ambience so these lamps are turned on. When desiring to turn in for the night, the operator can press the [Retire For The Night] button to switch off the family room, kitchen, lounge and hallway lights.

The Lounge Web Page

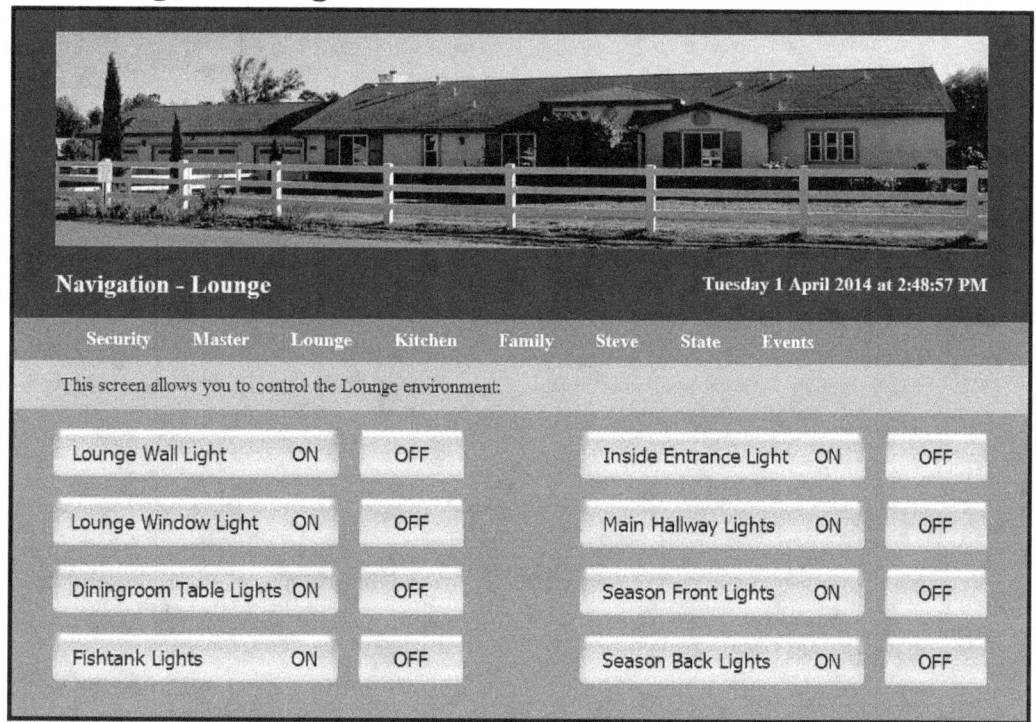

Navigation - Lounge   Tuesday 1 April 2014 at 2:48:57 PM

| Security | Master | Lounge | Kitchen | Family | Steve | State | Events |

This screen allows you to control the Lounge environment:

Lounge Wall Light	ON	OFF		Inside Entrance Light	ON	OFF
Lounge Window Light	ON	OFF		Main Hallway Lights	ON	OFF
Diningroom Table Lights	ON	OFF		Season Front Lights	ON	OFF
Fishtank Lights	ON	OFF		Season Back Lights	ON	OFF

The Lounge screen allows a multitude of different lights to be controlled. The lounge has two lights and each can be individually activated. The dining room table lamps can be turned on or off. The two fish tanks are also in the lounge and the fish tank lights can also be controlled. The front door inside lights and main hallway lights are accessible as are the outside seasonal lights. The power supplied by these controls terminates in switch boxes located under the eaves of the house. In winter the hanging icicle lights are installed and plugged into these receptacles. These controls then allow the front or the back seasonal lights to be activated. It should also be noted that various timed events are automatically installed when the system is powered up and these include the turning on and off of these seasonal lights (only during December and January, of course). The fish tank lights are also under timed control but the user is free to turn the lights on again after they had been previously turned off by the system (like when my father feeds the fish just before going to bed).

The Kitchen Web Page

This screen was the impetus for developing this entire package.

In our home, it is often the case that when someone comes into the family room to sit down and watch TV, it is only then when realization hits them that they have left the kitchen light (and other lights) still on. So with much muttering and complaining they would get up to turn off the lights and then return back to their seat. Now there are other home automation software packages out there (and I have used them) but they tend to provide generalized sequence setups and in particular cases there is nothing quite like creating dedicated software for driving the system in a very specific manner. But there is another underlying reason. It simply borders on the sacrilegious for an embedded software engineer to use a software package designed by some other person for an application that they themselves can (and should) develop on their own. Besides, to such persons as us, there is great enjoyment in watching the result of our handiwork as house lights turn on and off as people move through different parts of the home.

The Family Room Web Page

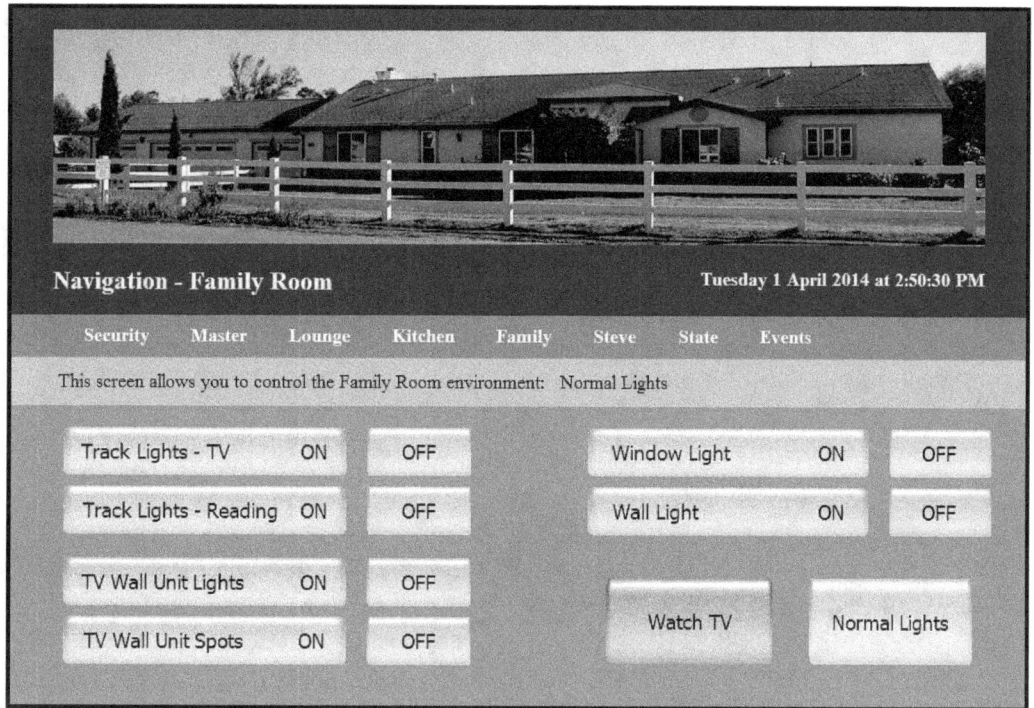

The family room has the television wall unit. In this unit there are some low wattage lights that illuminate various ornaments. These are the general purpose wall unit lights and the wall unit spot lights. There are also ceiling track lights with numerous spots. One set is turned towards the television wall unit whereas another set are turned towards the seats and are used while reading. Both these sets may be individually controlled. Two other lights remain. One is by the window and the other by the wall. The wall light gives some light ambience while viewing the television. The window light, while useful for reading, tends to provide refection off the TV (it doesn't affect my Mum or myself but my Dad gets the full brunt of it). So each evening various lights have to be turned on or off just to setup the lighting conditions (and also turn off the kitchen and hall lights in the process).

Wouldn't it be nice if we had just one button to do this. A button that tuddles (non-tech folk) could use without fear. This is what the [Watch TV] button does; and the [Normal Lights] does the opposite and turns on some lights.

Steve's Bedroom, Bathroom and Study Web Pages

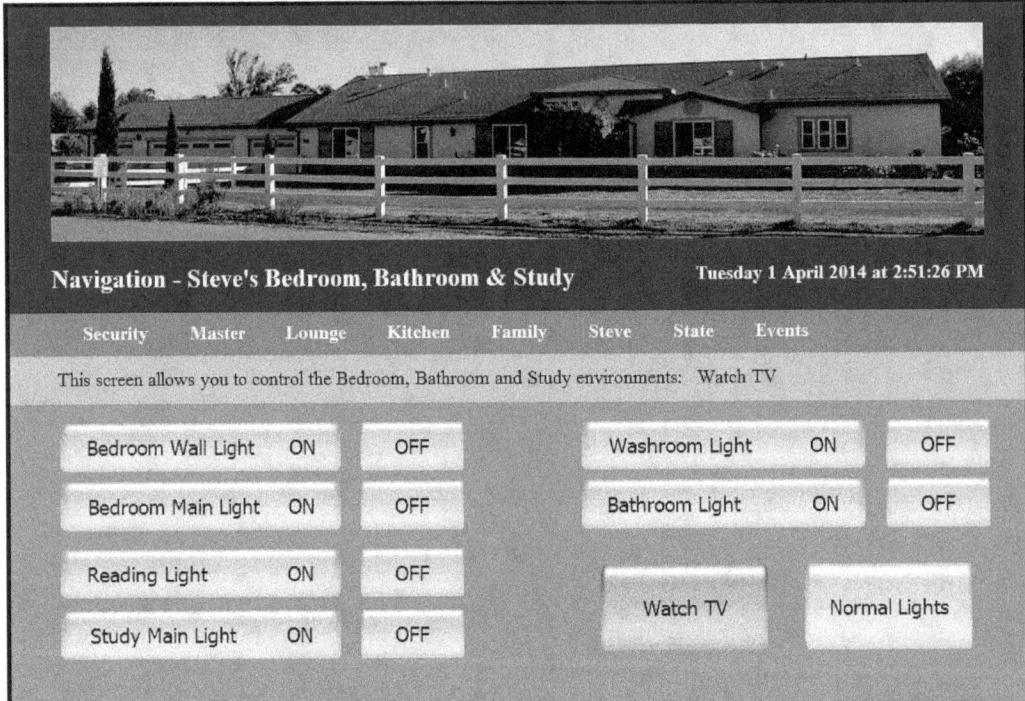

Steve (that's me) has his bedroom, bathroom and study at one end of the house. The bedroom has three main light controls, namely: wall lights, ceiling lights and a reading lamp. These can be individually controlled. The study also has a ceiling light. The washroom has its own light as does the bathroom, hence their own controls.

In the bedroom is a television and there is a need to turn off lights when it is desired to watch. But I may have just come from the study and walked through the washroom and so these lights are on until the predefined times have expired. But I want to turn these lights off right now. So for this we have our own [Watch TV] button. When pressed the study, washroom and bathroom lights are turned off as are the bedroom ceiling lamps, the reading lamp and one of the wall side lamps. The [Normal Lights] button restores the basic bedroom lights to their standard operation. If you have not figured it out yet, embedded software engineers are control-minded individuals.

The Device State Web Pages

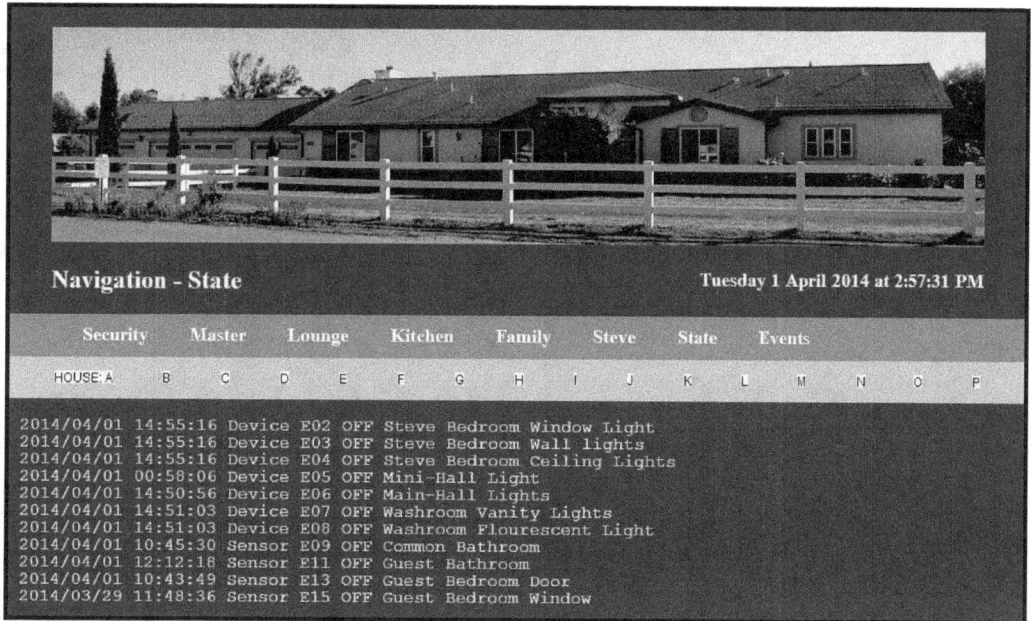

Navigation - State   Tuesday 1 April 2014 at 2:57:31 PM

Security	Master	Lounge	Kitchen	Family	Steve	State	Events

HOUSE: A	B	C	D	E	F	G	H	I	J	K	L	M	N	O	P

```
2014/04/01 14:55:16 Device E02 OFF Steve Bedroom Window Light
2014/04/01 14:55:16 Device E03 OFF Steve Bedroom Wall lights
2014/04/01 14:55:16 Device E04 OFF Steve Bedroom Ceiling Lights
2014/04/01 00:58:06 Device E05 OFF Mini-Hall Light
2014/04/01 14:50:56 Device E06 OFF Main-Hall Lights
2014/04/01 14:51:03 Device E07 OFF Washroom Vanity Lights
2014/04/01 14:51:03 Device E08 OFF Washroom Flourescent Light
2014/04/01 10:45:30 Sensor E09 OFF Common Bathroom
2014/04/01 12:12:18 Sensor E11 OFF Guest Bathroom
2014/04/01 10:43:49 Sensor E13 OFF Guest Bedroom Door
2014/03/29 11:48:36 Sensor E15 OFF Guest Bedroom Window
```

Every IR sensor transmits an RF coded signal when it detects someone (or something) moving in the house. Two minutes (or so) later it transmits another code to say that it has stopped sensing movement. These IR sensors are programmed with various (house, unit) codes in which the house code is usually represented by a letter ('A', 'B', 'C', .. , 'P') and the unit code by a number ('01', '02', '03', .. ,'16'). The code from these sensors is used to indicate if there was movement detected in a specific part of the house. The X10 system also provides devices such as appliance (on/off control) and lamp modules (on/off/brightness control). It would be nice to know when any sensor or device turned on or off. Hence the state screens. These screens, one for each house code ('A' thru 'P'), identify the various sensors and devices and show which ones are in the system along with the last date and time that they turned on or off.

Again, this satisfies the control aspects of our nature.

It is also a very useful screen in determining when to replace sensor batteries (they only last about six months (dependent upon usage).

The Events Log Web Page

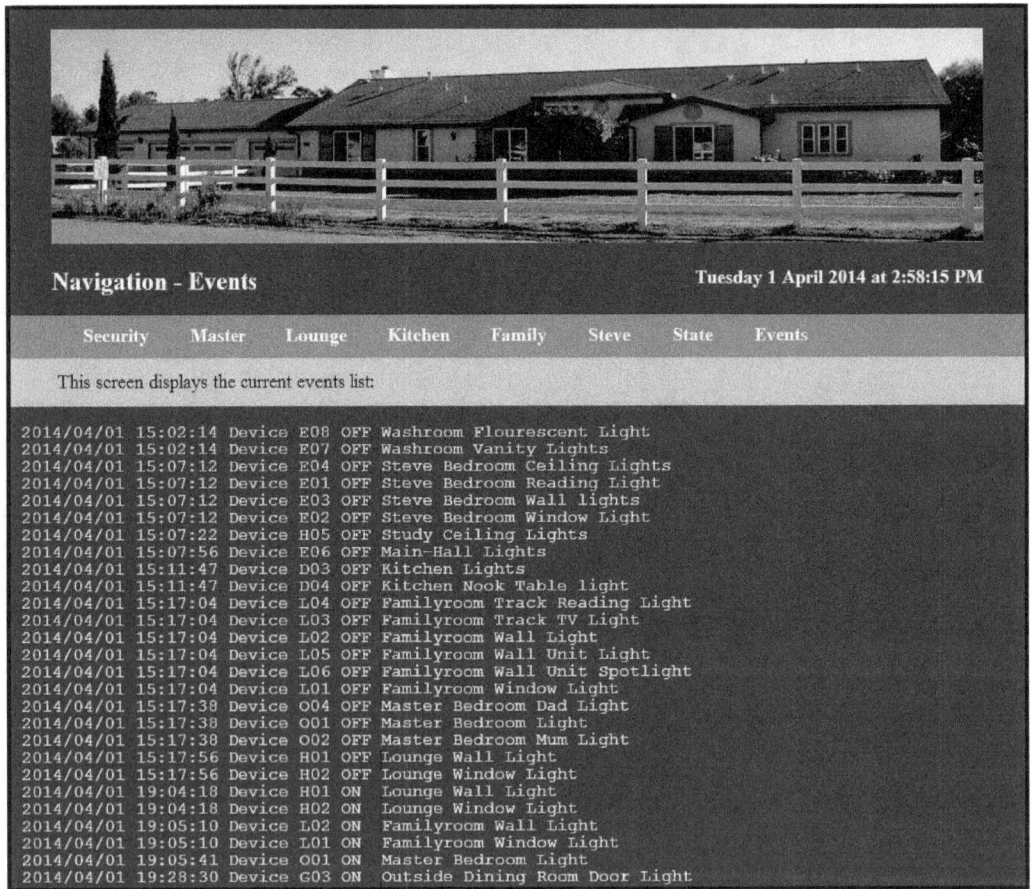

Navigation - Events   Tuesday 1 April 2014 at 2:58:15 PM

| Security | Master | Lounge | Kitchen | Family | Steve | State | Events |

This screen displays the current events list:

```
2014/04/01 15:02:14 Device E08 OFF Washroom Flourescent Light
2014/04/01 15:02:14 Device E07 OFF Washroom Vanity Lights
2014/04/01 15:07:12 Device E04 OFF Steve Bedroom Ceiling Lights
2014/04/01 15:07:12 Device E01 OFF Steve Bedroom Reading Light
2014/04/01 15:07:12 Device E03 OFF Steve Bedroom Wall lights
2014/04/01 15:07:12 Device E02 OFF Steve Bedroom Window Light
2014/04/01 15:07:22 Device H05 OFF Study Ceiling Lights
2014/04/01 15:07:56 Device E06 OFF Main-Hall Lights
2014/04/01 15:11:47 Device D03 OFF Kitchen Lights
2014/04/01 15:11:47 Device D04 OFF Kitchen Nook Table light
2014/04/01 15:17:04 Device L04 OFF Familyroom Track Reading Light
2014/04/01 15:17:04 Device L03 OFF Familyroom Track TV Light
2014/04/01 15:17:04 Device L02 OFF Familyroom Wall Light
2014/04/01 15:17:04 Device L05 OFF Familyroom Wall Unit Light
2014/04/01 15:17:04 Device L06 OFF Familyroom Wall Unit Spotlight
2014/04/01 15:17:04 Device L01 OFF Familyroom Window Light
2014/04/01 15:17:38 Device O04 OFF Master Bedroom Dad Light
2014/04/01 15:17:38 Device O01 OFF Master Bedroom Light
2014/04/01 15:17:38 Device O02 OFF Master Bedroom Mum Light
2014/04/01 15:17:56 Device H01 OFF Lounge Wall Light
2014/04/01 15:17:56 Device H02 OFF Lounge Window Light
2014/04/01 19:04:18 Device H01 ON  Lounge Wall Light
2014/04/01 19:04:18 Device H02 ON  Lounge Window Light
2014/04/01 19:05:10 Device L02 ON  Familyroom Wall Light
2014/04/01 19:05:10 Device L01 ON  Familyroom Window Light
2014/04/01 19:05:41 Device O01 ON  Master Bedroom Light
2014/04/01 19:28:30 Device G03 ON  Outside Dining Room Door Light
```

The Events page is another kind of log in which it provides a look inside the events database. This allows the developer the chance to check when the next timed event is set to occur. When the presence of a person is detected moving in a darkened room, an event entry to turn on a specific light might be generated and placed in this table (actually it is a table within a MySQL database). The time when the light should be turned off will also be determined and placed within this same table. By looking through the table entries we can quickly determine if all is well with the system.

The Systems Web Page

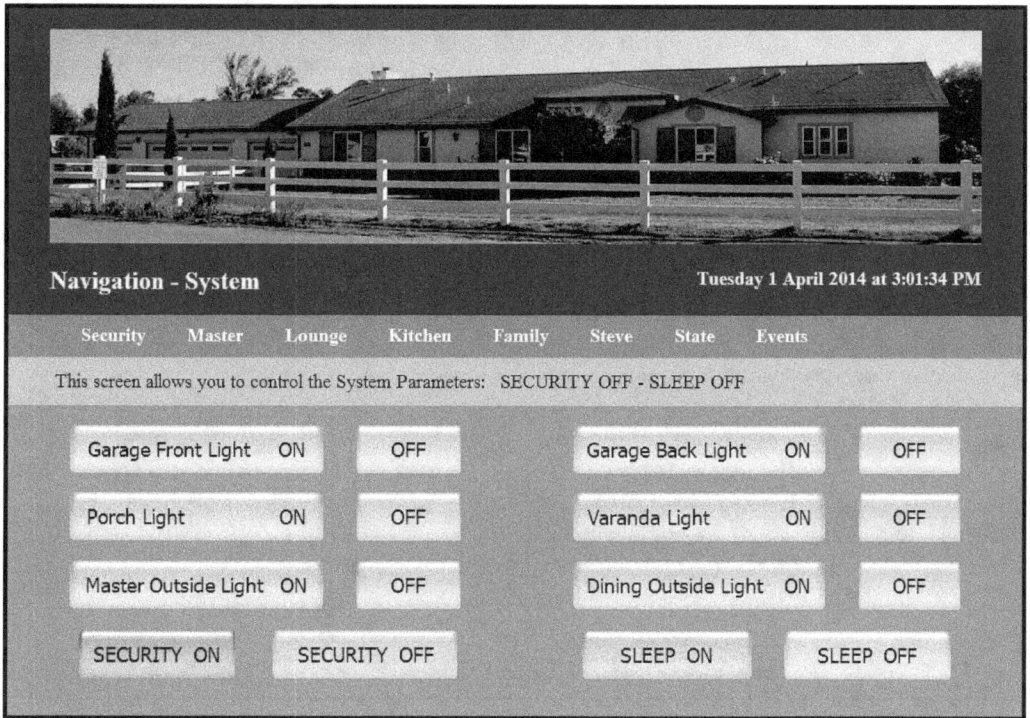

Now this is the screen to which we referred earlier but did not discuss. The reason being is because not all users should have access to this screen. For this is the page that is used to turn the security system on or off. Since there was some screen space I also placed all the outside light controls on this page along with the 'Sleep' control. When the [Sleep On] button is pressed my bedroom goes into sleep mode. The study, washroom, bathroom and my bedroom lights are turned off (after a short delay – long enough for me to hop into bed). The delay ends with the system telling me the time and date using an 'old time' format ('It is quarter past four in the morning on Tuesday the first of April 2014') and then the lights turn off. If I were to get up the lights will remain off (ie. the movement sensor in the room is ignored) until the [Sleep On] button is pressed (or until daybreak is detected).

Pressing the [Security On] button switches the system Security Mode on.

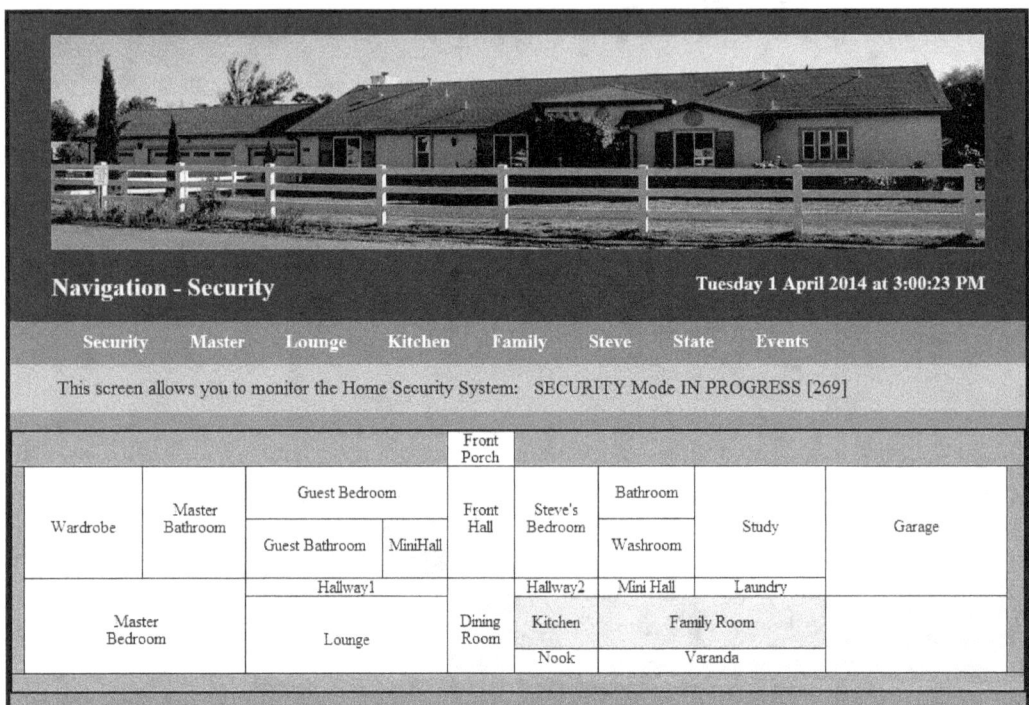

Navigation - Security   Tuesday 1 April 2014 at 3:00:23 PM

| Security | Master | Lounge | Kitchen | Family | Steve | State | Events |

This screen allows you to monitor the Home Security System: SECURITY Mode IN PROGRESS [269]

				Front Porch				
Wardrobe	Master Bathroom	Guest Bedroom		Front Hall	Steve's Bedroom	Bathroom	Study	Garage
		Guest Bathroom	MiniHall			Washroom		
		Hallway1			Hallway2	Mini Hall	Laundry	
Master Bedroom		Lounge		Dining Room	Kitchen	Family Room		
					Nook	Varanda		

Once the [Security On] button has been pressed, the home owner has five minutes to vacate the premises (of course, this time period can easily be changed in software).

As the time is decrementing, the Security screen will present an image showing the border of the house plan flashing two colors (blue and red). Once the security timeout has expired the border color will turn to a steady red (see the next screen shot). This simply indicates that the home is now in Secure mode and any detected movement will turn on the alarm and send an email to the home owner (and whoever else you wish). This information can then be accessed remotely via your phone, tablet, remote computer. If the unauthorized intruder walks into the study then a photograph is taken of them and sent off in an email as an attachment. This operation can easily be extended by having multiple cameras setup in various rooms. The code examples in this book clearly illustrate how this is achieved and provide the programmer with the information they need to easily extend this process as per their own requirements.

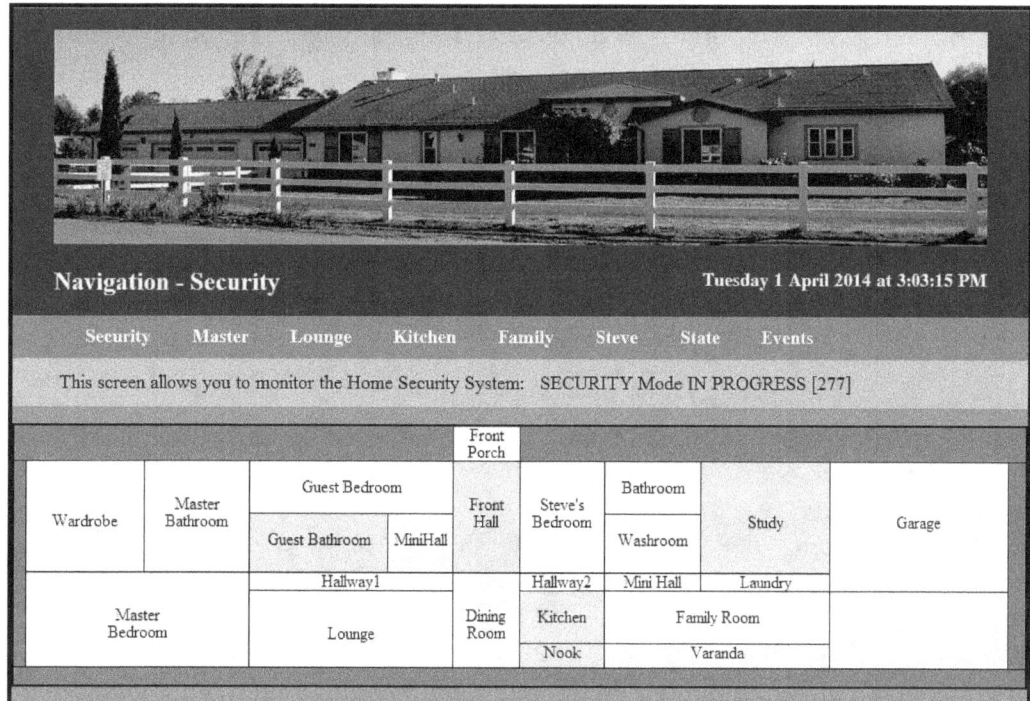

Home Automation / Home Security

So the sensors that were being used to identify presence for turning lights on and off are now serving a dual role in that of monitoring the security of the home.

As an additional feature, an alternative to detecting an intruder after they have entered the dwelling, the system also sets up an elaborate set of random time sequences for turning various lights on and off to simulate the home environment. This would provide the illusion that the home is still occupied and would make any would-be intruder think twice before entering the building.

Project Development System

Any IBM Personal Computer may be used and the Linux installation may be installed as either a single or dual boot system.

ORION-ITX System D2500CC

Since I wanted the end product to be small (and to take minimum power since it was to be powered continuously (ie. 24hrs/7days a week)) I opted for the Orion ITX system.

Such a system provided the following components:

1. Two core Intel Atom CPU D2500 @ 1.86GHz
2. 4GB DDR3 Memory (6.4GB/Sec)
3. 64 bit instruction set
4. 8 USB Ports
5. **2 SATA Ports**

However, any PC computer system with dual serial ports may be used.

IR and X-10 Interfaces

The application software was designed to use the following components:

WF800RF32A RF Receiver (www.wgldesigns.com, www.homeseer.com)
ACT TI103 Interface to transmit X10 signals over household mains wiring
        (Obtainable from www.act-remote.com, www.smarthomeusa.com)
MS13A X10 HawkEye Motion Detector (by X10 Active Home)
MS16A ActiveEye Motion Sensor (Outdoor sensor)
X10 Pro Universal Module (Alarm siren plus relay contacts)
X10 On Guard Barking Dog Alarm (SD20a) www.x10.com
X10 Appliance and X10 Lamp Modules

The application software may be modified to suit any interface of your choice.

Linux Installation (32-bit)

This section describes the Linux installation.

Purpose: To create a Linux Installation.

Program: Linux Mint 13 MATE 32-Bit Version (or later revision)

Obtained: http://linuxmint.com

Access the Download screen
Select Linux Mint 13 MATE 32-bit version (or later revision)
Take note of the MD5 value:
   eg. 43ca0be4501b9d1a46fea25ec2cd556e

Select the 'mirrorcatalogs.com' site and download and save the .iso file.

Once downloaded, verify the MD5 checksum number for accuracy

Equipment: Windows or Linux Computer System
DVD-Writer to create Linux Disk

Procedure: Use DVD Burning utility to burn disk with .iso file.

Insert Linux Disk into computer system for Linux Installation
Power on computer system (Boot from Linux DVD-ROM)
Start the Linux installation (overwrite any existing system)

Select timezone and English language options

Your name: orion
Your computer's name: orion-itx
Pick a user name: orion
Choose a password: rootpass

Select option: log in automatically

How to build a LAMP project

Do not check [ ] Encrypt home folder

Click [Restart Now] to exit and restart the system.
The DVD-ROM is ejected – Remove and store the disk.

Power down the computer system
Power up the computer system

ORION-ITX Linux Mint Components

Installed 32-bit version of Linux Maya

Start the Update Manager (Shield Symbol on bottom line at the right hand side).
1. Enter password
2. Updates are downloaded
3. Select 'Install Updates' (and accept further updates) as many times as are necessary to update the system
4. Replace any configuration files (as required)
5. Restart the system when completed updates (just to be safe)

However, the MySQL interface did not load in the correct 64-bit MySQL.h header files and the MySQL code would not compile (so resorted back to the 32-bit OS).
Image Backup – Completed

LAMP (Linux, Apache2, MySQL, PHP5)

The following Linux components are now manually installed:

Install apache2

Use the Terminal: **sudo apt-get install apache2**

Test installation by accessing the following web page: http://localhost/
(Displays "It Works!" message)

Install PHP

Use the Terminal: sudo apt-get install php5 libapache2-mod-php5
Use the Terminal: sudo /etc/init.d/apache2 restart

Test installation by creating the following 'php' web page...
Use the Terminal: sudo gedit /var/www/testphp.php
Place the following code in this file...
<?php phpinfo(); ?>

Save and close the file...

Test installation by accessing the following web page:

http://localhost/testphp.php
(Displays PHP information screen)

Install MySQL

Use the Terminal: sudo apt-get install mysql-server

Enter your 'root' password: datapass

Now change the bind address.

Use the Terminal:
sudo gedit /etc/mysql/my.cnf

Change the line:
bind-address = 127.0.0.1 to use your ip address (eg. 192.168.1.176)

Install phpMyAdmin

Use the Terminal:
sudo apt-get install libapache2-mod-auth-mysql php5-mysql phpmyadmin

Select webserver to reconfigure automatically: apache2

Configure database for phpmyadmin with dbconfig-common? <Yes>

Password of databases's administrative user: datapass
MySQL application password for phpmyadmin: datapass
Confirm: datapass

Edit php.ini file...
Use the Terminal: **gksudo gedit /etc/php5/apache2/php.ini**

Remove the ';' from the start of line: ' ; extension = mysql.so '

Restart apache2
Use the Terminal: sudo /etc/init.d/apache2 restart

Edit apache2.conf file...
Use the Terminal: sudo gedit /etc/apache2/apache2.conf

Add the following line to the bottom of the file...
Include /etc/phpmyadmin/apache.conf

Restart apache2
Use the Terminal: sudo /etc/init.d/apache2 restart

MySQL Administration

Using a Web Brouser:
Access the PHP MySQL Administration page: http://localhost/phpmyadmin

Sign in as 'root' using password 'rootpass'.

Navigate to Privileges.
Add new user 'steve', password 'william' (grant all privileges on wildcard name).

The following database was only used for test purposes:

Navigate to Database / Create New Database (use 'collation')
Created database: home_control with table 'state' User 'steve', password 'datapass'.
Created database: test with no tables.
Delete this database when finished testing.

Note: The home system database is created using the Linux program: hc_main.c

Keyring
When asked regarding the "Keyring", specify the password: 'keypass'.

Linux Image Backup

Purpose: To create an image of the Linux Hard Drive.

Program: qt4-fsarchiver

Obtained: sourceforge.net

Equipment: qt4-fsarchiver DVD-ROM (Live DVD)
              Linux Computer System
              Removable CD-ROM drive (USB Interface)
              Removable Hard Drive (USB Interface)

Procedure: Attach the removable CD-ROM to the Linux computer system.
              Attach the removable Hard Drive to the Linux computer system.
              Insert the qt4-fsarchiver disk into the CD-ROM drive
              Do not remove the CD-ROM until the backup is completed.

              Power up the Linux Computer System (Boot from the DVD-ROM)
              Ubuntu OS will automatically install.

              Select the qt-fsarchiver icon located at the top left.
                    Enter password: ubuntu

              Using the Ubuntu file manager:
              Create a folder in the removable Hard Drive

Using qt-fsarchiver:
        Enter the backup filename: eg. orion_121201_1950
        Select 'Partition Save'
        Select 'Notes to the backup'
        Select 'Available backup overwrite'

Select the relevant sda (ext4) drive to be backed up
    Store in backup directory 'media \ Vantec1N \ Steve123'
    Select the number of processor cores (orion_itx has 2 cores)
    Select 'gzip standard' compression setting
    Select [Save Partition]
    Enter notes in 'Description of the backup'
    Select [Back partition]

Backup process now starts.

When completed a 'success' dialog box is displayed.
Accept the dialog box and shut down the system.

Linux Image Restore

Purpose: To restore an image to the Linux Hard Drive.

Program: qt4-fsarchiver

Obtained: sourceforge.net

Equipment: qt4-fsarchiver DVD-ROM (Live DVD)
                Linux Computer System
                Removable CD-ROM drive (USB Interface)
                Removable Hard Drive (USB Interface)

Procedure: Attach the removable CD-ROM to the Linux computer system.
                Attach the removable Hard Drive to the Linux computer system.
                Insert the qt4-fsarchiver disk into the CD-ROM drive
                Do not remove the CD-ROM until the restore is completed.

                Power up the Linux Computer System (Boot from the DVD-ROM)
                Ubuntu OS will automatically install.

                Select the qt-fsarchiver icon located at the top left.
                      Enter password: ubuntu

Using qt-fsarchiver:
        Enter the backup filename: eg. orion_121201_1950
        Select 'Restore Partition'
        Select the relevant sda (ext4) partition to be restored
        Select backup file from 'media \ Vantec1N \ Steve123'
        Select the number of processor cores (orion_itx has 2 cores)
        Select [Partition Restore]

Partition restoration process now starts.
When completed a 'success' dialog box is displayed.

Project Implementation

Application Programs

There are two Linux application programs:

1. hc_main
2. hc_ti103

hc_main

This program creates the MySQL **'system_control'** Database (if it is required). The program also creates the following tables (if so required):

house_state [name, value]
house_code_events [house, unit, state, timestamp, description]
house_code_states [house, unit, state, timestamp, description]

If the tables are created, the 'states' table is populated with the currently utilized X-10 sevices (this includes their house and unit codes along with their descriptions).

The program then connects to the 'system_control' database as a user.

The program subsequently opens a serial port (4800,8,N,1) to the W800RF32A (RF X-10 Receiver).

All received X-10 commands are input via comms port '/dev/ttyS0' (Orion-ITX top RS232 Serial Port) as character strings which are then converted into their 'house / unit / state' codes.

The serial port receiver is configured to wait either for 4 characters or until an inter-character timeout of 100ms has expired.

A forever loop is then executed:

a) The serial port receiver waits for either 4 characters or the inter-character timeout to expire.
b) The 4 byte data is then converted into the true house / unit / state values. If this is a true valid code, the code parameters (house, unit and state) are displayed on the console.
c) A timestamp is then computed .
d) The 'house_code_states' table is then updated for the received X-10 house/ unit / state.

This program is built using the command line:

```
gcc hc_main.c -o hc_main `mysql_config --cflags --libs`
```

Sign in as SuperUser and issue the following commands:
```
chmod a+rw /dev/ttyS0
chmod a+rw /dev/ttyS1
```

This program is executed in a terminal window using the command:
./hc_main & (Use '&' if you want the task to execute in the background)

hc_ti103
This program connects to the MySQL 'system_control' database as a user.

The program subsequently opens a serial port (4800,8,N,1) to the TI103 (X-10 Line Interface).
All transmitted/received X-10 commands are via comms port '/dev/ttyS1' (Orion-ITX bottom RS232 Serial Port) as ASCII character strings.

The Web page utilizes PHP to build dynamic web pages. These pages include the ability to let the user press specific buttons to turn X-10 devices on or off. The PHP code executing on the web server detect the button presses and enter the device state changes into the MySQL 'house_code_events' table.

The hc_ti103 code connects to the 'system_control' database and monitors the 'house_code_events' table.

A forever loop is then executed:

a) When a MySQL table entry is detected it then uses the entry's house / unit / state information in order to build a TI103 command string.
b) The string if output over the comm port to the TI103 Line Interface when sends the command over the household wiring to the physical X-10 device.
c) The MySQL entry is then deleted from the 'house_code_events' table.

The transmit process is fully operational.
The receive process has still to be implemented.
This program is built using the command line:

```
gcc hc_ti103.c -o hc_ti103 `mysql_config --cflags --libs`
```

Sign in as SuperUser and issue the following commands:
chmod a+rw /dev/ttyS0
chmod a+rw /dev/ttyS1

This program is executed in a terminal window using the command:
./hc_ti103 &   (Use '&' if you want the task to execute in the background)
                        (Use '>' to re-direct the task output to a separate file for storage)

Miscellaneous

Web Pages
The Web pages utilize the following tools:
   a) JavaScript
   b) PHP
   c) SQL

The following web site provides various examples: http://www.w3schools.com/

How to build a LAMP project

JavaScript

JavaScript is used to provide code that executes on the browser itself (on the PC or iPAD).

This code provides the real-time display of the system calendar/time. The code is started when the page is loaded and is set to repeatedly execute every 500ms.

PHP

PHP (PHP: Hypertext Preprocessor) is a server-side scripting language and supports access to MySQL).

PHP is used to perform the following operations:
   a) Connect to the MySQL Database Environment
   b) Access the 'system_control' database
   c) POST button states to the server to insert entries into the database tables

A 'form' is created in which various 'buttons' are created. This includes the button variable's name and value if it is pressed along with any associated display label. When this button is pressed, the data value associated with the button is 'posted' to the web page (ie. action="web_page_name.php" method="post"). The 'php' file is accessed on the web server and the php code executed.

Each time this php code is executed it accesses the MySQL database and updates the tables accordingly.

SQL

MySQL provides the Database Tables used by the Home Control system.
PHP interfaces via MySQL commands.

Serial Comms Port

The serial communications port is used to transfer data serially as per the RS232 standard.

Source Code

Directory: CSS (Cascading Style Sheets)

File: reset.css

The 'reset.css' file is a cascading style sheet and contains styles to reset the browser to a standard format.

```css
/* http://meyerweb.com/eric/tools/css/reset/
   v2.0 | 20110126
   License: none (public domain)
*/

html, body, div, span, applet, object, iframe,
h1, h2, h3, h4, h5, h6, p, blockquote, pre,
a, abbr, acronym, address, big, cite, code,
del, dfn, em, img, ins, kbd, q, s, samp,
small, strike, strong, sub, sup, tt, var,
b, u, i, center,
dl, dt, dd, ol, ul, li,
fieldset, form, label, legend,
table, caption, tbody, tfoot, thead, tr, th, td,
article, aside, canvas, details, embed,
figure, figcaption, footer, header, hgroup,
menu, nav, output, ruby, section, summary,
time, mark, audio, video {
    margin: 0;
    padding: 0;
    border: 0;
    font-size: 100%;
    font: inherit;
    vertical-align: baseline;
}
/* HTML5 display-role reset for older browsers */
article, aside, details, figcaption, figure,
footer, header, hgroup, menu, nav, section {
    display: block;
}
body {
    line-height: 1;
}
ol, ul {
    list-style: none;
}
blockquote, q {
    quotes: none;
}
blockquote:before, blockquote:after,
```

```css
q:before, q:after {
    content: '';
    content: none;
}
table {
    border-collapse: collapse;
    border-spacing: 0;
}
```

File: styles.css

The 'styles.css' file is an additional cascading style sheet used to reset the browser to a standard format.

```
/*
// File name: styles.css
// Author: Steve McClure
// Book: Designing Embedded Sytems
// Description: This styles file is used by the Home Control /
//    Security application.
*/

/* Full Reset */
* { font-family:Arial, Helvetica, sans-serif;
    font-size:12px;
    color:#000000;
    font-weight:normal;
    font-style:normal;
    margin:0;
    padding:0;
    border:0;
  }

/* Global */

html    {   }

body    { background-color:#eeeeee;          }



h1 {
      font-family:Arial, Helvetica, sans-serif;
      font-size:36px;
      color:#99FF99;
    }

h2 {
      color:yellow;
    }

h3 {
      color:blue;
    }

#top { background-color:#073EF8;
       padding:20px 40px 10px 40px;
}
```

```css
#navigation
{
    color:white;
    background-color:#010EA9;
/*  font-weight:bold; */
}

#navigation_picture
{
    font-size: large;
    color:white;
    background-color:#010EA9;
    padding:20px 40px 0px 40px;
}


#navigation_heading
{
    color:white;
    font-size:x-large;
    background-color:#010EA9;       /* Dark Blue */
    padding:20px 40px 20px 40px;
    float:left;
}

#navigation_time  /* Works */
{
    color:white;
    font-size: large;
    background-color:#010EA9;
    padding:20px 40px 20px 40px;
    float:right;
}


#navigation_links   /* Works */
{
    color:white;
    background-color:#0780F8;  /* Light Blue */
    clear:both;
    font-size:large;
       padding:10px 10px 30px 50px;   /* Border around navigation buttons
*/
}


#mainNav   /* Works */
{
    color:white;
    background-color:#0780F8;
    clear:both;
    padding:10px 10px 30px 50px;   /* Border around navigation buttons */
```

```
}

#dddmainNav ul li a    { display:inline; text-decoration: none;}

#mainNav ul li a    { text-decoration: none; float:left; padding:0px 20px
10px 20px; display:inline; }

#mainNav  a:link     { color:#ffffff;  }
#mainNav  a:visited  { color:#ffffff;  }
#mainNav  a:active   { color:#ffffff;  }
#mainNav  a:hover    { color:#ffffff; background-color:#777777; }
#mainNav  a:focus    { color:#ffffff;  }


#main_stuff
{
    font-size:large;
}

#event_labels
{
    font-size:large;
}


#state_stuff
{
    font-size:x-small;
    font-family:"Courier New", Courier, monospace;
    color:white;
}


#navigation_links ul li a    { text-decoration: none; float:left;
padding:0px 20px 10px 20px; display:inline;}

#navigation_links a:link     { color:#ffffff;  }
#navigation_links a:visited  { color:#ffffff;  }
#navigation_links a:active   { color:#ffffff;  }
#navigation_links a:hover    { color:#ffffff; background-color:#777777; }
#navigation_links a:focus    { color:#ffffff;  }


#banner { background-color:#FFCC99;
        padding:30px 60px 50px 60px;
        border-bottom:2px #000000 solid;
}


subbanner {
    color:blue;
```

```
}

#test1
{
    font-size: large;
    color:maroon;
    background-color:#010EA9;
}

#key_background
{
    background-color:#808080;
}

#sensor_background
{
    background-color:#E7E7E7;              /* Light gray */
/*  background-color:#F7F7F7; */           /* Almost white */
}


#general_text
{
font-family:"Courier New", Courier, monospace;
    font-size:medium;
    color:white;
    background-color:#010EA9;
}


#event_list
{
font-family:"Courier New", Courier, monospace;
    font-size:medium;
    color:white;
    background-color:#010EA9;
}

#state_list
{
font-family:"Courier New", Courier, monospace;
    font-size:medium;
    color:white;
    background-color:#010EA9;
}

#wrapper {    background-color:#AAAAAA;
    width:980px;
    margin:0px auto;}
```

Directory: Images
This directory contains the house picture and the button images.
The user is required to build these images themselves.

Directory: js (Java Script)
The js directory contains the following files:

File: calendar.js
This file is used to provide the calendar data and time that is displayed
continuously of the web page.

```
// File name:
//    calendar.js
// Author:
//    Steve McClure
// Book:
//    Designing Embedded Sytems
// Description:
//    This Java Script file is used by the Home Control / Security
//    application to display the system date and time on the Security
//    web page.  It also changes/flashes the border color of the
//    home layout table.

var home_security_state_js = 0;

function startTime()
{
// Get the current time and date
var today=new Date();

// Create a list of day names
var weekday=new Array(7);
weekday[0]="Sunday";
weekday[1]="Monday";
weekday[2]="Tuesday";
weekday[3]="Wednesday";
weekday[4]="Thursday";
weekday[5]="Friday";
weekday[6]="Saturday";

// Create a list of month names
var month_name=new Array(12);
month_name[0] = "January";
month_name[1] = "February";
month_name[2] = "March";
month_name[3] = "April";
```

```
month_name[4]  = "May";
month_name[5]  = "June";
month_name[6]  = "July";
month_name[7]  = "August";
month_name[8]  = "September";
month_name[9]  = "October";
month_name[10]= "November";
month_name[11]= "December";

// Extract the time and date parameters
var hours   = today.getHours();
var minutes = today.getMinutes();
var seconds = today.getSeconds();

var dd=today.getDate();
var mm=today.getMonth();
var yy=today.getFullYear();

// Determine AM or PM indicator
var tt;
if (hours < 12)
    tt = "AM";
else
{
    tt = "PM";
    if (hours > 12)
        hours -= 12;
}

// Add a zero in front of single digit numbers
minutes = check_time(minutes);
seconds = check_time(seconds);

// Build the calendar date, for example: Thursday 28 March 2013 at 2:58
PM
document.getElementById("navigation_time").innerHTML=weekday[today.getDay
()]+" "+dd+" "+month_name[mm]+" "+yy+" at
"+hours+":"+minutes+":"+seconds+" "+tt;

if (home_security_state_js == 0)
{
    document.getElementById("smc1").style.backgroundColor = "#009933";
//"#00FF00";
    document.getElementById("smc2").style.backgroundColor = "#009933";
//"#00FF00";
    document.getElementById("smc3").style.backgroundColor = "#009933";
//"#00FF00";
    document.getElementById("smc4").style.backgroundColor = "#009933";
//"#00FF00";
    document.getElementById("smc5").style.backgroundColor = "#009933";
//"#00FF00";
}
```

```
else if (home_security_state_js == 1)
{
    document.getElementById("smc1").style.backgroundColor = "#6699FF";
//"#0000FF";
    document.getElementById("smc2").style.backgroundColor = "#6699FF";
//"#0000FF";
    document.getElementById("smc3").style.backgroundColor = "#6699FF";
//"#0000FF";
    document.getElementById("smc4").style.backgroundColor = "#6699FF";
//"#0000FF";
    document.getElementById("smc5").style.backgroundColor = "#6699FF";
//"#0000FF";
}
else if (home_security_state_js == 2)
{
    if ((seconds % 2) == 0)
    {
        document.getElementById("smc1").style.backgroundColor = "#6699FF";
//"#0000FF";
        document.getElementById("smc2").style.backgroundColor = "#6699FF";
//"#0000FF";
        document.getElementById("smc3").style.backgroundColor = "#6699FF";
//"#0000FF";
        document.getElementById("smc4").style.backgroundColor = "#6699FF";
//"#0000FF";
        document.getElementById("smc5").style.backgroundColor = "#6699FF";
//"#0000FF";
    }
    else
    {
        document.getElementById("smc1").style.backgroundColor = "#CC3300";
//"#00FF00";
        document.getElementById("smc2").style.backgroundColor = "#CC3300";
//"#00FF00";
        document.getElementById("smc3").style.backgroundColor = "#CC3300";
//"#00FF00";
        document.getElementById("smc4").style.backgroundColor = "#CC3300";
//"#00FF00";
        document.getElementById("smc5").style.backgroundColor = "#CC3300";
//"#00FF00";
    }
}
else if (home_security_state_js == 3)
{
    document.getElementById("smc1").style.backgroundColor = "#FF0000";
    document.getElementById("smc2").style.backgroundColor = "#FF0000";
    document.getElementById("smc3").style.backgroundColor = "#FF0000";
    document.getElementById("smc4").style.backgroundColor = "#FF0000";
    document.getElementById("smc5").style.backgroundColor = "#FF0000";
}

//  Execute the function in another 500ms
```

```
var t=setTimeout(function(){startTime()},500);
}
//============================================================
// check_time
//
// This function prefixes a '0' before single digit numbers
//============================================================
function check_time(i)
{
if (i < 10)
    {
        i="0" + i;
    }
return i;
}
```

File: calendar2.js

This file is used to provide the calendar data and time that is displayed continuously on the web page.

```
// File name:
//    calendar2.js
// Author:
//    Steve McClure
// Book:
//    Designing Embedded Sytems
// Description:
//    This Java Script file is used by the Home
//    Control / Security application to display the
//    system date and time on the System, State and
//    Event web pages.

var home_security_state_js = 0;

function startTime()
{
// Get the current time and date
var today=new Date();

// Create a list of day names
var weekday=new Array(7);
weekday[0]="Sunday";
weekday[1]="Monday";
weekday[2]="Tuesday";
weekday[3]="Wednesday";
weekday[4]="Thursday";
weekday[5]="Friday";
weekday[6]="Saturday";

// Create a list of month names
var month_name=new Array(12);
month_name[0]  = "January";
month_name[1]  = "February";
month_name[2]  = "March";
month_name[3]  = "April";
month_name[4]  = "May";
month_name[5]  = "June";
month_name[6]  = "July";
month_name[7]  = "August";
month_name[8]  = "September";
month_name[9]  = "October";
month_name[10]= "November";
month_name[11]= "December";
// Extract the time and date parameters
var hour    = today.getHours();
var hours   = today.getHours();
```

```
var minutes = today.getMinutes();
var seconds = today.getSeconds();

var dd=today.getDate();
var mm=today.getMonth();
var yy=today.getFullYear();

// Determine AM or PM indicator
var tt;
if (hours < 12)
    tt = "AM";
else
    {
        tt = "PM";
        if (hours > 12)
            hours -= 12;
    }

// Add a zero in front of single digit numbers
minutes = check_time(minutes);
seconds = check_time(seconds);

// Build the calendar date, for example: Thursday 28 March 2013 at 2:58
PM
document.getElementById("navigation_time").innerHTML=weekday[today.getDay
()]+" "+dd+" "+month_name[mm]+" "+yy+" at
"+hours+":"+minutes+":"+seconds+" "+tt;

var hour  = check_time(hour);
var day   = check_time(dd);
var month = check_time(mm + 1);

// Build the calendar time that will timestamp each entry recorded in the
state able
var calendar_date = yy +"/" + month + "/" + day;
var calendar_time = hour + ":" + minutes + ":" + seconds;
var calendar_full = yy +"/" + month + "/" + day + "%20" + hour + ":" +
minutes + ":" + seconds;

//  Execute the function in another 500ms
var t=setTimeout(function(){startTime()},500);
}
```

```
//=========================================================
// check_time
//
// This function prefixes a '0' before single digit numbers
//=========================================================
function check_time(i)
{
if (i < 10)
   {
     i="0" + i;
   }
return i;
}




//=========================================================
// get_datetime
//
// This function gets the calendar date time and inserts it
// into the html page request.
//=========================================================
function get_datetime()
{
document.getElementById("navigation_time").innerHTML= calendar_time;
}
```

File: master_calendar.js

This file is used to provide the calendar data and time that is displayed continuously on the Master web page.

```javascript
// File name:
//    master_calendar.js
// Author:
//    Steve McClure
// Book:
//    Designing Embedded Sytems
// Description:
//    This Java Script file is used by the Home
//    Control / Security application Master web page.

var home_security_state_js = 0;

function startTime()
{
// Get the current time and date
var today=new Date();

// Create a list of day names
var weekday=new Array(7);
weekday[0]="Sunday";
weekday[1]="Monday";
weekday[2]="Tuesday";
weekday[3]="Wednesday";
weekday[4]="Thursday";
weekday[5]="Friday";
weekday[6]="Saturday";

// Create a list of month names
var month_name=new Array(12);
month_name[0]  = "January";
month_name[1]  = "February";
month_name[2]  = "March";
month_name[3]  = "April";
month_name[4]  = "May";
month_name[5]  = "June";
month_name[6]  = "July";
month_name[7]  = "August";
month_name[8]  = "September";
month_name[9]  = "October";
month_name[10]= "November";
month_name[11]= "December";

// Extract the time and date parameters
var hour    = today.getHours();
var hours   = today.getHours();
var minutes = today.getMinutes();
```

```
var seconds = today.getSeconds();

var dd=today.getDate();
var mm=today.getMonth();
var yy=today.getFullYear();

// Determine AM or PM indicator
var tt;
if (hours < 12)
  tt = "AM";
else
{
  tt = "PM";
  if (hours > 12)
    hours -= 12;
}

// Add a zero in front of single digit numbers
minutes = check_time(minutes);
seconds = check_time(seconds);

// Build the calendar date, for example: Thursday 28 March 2013 at 2:58
PM
document.getElementById("navigation_time").innerHTML=weekday[today.getDay
()]+" "+dd+" "+month_name[mm]+" "+yy+" at
"+hours+":"+minutes+":"+seconds+" "+tt;


// Build the calendar time that will timestamp each entry recorded in the
state able
var hour  = check_time(hour);
var day   = check_time(dd);
var month = check_time(mm + 1);

var calendar_date = yy +"/" + month + "/" + day;
var calendar_time = hour + ":" + minutes + ":" + seconds;

var calendar_full = yy +"/" + month + "/" + day + "%20" + hour + ":" +
minutes + ":" + seconds;
```

```
// Reconfigure the buttons to include the full calendar
document.getElementById("smc1a").href =
"master.php?mums_bedside_light_on=1&calendar="  + calendar_full;
document.getElementById("smc1b").href =
"master.php?mums_bedside_light_off=1&calendar=" + calendar_full;
document.getElementById("smc2a").href =
"master.php?dads_bedside_light_on=1&calendar="  + calendar_full;
document.getElementById("smc2b").href =
"master.php?dads_bedside_light_off=1&calendar=" + calendar_full;

document.getElementById("smc3").href  = "master.php?watch_tv=1&calendar="
+ calendar_full;

document.getElementById("smc4a").href =
"master.php?bedroom_light_on=1&calendar="  + calendar_full;
document.getElementById("smc4b").href =
"master.php?bedroom_light_off=1&calendar=" + calendar_full;
document.getElementById("smc5a").href =
"master.php?closet_light_on=1&calendar="   + calendar_full;
document.getElementById("smc5b").href =
"master.php?closet_light_off=1&calendar="  + calendar_full;

document.getElementById("smc6").href  =
"master.php?retire_for_the_night=1&calendar=" + calendar_full;

//  Execute the function in another 500ms
var t=setTimeout(function(){startTime()},500);
}




//============================================================
// check_time
//
// This function prefixes a '0' before single digit numbers
//============================================================
function check_time(i)
{
if (i < 10)
   {
     i="0" + i;
   }
return i;
}
```

File: lounge_calendar.js
This file is used to provide the calendar data and time that is displayed continuously on the Lounge web page.

```
// File name:
//    lounge_calendar.js
// Author:
//    Steve McClure
// Book:
//    Designing Embedded Sytems
// Description:
//    This Java Script file is used by the Home
//    Control / Security application Lounge web page.

var home_security_state_js = 0;

function startTime()
{
// Get the current time and date
var today=new Date();

// Create a list of day names
var weekday=new Array(7);
weekday[0]="Sunday";
weekday[1]="Monday";
weekday[2]="Tuesday";
weekday[3]="Wednesday";
weekday[4]="Thursday";
weekday[5]="Friday";
weekday[6]="Saturday";

// Create a list of month names
var month_name=new Array(12);
month_name[0]  = "January";
month_name[1]  = "February";
month_name[2]  = "March";
month_name[3]  = "April";
month_name[4]  = "May";
month_name[5]  = "June";
month_name[6]  = "July";
month_name[7]  = "August";
month_name[8]  = "September";
month_name[9]  = "October";
month_name[10] = "November";
month_name[11] = "December";

// Extract the time and date parameters
var hour    = today.getHours();
var hours   = today.getHours();
var minutes = today.getMinutes();
```

```
var seconds = today.getSeconds();

var dd=today.getDate();
var mm=today.getMonth();
var yy=today.getFullYear();

// Determine AM or PM indicator
var tt;
if (hours < 12)
  tt = "AM";
else
{
  tt = "PM";
  if (hours > 12)
    hours -= 12;
}


// Add a zero in front of single digit numbers
minutes = check_time(minutes);
seconds = check_time(seconds);


// Build the calendar date, for example: Thursday 28 March 2013 at 2:58
PM
document.getElementById("navigation_time").innerHTML=weekday[today.getDay
()]+" "+dd+" "+month_name[mm]+" "+yy+" at
"+hours+":"+minutes+":"+seconds+" "+tt;


// Build the calendar time that will timestamp each entry recorded in the
state able
var hour  = check_time(hour);
var day   = check_time(dd);
var month = check_time(mm + 1);

var calendar_date = yy +"/" + month + "/" + day;
var calendar_time = hour + ":" + minutes + ":" + seconds;

var calendar_full = yy +"/" + month + "/" + day + "%20" + hour + ":" +
minutes + ":" + seconds;

// Reconfigure the buttons to include the full calendar
document.getElementById("smc1a").href =
"lounge.php?lounge_wall_light_on=1&calendar="    + calendar_full;
document.getElementById("smc1b").href =
"lounge.php?lounge_wall_light_off=1&calendar="    + calendar_full;
document.getElementById("smc2a").href =
"lounge.php?lounge_window_light_on=1&calendar="   + calendar_full;
document.getElementById("smc2b").href =
"lounge.php?lounge_window_light_off=1&calendar=" + calendar_full;
```

```
document.getElementById("smc3a").href =
"lounge.php?diningroom_table_lights_on=1&calendar="  + calendar_full;
document.getElementById("smc3b").href =
"lounge.php?diningroom_table_lights_off=1&calendar=" + calendar_full;
document.getElementById("smc4a").href =
"lounge.php?fishtank_lights_on=1&calendar="          + calendar_full;
document.getElementById("smc4b").href =
"lounge.php?fishtank_lights_off=1&calendar="         + calendar_full;

document.getElementById("smc5a").href =
"lounge.php?inside_entrance_light_on=1&calendar="  + calendar_full;
document.getElementById("smc5b").href =
"lounge.php?inside_entrance_light_off=1&calendar=" + calendar_full;
document.getElementById("smc6a").href =
"lounge.php?main_hallway_lights_on=1&calendar="      + calendar_full;
document.getElementById("smc6b").href =
"lounge.php?main_hallway_lights_off=1&calendar="     + calendar_full;

document.getElementById("smc7a").href =
"lounge.php?season_front_lights_on=1&calendar="  + calendar_full;
document.getElementById("smc7b").href =
"lounge.php?season_front_lights_off=1&calendar=" + calendar_full;
document.getElementById("smc8a").href =
"lounge.php?season_back_lights_on=1&calendar="   + calendar_full;
document.getElementById("smc8b").href =
"lounge.php?season_back_lights_off=1&calendar="  + calendar_full;


//  Execute the function in another 500ms
var t=setTimeout(function(){startTime()},500);
}



//=============================================================
// check_time
//
// This function prefixes a '0' before single digit numbers
//=============================================================
function check_time(i)
{
if (i < 10)
  {
    i="0" + i;
  }
return i;
}
```

File: kitchen_calendar.js

This file is used to provide the calendar data and time that is displayed continuously on the Kitchen web page.

```javascript
// File name:
//    kitchen_calendar.js
// Author:
//    Steve McClure
// Book:
//    Designing Embedded Sytems
// Description:
//    This Java Script file is used by the Home
//    Control / Security application Kitchen web page.

var home_security_state_js = 0;

function startTime()
{
// Get the current time and date
var today=new Date();

// Create a list of day names
var weekday=new Array(7);
weekday[0]="Sunday";
weekday[1]="Monday";
weekday[2]="Tuesday";
weekday[3]="Wednesday";
weekday[4]="Thursday";
weekday[5]="Friday";
weekday[6]="Saturday";

// Create a list of month names
var month_name=new Array(12);
month_name[0]  = "January";
month_name[1]  = "February";
month_name[2]  = "March";
month_name[3]  = "April";
month_name[4]  = "May";
month_name[5]  = "June";
month_name[6]  = "July";
month_name[7]  = "August";
month_name[8]  = "September";
month_name[9]  = "October";
month_name[10]= "November";
month_name[11]= "December";
// Extract the time and date parameters
var hour    = today.getHours();
var hours   = today.getHours();
var minutes = today.getMinutes();
var seconds = today.getSeconds();
```

```
var dd=today.getDate();
var mm=today.getMonth();
var yy=today.getFullYear();

// Determine AM or PM indicator
var tt;
if (hours < 12)
  tt = "AM";
else
{
  tt = "PM";
  if (hours > 12)
    hours -= 12;
}


// Add a zero in front of single digit numbers
minutes = check_time(minutes);
seconds = check_time(seconds);

// Build the calendar date, for example: Thursday 28 March 2013 at 2:58
PM
document.getElementById("navigation_time").innerHTML=weekday[today.getDay
()]+" "+dd+" "+month_name[mm]+" "+yy+" at
"+hours+":"+minutes+":"+seconds+" "+tt;


// Build the calendar time that will timestamp each entry recorded in the
state able
var hour  = check_time(hour);
var day   = check_time(dd);
var month = check_time(mm + 1);

var calendar_date = yy +"/" + month + "/" + day;
var calendar_time = hour + ":" + minutes + ":" + seconds;

var calendar_full = yy +"/" + month + "/" + day + "%20" + hour + ":" +
minutes + ":" + seconds;


// Reconfigure the buttons to include the full calendar
document.getElementById("smc1a").href="kitchen.php?kitchen_main_lights_on
=1&calendar="    + calendar_full;
document.getElementById("smc1b").href="kitchen.php?kitchen_main_lights_of
f=1&calendar="    + calendar_full;
document.getElementById("smc2a").href="kitchen.php?kitchen_counter_lights
_on=1&calendar="  + calendar_full;
document.getElementById("smc2b").href="kitchen.php?kitchen_counter_lights
_off=1&calendar=" + calendar_full;
```

```
document.getElementById("smc3a").href="kitchen.php?kitchen_sink_light_on=
1&calendar="  + calendar_full;
document.getElementById("smc3b").href="kitchen.php?kitchen_sink_light_off
=1&calendar=" + calendar_full;
document.getElementById("smc4a").href="kitchen.php?kitchen_nook_light_on=
1&calendar="  + calendar_full;
document.getElementById("smc4b").href="kitchen.php?kitchen_nook_light_off
=1&calendar=" + calendar_full;

document.getElementById("smc5a").href="kitchen.php?diningroom_table_light
s_on=1&calendar="  + calendar_full;
document.getElementById("smc5b").href="kitchen.php?diningroom_table_light
s_off=1&calendar=" + calendar_full;
document.getElementById("smc6a").href="kitchen.php?main_hallway_lights_on
=1&calendar="       + calendar_full;
document.getElementById("smc6b").href="kitchen.php?main_hallway_lights_of
f=1&calendar="       + calendar_full;

document.getElementById("smc7a").href="kitchen.php?pantry_light_on=1&cale
ndar="   + calendar_full;
document.getElementById("smc7b").href="kitchen.php?pantry_light_off=1&cal
endar="   + calendar_full;
document.getElementById("smc8a").href="kitchen.php?laundry_light_on=1&cal
endar="   + calendar_full;
document.getElementById("smc8b").href="kitchen.php?laundry_light_off=1&ca
lendar=" + calendar_full;

//  Execute the function in another 500ms
var t=setTimeout(function(){startTime()},500);
}




//============================================================
// check_time
//
// This function prefixes a '0' before single digit numbers
//============================================================
function check_time(i)
{
if (i < 10)
  {
    i="0" + i;
  }
return i;
}
```

File: family_calendar.js

This file is used to provide the calendar data and time that is displayed continuously on the Family web page.

```
// File name:
//    family_calendar.js
// Author:
//    Steve McClure
// Book:
//    Designing Embedded Sytems
// Description:
//    This Java Script file is used by the Home
//    Control / Security application Family web page.

var home_security_state_js = 0;

function startTime()
{
// Get the current time and date
var today=new Date();

// Create a list of day names
var weekday=new Array(7);
weekday[0]="Sunday";
weekday[1]="Monday";
weekday[2]="Tuesday";
weekday[3]="Wednesday";
weekday[4]="Thursday";
weekday[5]="Friday";
weekday[6]="Saturday";

// Create a list of month names
var month_name=new Array(12);
month_name[0]  = "January";
month_name[1]  = "February";
month_name[2]  = "March";
month_name[3]  = "April";
month_name[4]  = "May";
month_name[5]  = "June";
month_name[6]  = "July";
month_name[7]  = "August";
month_name[8]  = "September";
month_name[9]  = "October";
month_name[10]= "November";
month_name[11]= "December";
// Extract the time and date parameters
var hour    = today.getHours();
var hours   = today.getHours();
var minutes = today.getMinutes();
var seconds = today.getSeconds();
```

```
var dd=today.getDate();
var mm=today.getMonth();
var yy=today.getFullYear();

// Determine AM or PM indicator
var tt;
if (hours < 12)
  tt = "AM";
else
{
  tt = "PM";
  if (hours > 12)
    hours -= 12;
}


// Add a zero in front of single digit numbers
minutes = check_time(minutes);
seconds = check_time(seconds);

// Build the calendar date, for example: Thursday 28 March 2013 at 2:58
PM
document.getElementById("navigation_time").innerHTML=weekday[today.getDay
()]+" "+dd+" "+month_name[mm]+" "+yy+" at
"+hours+":"+minutes+":"+seconds+" "+tt;


// Build the calendar time that will timestamp each entry recorded in the
state able
var hour  = check_time(hour);
var day   = check_time(dd);
var month = check_time(mm + 1);

var calendar_date = yy +"/" + month + "/" + day;
var calendar_time = hour + ":" + minutes + ":" + seconds;

var calendar_full = yy +"/" + month + "/" + day + "%20" + hour + ":" +
minutes + ":" + seconds;


// Reconfigure the buttons to include the full calendar
document.getElementById("smc1a").href="family.php?track_lights_tv_on=1&ca
lendar="       + calendar_full;
document.getElementById("smc1b").href="family.php?track_lights_tv_off=1&c
alendar="       + calendar_full;
document.getElementById("smc2a").href="family.php?track_lights_reading_on
=1&calendar="  + calendar_full;
document.getElementById("smc2b").href="family.php?track_lights_reading_of
f=1&calendar=" + calendar_full;
```

```
document.getElementById("smc3a").href="family.php?tv_wall_unit_lights_on=
1&calendar="  + calendar_full;
document.getElementById("smc3b").href="family.php?tv_wall_unit_lights_off
=1&calendar=" + calendar_full;
document.getElementById("smc4a").href="family.php?tv_wall_unit_spots_on=1
&calendar="   + calendar_full;
document.getElementById("smc4b").href="family.php?tv_wall_unit_spots_off=
1&calendar="  + calendar_full;

document.getElementById("smc5a").href="family.php?window_light_on=1&calen
dar="  + calendar_full;
document.getElementById("smc5b").href="family.php?window_light_off=1&cale
ndar=" + calendar_full;
document.getElementById("smc6a").href="family.php?wall_light_on=1&calenda
r="    + calendar_full;
document.getElementById("smc6b").href="family.php?wall_light_off=1&calend
ar="    + calendar_full;

document.getElementById("smc7").href="family.php?watch_tv=1&calendar="
+ calendar_full;
document.getElementById("smc8").href="family.php?normal_lights=1&calendar
=" + calendar_full;

//  Execute the function in another 500ms
var t=setTimeout(function(){startTime()},500);
}




//============================================================
// check_time
//
// This function prefixes a '0' before single digit numbers
//============================================================
function check_time(i)
{
if (i < 10)
  {
    i="0" + i;
  }
return i;
}
```

File: steve_calendar.js

This file is used to provide the calendar data and time that is displayed continuously on the Steve web page.

```javascript
// File name:
//     steve_calendar.js
// Author:
//     Steve McClure
// Book:
//     Designing Embedded Sytems
// Description:
//     This Java Script file is used by the Home
//     Control / Security application Steve web page.

var home_security_state_js = 0;

function startTime()
{
// Get the current time and date
var today=new Date();

// Create a list of day names
var weekday=new Array(7);
weekday[0]="Sunday";
weekday[1]="Monday";
weekday[2]="Tuesday";
weekday[3]="Wednesday";
weekday[4]="Thursday";
weekday[5]="Friday";
weekday[6]="Saturday";

// Create a list of month names
var month_name=new Array(12);
month_name[0]  = "January";
month_name[1]  = "February";
month_name[2]  = "March";
month_name[3]  = "April";
month_name[4]  = "May";
month_name[5]  = "June";
month_name[6]  = "July";
month_name[7]  = "August";
month_name[8]  = "September";
month_name[9]  = "October";
month_name[10]= "November";
month_name[11]= "December";

// Extract the time and date parameters
var hour     = today.getHours();
var hours    = today.getHours();
var minutes = today.getMinutes();
```

```
var seconds = today.getSeconds();

var dd=today.getDate();
var mm=today.getMonth();
var yy=today.getFullYear();

// Determine AM or PM indicator
var tt;
if (hours < 12)
  tt = "AM";
else
{
  tt = "PM";
  if (hours > 12)
    hours -= 12;
}


// Add a zero in front of single digit numbers
minutes = check_time(minutes);
seconds = check_time(seconds);

// Build the calendar date, for example: Thursday 28 March 2013 at 2:58
PM
document.getElementById("navigation_time").innerHTML=weekday[today.getDay
()]+" "+dd+" "+month_name[mm]+" "+yy+" at
"+hours+":"+minutes+":"+seconds+" "+tt;


// Build the calendar time that will timestamp each entry recorded in the
state able
var hour  = check_time(hour);
var day   = check_time(dd);
var month = check_time(mm + 1);

var calendar_date = yy +"/" + month + "/" + day;
var calendar_time = hour + ":" + minutes + ":" + seconds;

var calendar_full = yy +"/" + month + "/" + day + "%20" + hour + ":" +
minutes + ":" + seconds;


// Reconfigure the buttons to include the full calendar
document.getElementById("smc1a").href="steve.php?bedroom_wall_light_on=1&
calendar="  + calendar_full;
document.getElementById("smc1b").href="steve.php?bedroom_wall_light_off=1
&calendar=" + calendar_full;
document.getElementById("smc2a").href="steve.php?bedroom_main_light_on=1&
calendar="  + calendar_full;
document.getElementById("smc2b").href="steve.php?bedroom_main_light_off=1
&calendar=" + calendar_full;
```

```
document.getElementById("smc3a").href="steve.php?reading_light_on=1&calen
dar="    + calendar_full;
document.getElementById("smc3b").href="steve.php?reading_light_off=1&cale
ndar="    + calendar_full;
document.getElementById("smc4a").href="steve.php?study_main_light_on=1&ca
lendar="   + calendar_full;
document.getElementById("smc4b").href="steve.php?study_main_light_off=1&c
alendar=" + calendar_full;

document.getElementById("smc5a").href="steve.php?washroom_light_on=1&cale
ndar="   + calendar_full;
document.getElementById("smc5b").href="steve.php?washroom_light_off=1&cal
endar=" + calendar_full;
document.getElementById("smc6a").href="steve.php?bathroom_light_on=1&cale
ndar="   + calendar_full;
document.getElementById("smc6b").href="steve.php?bathroom_light_off=1&cal
endar=" + calendar_full;

document.getElementById("smc7").href="steve.php?watch_tv=1&calendar="
+ calendar_full;
document.getElementById("smc8").href="steve.php?normal_lights=1&calendar=
" + calendar_full;

//  Execute the function in another 500ms
var t=setTimeout(function(){startTime()},500);
}




//============================================================
// check_time
//
// This function prefixes a '0' before single digit numbers
//============================================================
function check_time(i)
{
if (i < 10)
  {
    i="0" + i;
  }
return i;
}
```

Directory: php

This directory contains a number of html web pages that each contain php constructs. PHP (Hypertext Preprocessor) instructions are a server-side scripting language that permits the web server to dynamically build/process the web page.

The php directory contains the following PHP files:

1. security.php
2. master.php
3. lounge.php
4. kitchen.php
5. family.php
6. steve.php
7. state.php
8. events.php
9. system.php

Please Note: For obvious reasons the button image '.gif' files and the house .jpg file has not been provided in this book (would you really want to type in all the data bytes pertaining to an image file?). Please use Microsoft Expression 4 (or some other web building package) in order to build your web application buttons.

To display the Security web page the tablet device would be set to access the Internet address: 192.168.1.176/HomeControl/php/security.php

To display the Master web page the tablet device would be set to access the Internet address: 192.168.1.176/HomeControl/php/master.php

File: security.php

```
<!DOCTYPE HTML>
<html>
<head>
<meta http-equiv="refresh" content="4">
<title>HC-Security</title>

<!--
File name:
    security.php
Author:
    Steve McClure
Book:
    Designing Embedded Sytems
Description:
    This file is used by the Home Control / Security
    application to build the Security Web page.
-->


<link href="../css/reset.css" rel="stylesheet" type="text/css"
media="screen">
<link href="../css/styles.css" rel="stylesheet" type="text/css"
media="screen">

<script type="text/javascript" src="../js/calendar.js"> </script>

<style type="text/css">
.auto-style1 {
    color: #FFFFFF;
}
</style>


<style>
table,th,td
{
border:1px solid black
}
</style>

<style>
table,th,td
{
padding:500
}
.auto-style2 {
    border-style: solid;
    border-width: 2px;
}
```

```
.auto-style3 {
   text-align: center;
}
.auto-style4 {
   font-size: small;
}
.auto-style5 {
   font-size: large;
}

</style>



</head>

<body onload=" startTime()">
<div style="width:980px; margin: 0 auto; overflow: hidden;">
<div id="wrapper">
  <div id="navigation">
    <div id="navigation_picture">
      <img src="../images/HouseFront1.jpg" height="200" width="900" />
    </div>

    <div id="navigation_heading">
      <p><span class="auto-style1">Navigation</span> <span class="auto-
style1">- Security</span></p>
    </div>

    <div id="navigation_time">
      <p>Date and Time</p>
    </div>

    <div id="navigation_links">
      <ul>
         <li><a href="security.php">Security</a></li>
         <li><a href="master.php">Master</a></li>
         <li><a href="lounge.php">Lounge</a></li>
         <li><a href="kitchen">Kitchen</a></li>

         <li><a href="family.php">Family</a></li>
         <li><a href="steve.php">Steve</a></li>
         <li><a href="state.php">State</a></li>
         <li><a href="events.php">Events</a></li>
      </ul>
    </div>
  </div>


    <?php

    // Connect to the MySQL Database Environment
```

```
//==========================================
    $con = mysql_connect("192.168.1.176","steve","william");    // This
works on Archimedes
    if (!$con)
    {
      die('Could not connect as: ' . mysql_error());
      echo "<br />";
    }



    // Access the 'system_control' database
    //===================================
      mysql_select_db("system_control", $con);


    // Insert data into the 'house_state' table
    //===================================

    if ($_POST["home_button"] == 1)
    {
        mysql_query ("UPDATE house_state SET security = 0, security_delay
= 0");         // Zero or NULL is 'Home' Mode
    }


    if ($_POST["security_button"] == 1)
    {
        $result = mysql_query("SELECT * FROM house_state");

        $row = mysql_fetch_array($result);

        // Enter SECURITY mode ONLY if we are currently in HOME mode
        if ($row['security'] == 0)
        {
          mysql_query ("UPDATE house_state SET security = 1,
security_delay = 0");  // Zero or NULL is 'Home' Mode
        }
    }



    $presence_detected = 1;
    $no_one_detected   = 0;

    $steve_bedroom_sensor_house_code    = 1;
    $steve_bedroom_sensor_unit_code     = 2;
    $mini_hallway_sensor_house_code     = 1;
    $mini_hallway_sensor_unit_code      = 5;
    $study_sensor_house_code            = 1;
    $study_sensor_unit_code             = 7;
```

```
$master_bedroom_sensor_house_code     = 1;
$master_bedroom_sensor_unit_code      = 9;
$family_room_sensor_house_code        = 1;
$family_room_sensor_unit_code         = 11;
$inside_front_door_sensor_house_code  = 1;
$inside_front_door_sensor_unit_code   = 13;

$main_hallway_sensor_house_code       = 2;
$main_hallway_sensor_unit_code        = 5;
$lounge_hallway_sensor_house_code     = 2;
$lounge_hallway_sensor_unit_code      = 7;
$master_hallway_sensor_house_code     = 2;
$master_hallway_sensor_unit_code      = 9;

$pantry_sensor_house_code             = 3;
$pantry_sensor_unit_code              = 1;
$kitchen_sensor_house_code            = 3;
$kitchen_sensor_unit_code             = 3;
$kitchen_nook_sensor_house_code       = 3;
$kitchen_nook_sensor_unit_code        = 11;
$master_closet_sensor_house_code      = 3;
$master_closet_sensor_unit_code       = 13;
$garage_fridge_sensor_house_code      = 3;
$garage_fridge_sensor_unit_code       = 15;

$laundry_sensor_house_code            = 4;
$laundry_sensor_unit_code             = 11;
$common_washroom_sensor_house_code    = 4;
$common_washroom_sensor_unit_code     = 13;
$front_porch_sensor_house_code        = 4;
$front_porch_sensor_unit_code         = 15;

$common_bathroom_sensor_house_code    = 5;
$common_bathroom_sensor_unit_code     = 9;
$guest_bathroom_sensor_house_code     = 5;
$guest_bathroom_sensor_unit_code      = 11;
$guest_bedroom_sensor_house_code      = 5;
$guest_bedroom_sensor_unit_code       = 13;

$master_bathroom_sensor_house_code    = 8;
$master_bathroom_sensor_unit_code     = 9;


$result = mysql_query("SELECT * FROM house_code_states");

while($row = mysql_fetch_array($result))
   {

       if ($row['description'] == "No Description")
         continue;

       // A1 - Steve's Room
```

```
if (($row['house'] == $steve_bedroom_sensor_house_code) &&
    ($row['unit']  == $steve_bedroom_sensor_unit_code))
{
    if ($row['state'] == $no_one_detected)
        $steve_color = "#FFFFFF";  // Off
    elseif ($row['state'] == $presence_detected)
        $steve_color = "#FFCC66";  // On
    else
        $steve_color = "#FFFFFF";  // ---
}

// A5 - Mini Hall
if (($row['house'] == $mini_hallway_sensor_house_code) &&
    ($row['unit']  == $mini_hallway_sensor_unit_code))
{
    if ($row['state'] == $no_one_detected)
        $mini_hall_color = "#FFFFFF";  // Off
    elseif ($row['state'] == $presence_detected)
        $mini_hall_color = "#FFCC66";  // On
    else
        $mini_hall_color = "#FFFFFF";  // ---
}

// A7 - Lab
if (($row['house'] == $study_sensor_house_code) &&
    ($row['unit']  == $study_sensor_unit_code))
{
    if ($row['state'] == $no_one_detected)
        $lab_color = "#FFFFFF";  // Off
    elseif ($row['state'] == $presence_detected)
        $lab_color = "#FFCC66";  // On
    else
        $lab_color = "#FFFFFF";  // ---
}

// A9 - Master Bedroom
if (($row['house'] == $master_bedroom_sensor_house_code) &&
    ($row['unit']  == $master_bedroom_sensor_unit_code))
{
    if ($row['state'] == $no_one_detected)
        $master_bedroom_color = "#FFFFFF";  // Off
    elseif ($row['state'] == $presence_detected)
        $master_bedroom_color = "#FFCC66";  // On
    else
        $master_bedroom_color = "#FFFFFF";  // ---
}

// A11 - Family Room
if (($row['house'] == $family_room_sensor_house_code) &&
    ($row['unit']  == $family_room_sensor_unit_code))
{
    if ($row['state'] == $no_one_detected)
```

```
        $family_color = "#FFFFFF";  // Off
    elseif ($row['state'] == $presence_detected)
        $family_color = "#FFCC66";  // On
    else
        $family_color = "#FFFFFF";  // ---
}


// A13 - Front Hall
if (($row['house'] == $inside_front_door_sensor_house_code) &&
    ($row['unit']  == $inside_front_door_sensor_unit_code))
{
    if ($row['state'] == $no_one_detected)
        $front_hall_color = "#FFFFFF";  // Off
    elseif ($row['state'] == $presence_detected)
        $front_hall_color = "#FFCC66";  // On
    else
        $front_hall_color = "#FFFFFF";  // ---
}


// B5 - Main Hallway 'Hallway2'
if (($row['house'] == $main_hallway_sensor_house_code) &&
    ($row['unit']  == $main_hallway_sensor_unit_code))
{
    if ($row['state'] == $no_one_detected)
        $hallway2_color = "#FFFFFF";  // Off
    elseif ($row['state'] == $presence_detected)
        $hallway2_color = "#FFCC66";  // On
    else
        $hallway2_color = "#FFFFFF";  // ---
}

// B7 - Lounge Hallway 'Lounge'
if (($row['house'] == $lounge_hallway_sensor_house_code) &&
    ($row['unit']  == $lounge_hallway_sensor_unit_code))
{
    if ($row['state'] == $no_one_detected)
        $lounge_color = "#FFFFFF";  // Off
    elseif ($row['state'] == $presence_detected)
        $lounge_color = "#FFCC66";  // On
    else
        $lounge_color = "#FFFFFF";  // ---
}

// B9 - Master Hallway 'Hallway1'
if (($row['house'] == $master_hallway_sensor_house_code) &&
    ($row['unit']  == $master_hallway_sensor_unit_code))
{
    if ($row['state'] == $no_one_detected)
        $hallway1_color = "#FFFFFF";  // Off
    elseif ($row['state'] == $presence_detected)
```

```
            $hallway1_color = "#FFCC66";   // On
        else
            $hallway1_color = "#FFFFFF";   // ---
}


// C3 - Kitchen
if (($row['house'] == $kitchen_sensor_house_code) &&
    ($row['unit']  == $kitchen_sensor_unit_code))
{

    if ($row['state'] == $no_one_detected)
        $kitchen_color = "#FFFFFF";   // Off
    elseif ($row['state'] == $presence_detected)
        $kitchen_color = "#FFCC66";   // On
    else
        $kitchen_color = "#FFFFFF";   // ---
}


// C11 - Nook
if (($row['house'] == $kitchen_nook_sensor_house_code) &&
    ($row['unit']  == $kitchen_nook_sensor_unit_code))
{

    if ($row['state'] == $no_one_detected)
        $nook_color = "#FFFFFF";   // Off
    elseif ($row['state'] == $presence_detected)
        $nook_color = "#FFCC66";   // On
    else
        $nook_color = "#FFFFFF";   // ---
}


// C13 - Master Closet
if (($row['house'] == $master_closet_sensor_house_code) &&
    ($row['unit']  == $master_closet_sensor_unit_code))
{

    if ($row['state'] == $no_one_detected)
        $master_closet_color = "#FFFFFF";   // Off
    elseif ($row['state'] == $presence_detected)
        $master_closet_color = "#FFCC66";   // On
    else
        $master_closet_color = "#FFFFFF";   // ---
}


// C15 - Garage Fridge
if (($row['house'] == $garage_fridge_sensor_house_code) &&
    ($row['unit']  == $garage_fridge_sensor_unit_code))
{

    if ($row['state'] == $no_one_detected)
        $garage_fridge_color = "#FFFFFF";   // Off
    elseif ($row['state'] == $presence_detected)
        $garage_fridge_color = "#FFCC66";   // On
    else
        $garage_fridge_color = "#FFFFFF";   // ---
}
```

```
// D11 - Laundry
if (($row['house'] == $laundry_sensor_house_code) &&
    ($row['unit']  == $laundry_sensor_unit_code))
{
    if ($row['state'] == $no_one_detected)
        $laundry_color = "#FFFFFF";  // Off
    elseif ($row['state'] == $presence_detected)
        $laundry_color = "#FFCC66";  // On
    else
        $laundry_color = "#FFFFFF";  // ---
}


// D13 - Common Washroom
if (($row['house'] == $common_washroom_sensor_house_code) &&
    ($row['unit']  == $common_washroom_sensor_unit_code))
{
    if ($row['state'] == $no_one_detected)
        $common_washroom_color = "#FFFFFF";  // Off
    elseif ($row['state'] == $presence_detected)
        $common_washroom_color = "#FFCC66";  // On
    else
        $common_washroom_color = "#FFFFFF";  // ---
}


// D15 - Outside Front Porch
if (($row['house'] == $front_porch_sensor_house_code) &&
    ($row['unit']  == $front_porch_sensor_unit_code))
{
    if ($row['state'] == $no_one_detected)
        $front_porch_color = "#FFFFFF";  // Off
    elseif ($row['state'] == $presence_detected)
        $front_porch_color = "#FFCC66";  // On
    else
        $front_porch_color = "#FFFFFF";  // ---
}


// E9 - Common Bathroom
if (($row['house'] == $common_bathroom_sensor_house_code) &&
    ($row['unit']  == $common_bathroom_sensor_unit_code))
{
    if ($row['state'] == $no_one_detected)
        $common_bathroom_color = "#FFFFFF";  // Off
    elseif ($row['state'] == $presence_detected)
        $common_bathroom_color = "#FFCC66";  // On
    else
        $common_bathroom_color = "#FFFFFF";  // ---
}


// E11 - Guest Bathroom
if (($row['house'] == $guest_bathroom_sensor_house_code) &&
    ($row['unit']  == $guest_bathroom_sensor_unit_code))
```

```php
    {
        if ($row['state'] == $no_one_detected)
            $guest_bathroom_color = "#FFFFFF";  // Off
        elseif ($row['state'] == $presence_detected)
            $guest_bathroom_color = "#FFCC66";  // On
        else
            $guest_bathroom_color = "#FFFFFF";  // ---
    }

    // E13 - Guest Bedroom Door
    if (($row['house'] == $guest_bedroom_sensor_house_code) &&
        ($row['unit']  == $guest_bedroom_sensor_unit_code))
    {
        if ($row['state'] == $no_one_detected)
            $guest_bedroom_color = "#FFFFFF";  // Off
        elseif ($row['state'] == $presence_detected)
            $guest_bedroom_color = "#FFCC66";  // On
        else
            $guest_bedroom_color = "#FFFFFF";  // ---
    }

    // H9 - Master Bathroom
    if (($row['house'] == $master_bathroom_sensor_house_code) &&
        ($row['unit']  == $master_bathroom_sensor_unit_code))
    {
        if ($row['state'] == $no_one_detected)
            $master_bathroom_color = "#FFFFFF";  // Off
        elseif ($row['state'] == $presence_detected)
            $master_bathroom_color = "#FFCC66";  // On
        else
            $master_bathroom_color = "#FFFFFF";  // ---
    }

    }

    ?>

<div id="main_stuff">
  <?php
$result = mysql_query("SELECT * FROM house_state");

$row = mysql_fetch_array($result);

if ($row['security'] == 0)
{
  ?><p class="auto-style4"> </p><?php
  ?><p class="auto-
style5">         This screen
allows you to monitor the Home Security System:   SECURITY
OFF</p><?php
  ?><p class="auto-style4"> </p><?php
  $home_security_state = 0;
```

64

```php
      $home_security_color = "#009933";    // "#00FF00";
   }

   elseif ($row['security'] == 1)
   {
      ?><p class="auto-style4"> </p><?php
      ?><p class="auto-
style5">         This screen
allows you to monitor the Home Security System:   SECURITY
Mode INITIATED...</p><?php
      ?><p class="auto-style4"> </p><?php
      $home_security_state = 1;
      $home_security_color = "#6699FF";
   }

   elseif ($row['security'] == 2)
   {
      ?><p class="auto-style4"> </p><?php
      echo "         This
screen allows you to monitor the Home Security
System:   ";
      if ($row['security_delay'] > 0)
      {
         echo "SECURITY Mode IN PROGRESS [";
         echo ($row['security_delay']);
          echo "]";
      }
      else
      {
         echo "SECURITY Mode IN PROGRESS...";
      }
      ?><p class="auto-style4"> </p><?php
      $home_security_state = 2;
      $home_security_color = "#CC3300";
   }


   elseif ($row['security'] == 3)
   {
      ?><p class="auto-style4"> </p><?php
      echo "         This
screen allows you to monitor the Home Security
System:   SECURITY ACTIVE";
      ?><p class="auto-style4"> </p><?php
      $home_security_state = 3;
      $home_security_color = "#CC3300";
   }

// Close the 'home_control' database
//=================================
mysql_close($con);
```

```
      ?>
    </div>

    <script>
    home_security_state_js = <?php echo $home_security_state ?>;
    </script>


<div id="key_background">
<p> </p>
</div>
<div id="sensor_background">

<table align="center" cellpadding="10" cellspacing="5" class="auto-
style2" style="width: 100%">
    <tr>
<!--        <td id="smc1" colspan="5" style="background-color: <?php echo
$home_security_color; ?>">   </td>
-->
        <td id="smc1" colspan="5" style="background-color: <?php echo
$home_security_color; ?>">   </td>

<!--        <td id="smc1" colspan="5" style="background-color: <?php echo
$home_security_color; ?>">   </td>
-->
        <td class="auto-style3" style="width: 71px; background-color:
<?php echo $front_porch_color; ?>">Front Porch</td>
        <td id="smc2" colspan="5" style="background-color: <?php echo
$home_security_color; ?>">   </td>
    </tr>
    <tr>
        <td id="smc3" rowspan="5" style="width: 14px; background-color:
<?php echo $home_security_color; ?>">
         </td>
        <td class="auto-style3" rowspan="2" style="width: 131px;
background-color: <?php echo $master_closet_color; ?>"><br><br>
        <br>Wardrobe</td>
        <td class="auto-style3" rowspan="2" style="width: 114px;
background-color: <?php echo $master_bathroom_color;
?>"><br><br>Master<br>
        Bathroom</td>
        <td class="auto-style3" colspan="2" style="background-color: <?php
echo $guest_bedroom_color; ?>"><br>Guest Bedroom<br><br></td>
        <td class="auto-style3" rowspan="2" style="width: 71px;
background-color: <?php echo $front_hall_color; ?>"><br><br>Front<br>
        Hall<br></td>
        <td class="auto-style3" rowspan="2" style="width: 89px;
background-color: <?php echo $steve_color; ?>"><br><br>Steve's<br>
        Bedroom</td>
        <td class="auto-style3" style="width: 100px; background-color:
<?php echo $common_bathroom_color; ?>"><br>Bathroom</td>
```

```
        <td class="auto-style3" rowspan="2" style="width: 151px;
background-color: <?php echo $lab_color; ?>">
        <br><br><br>Study</td>
        <td class="auto-style3" rowspan="3" style="width: 220px;
background-color: <?php echo $garage_fridge_color;
?>"><br><br><br>Garage</td>
        <td id="smc4" rowspan="5" style="width: 20px; background-color:
<?php echo $home_security_color; ?>">
         </td>
    </tr>
    <tr>
        <td class="auto-style3" style="width: 158px; height: 54px;
background-color: <?php echo $guest_bathroom_color; ?>"><br>Guest
Bathroom<br><br>
        </td>
        <td class="auto-style3" style="width: 66px; height:
54px;"><br>MiniHall</td>
        <td class="auto-style3" style="width: 100px; height: 54px;
background-color: <?php echo $common_washroom_color;
?>"><br>Washroom</td>
    </tr>
    <tr>
        <td colspan="2" rowspan="3" class="auto-style3" style="background-
color: <?php echo $master_bedroom_color;
?>"><br><br>Master<br>Bedroom</td>
        <td class="auto-style3" colspan="2" style="background-color: <?php
echo $hallway1_color; ?>">Hallway1</td>
        <td class="auto-style3" rowspan="3" style="width:
71px"><br><br>Dining<br>Room</td>
        <td class="auto-style3" style="width: 89px;  background-color:
<?php echo $hallway2_color;  ?>">Hallway2</td>
        <td class="auto-style3" style="width: 100px; background-color:
<?php echo $mini_hall_color; ?>">Mini Hall</td>
        <td class="auto-style3" style="width: 151px; background-color:
<?php echo $laundry_color;    ?>">Laundry</td>
    </tr>
    <tr>
        <td colspan="2" class="auto-style3" rowspan="2" style="background-
color: <?php echo $lounge_color; ?>"><br><br>Lounge</td>
        <td class="auto-style3" style="width: 89px; background-color:
<?php echo $kitchen_color; ?>"><br>Kitchen<br><br></td>
        <td class="auto-style3" colspan="2" ; style="background-color:
<?php echo $family_color; ?>"><br>Family Room</td>
        <td rowspan="2" style="width: 22px"> </td>
    </tr>
    <tr>
        <td class="auto-style3" style="height: 22px; width: 89px;
background-color: <?php echo $nook_color; ?>">Nook</td>
        <td class="auto-style3" colspan="2" style="height:
22px">Varanda</td>
    </tr>
    <tr>
```

```
        <td id="smc5" colspan="11" style="background-color: <?php echo
$home_security_color; ?>">
         </td>
    </tr>
</table>
</div>
<div id="key_background">
<p> </p>
</div>
</div>
</div>
</body>
</html>
```

File: master.php

```
<!DOCTYPE HTML>
<html>
<head>
<title>HC-Master</title>

<!--
File name:
    master.php
Author:
    Steve McClure
Book:
    Designing Embedded Sytems
Description:
    This file is used by the Home Control / Security application
    to build the Master Web page.
-->

<link href="../css/reset.css" rel="stylesheet" type="text/css"
media="screen">
<link href="../css/styles.css" rel="stylesheet" type="text/css"
media="screen">

<script type="text/javascript" src="../js/master_calendar.js"> </script>

<style type="text/css">
.auto-style1 {
    color: #FFFFFF;
}
.auto-style2 {
    text-align: center;
}
.auto-style3 {
    font-size: large;
}
.auto-style4 {
    font-size: small;
}
</style>
</head>

<body onload=" startTime()">

<div style="width:980px; margin: 0 auto; overflow: hidden;">
<div id="wrapper">
  <div id="navigation">
    <div id="navigation_picture">
      <img src="../images/HouseFront1.jpg" height="200" width="900" />
    </div>
```

```
    <div id="navigation_heading">
      <p><span class="auto-style1">Navigation</span> <span class="auto-
style1">- Master Bedroom</span></p>
    </div>
    <div id="navigation_time">
      <p>Date and Time</p>
    </div>

    <div id="navigation_links">
      <ul>
          <li><a href="security.php">Security</a></li>
          <li><a href="master.php">Master</a></li>
          <li><a href="lounge.php">Lounge</a></li>
          <li><a href="kitchen">Kitchen</a></li>
          <li><a href="family.php">Family</a></li>
          <li><a href="steve.php">Steve</a></li>
          <li><a href="state.php">State</a></li>
          <li><a href="events.php">Events</a></li>
      </ul>
    </div>
  </div>

  <div id="main_stuff">
    <p class="auto-style4"> </p>
    <p><strong>         This
screen allows you to control the Master Bedroom environment:</strong></p>
      <p class="auto-style4"> </p>
  </div>
</div>

    <?php

    // Connect to the MySQL Database Environment
    //=========================================
    $con = mysql_connect("192.168.1.176","steve","william");    // This
works on Archimedes

    if (!$con)
    {
      die('Could not connect as: ' . mysql_error());
      echo "<br />";
    }

    // Access the 'system_control' database
    //=================================
    mysql_select_db("system_control", $con);


    // Insert data into the 'house_state' table
    //=================================

    if ($_GET["watch_tv"] == 1)
```

```
   {
      mysql_query ("UPDATE house_state SET master_watch_tv = 1");
    }

   if ($_GET["retire_for_the_night"] == 1)
    {
      mysql_query ("UPDATE house_state SET go_to_bed = 1");
    }


   // Insert data into the 'house_code_events' table
   //=================================================

   // Mum's Bedside Light ON
   if ($_GET["mums_bedside_light_on"] == 1)
    {
      mysql_query ("INSERT INTO house_code_events (house, unit, type,
state, timeout, timestamp) VALUES (15, 2, 1, 1, 777,
'".$_GET["calendar"]."')");
     }

   // Mum's Bedside Light OFF
   if ($_GET["mums_bedside_light_off"] == 1)
    {
      mysql_query ("INSERT INTO house_code_events (house, unit, type,
state, timeout, timestamp) VALUES (15, 2, 1, 0, 777,
'".$_GET["calendar"]."')");
     }


   // Dad's Bedside Light ON
   if ($_GET["dads_bedside_light_on"] == 1)
    {
      mysql_query ("INSERT INTO house_code_events (house, unit, type,
state, timeout, timestamp) VALUES (15, 4, 1, 1, 777,
'".$_GET["calendar"]."')");
     }

   // Dad's Bedside Light OFF
   if ($_GET["dads_bedside_light_off"] == 1)
    {
      mysql_query ("INSERT INTO house_code_events (house, unit, type,
state, timeout, timestamp) VALUES (15, 4, 1, 0, 777,
'".$_GET["calendar"]."')");
     }


   // Bedroom Light ON
   if ($_GET["bedroom_light_on"] == 1)
    {
```

```
     mysql_query ("INSERT INTO house_code_events (house, unit, type,
state, timeout, timestamp) VALUES (15, 1, 1, 1, 777,
'".$_GET["calendar"]."')");
    }

   // Bedroom Light OFF
   if ($_GET["bedroom_light_off"] == 1)
   {
     mysql_query ("INSERT INTO house_code_events (house, unit, type,
state, timeout, timestamp) VALUES (15, 1, 1, 0, 777,
'".$_GET["calendar"]."')");
    }


   // Closet Light ON
   if ($_GET["closet_light_on"] == 1)
   {
     mysql_query ("INSERT INTO house_code_events (house, unit, type,
state, timeout, timestamp) VALUES (15, 3, 1, 1, 777,
'".$_GET["calendar"]."')");
    }

   // Closet Light OFF
   if ($_GET["closet_light_off"] == 1)
   {
     mysql_query ("INSERT INTO house_code_events (house, unit, type,
state, timeout, timestamp) VALUES (15, 3, 1, 0, 777,
'".$_GET["calendar"]."')");
    }


   // Close the 'home_control' database
   //===================================
   mysql_close($con);
   ?>

<div id="key_background">
    <form action="family.php" method="post">
       <div class="auto-style2">
          <span class="auto-style3">  </span><br class="auto-
style3"> <a id="smc1a"
href="master.php?mums_bedside_light_on=1"><img id="img42" alt="Mum's
Bedside Light   ON" fp-style="fp-btn: Embossed Rectangle 6; fp-font-size:
14; fp-img-hover: 0; fp-img-press: 0; fp-preload: 0; fp-transparent: 1;
fp-proportional: 0" fp-title="Mum's Bedside Light   ON" height="45"
src="../images/buttonD1.gif" style="border: 0"
width="244"></a>    
          <a id="smc1b" href="master.php?mums_bedside_light_off=1">
    <img id="img43" alt="OFF" fp-style="fp-btn: Embossed Rectangle 6; fp-
font-size: 14; fp-img-hover: 0; fp-img-press: 0; fp-preload: 0; fp-
transparent: 1; fp-proportional: 0" fp-title="OFF" height="45"
src="../images/buttonD3.gif" style="border: 0"
```

```
width="100"></a>         &nb
sp;           &nbs
p;            
;   
        <a id="smc4a" href="master.php?bedroom_light_on=1">
    <img id="img44" alt="Bedroom Light   ON" fp-style="fp-btn: Embossed
Rectangle 6; fp-font-size: 14; fp-font-color-hover: #FF0000; fp-font-
color-press: #0000FF; fp-img-hover: 0; fp-img-press: 0; fp-preload: 0;
fp-transparent: 1; fp-proportional: 0" fp-title="Bedroom Light   ON"
height="45" src="../images/buttonD6.gif" style="border: 0"
width="244"></a>    
        <a id="smc4b" href="master.php?bedroom_light_off=1">
    <img id="img45" alt="OFF" fp-style="fp-btn: Embossed Rectangle 6; fp-
font-size: 14; fp-font-color-hover: #FF0000; fp-font-color-press:
#0000FF; fp-img-hover: 0; fp-img-press: 0; fp-preload: 0; fp-transparent:
1; fp-proportional: 0" fp-title="OFF" height="45"
src="../images/buttonD8.gif" style="border: 0" width="100"></a><br><br>
        <a id="smc2a" href="master.php?dads_bedside_light_on=1">
    <img id="img46" alt="Dad's Bedside Light   ON" fp-style="fp-btn:
Embossed Rectangle 6; fp-font-size: 14; fp-img-hover: 0; fp-img-press: 0;
fp-preload: 0; fp-transparent: 1; fp-proportional: 0" fp-title="Dad's
Bedside Light   ON" height="45" src="../images/buttonD2.gif"
style="border: 0" width="244"></a>    
        <a id="smc2b" href="master.php?dads_bedside_light_off=1">
    <img id="img52" alt="OFF" fp-style="fp-btn: Embossed Rectangle 6; fp-
font-size: 14; fp-img-hover: 0; fp-img-press: 0; fp-preload: 0; fp-
transparent: 1; fp-proportional: 0" fp-title="OFF" height="45"
src="../images/buttonD4.gif" style="border: 0"
width="100"></a>         &nb
sp;           &nbs
p;            
;   
        <a id="smc5a" href="master.php?closet_light_on=1">
    <img id="img48" alt="Closet Light     ON" fp-style="fp-btn:
Embossed Rectangle 6; fp-font-size: 14; fp-font-color-hover: #FF0000; fp-
img-hover: 0; fp-img-press: 0; fp-preload: 0; fp-transparent: 1; fp-
proportional: 0" fp-title="Closet Light       ON" height="45"
src="../images/buttonD7.gif" style="border: 0"
width="244"></a>    
        <a id="smc5b" href="master.php?closet_light_off=1">
    <img id="img49" alt="OFF" fp-style="fp-btn: Embossed Rectangle 6; fp-
font-size: 14; fp-font-color-hover: #FF0000; fp-img-hover: 0; fp-img-
press: 0; fp-preload: 0; fp-transparent: 1; fp-proportional: 0" fp-
title="OFF" height="45" src="../images/buttonD9.gif" style="border: 0"
width="100"></a><br><br><br>
        <a id="smc3" href="master.php?watch_tv=1">
    <img id="img50" alt="Watch TV" fp-style="fp-btn: Embossed Rectangle
9; fp-font-size: 14; fp-img-hover: 0; fp-img-press: 0; fp-preload: 0; fp-
transparent: 1; fp-proportional: 0" fp-title="Watch TV" height="80"
src="../images/buttonD5.gif" style="border: 0"
width="365"></a>         &nb
sp;           &nbs
```

```
p;            
;   
          <a id="smc6" href="master.php?retire_for_the_night=1">
   <img id="img51" alt="Retire For The Night" fp-style="fp-btn: Embossed
Rectangle 4; fp-font-size: 14; fp-img-hover: 0; fp-img-press: 0; fp-
preload: 0; fp-transparent: 1; fp-proportional: 0" fp-title="Retire For
The Night" height="80" src="../images/buttonDA.gif" style="border: 0"
width="365"></a><br><br>
   </div>
   <p> </p>
   <p> </p>

</form>
</div>
</div>
</body>
</html>
```

File: lounge.php

```
<!DOCTYPE HTML>
<html>
<head>
<title>HC-Lounge</title>

<!--
File name:
    lounge.php
Author:
    Steve McClure
Book:
    Designing Embedded Sytems
Description:
    This file is used by the Home Control / Security application
    to build the Lounge Web page.
  -->

<link href="../css/reset.css" rel="stylesheet" type="text/css"
media="screen">
<link href="../css/styles.css" rel="stylesheet" type="text/css"
media="screen">

<script type="text/javascript" src="../js/lounge_calendar.js">
</script>

<style type="text/css">
.auto-style1 {
    color: #FFFFFF;
}
.auto-style2 {
    text-align: center;
}
.auto-style3 {
    font-size: large;
}
.auto-style4 {
    font-size: small;
}
</style>

</head>

<body onload=" startTime()">
<div style="width:980px; margin: 0 auto; overflow: hidden;">
<div id="wrapper">

  <div id="navigation">
    <div id="navigation_picture">
      <img src="../images/HouseFront1.jpg" height="200" width="900" />
```

```
      </div>

      <div id="navigation_heading">
        <p><span class="auto-style1">Navigation</span> <span class="auto-
style1">- Lounge</span></p>
      </div>

      <div id="navigation_time">
        <p>Date and Time</p>
      </div>

      <div id="navigation_links">
        <ul>
          <li><a href="security.php">Security</a></li>
          <li><a href="master.php">Master</a></li>
          <li><a href="lounge.php">Lounge</a></li>
          <li><a href="kitchen">Kitchen</a></li>
          <li><a href="family.php">Family</a></li>
          <li><a href="steve.php">Steve</a></li>
          <li><a href="state.php">State</a></li>
          <li><a href="events.php">Events</a></li>
        </ul>
      </div>
    </div>

    <div id="main_stuff">
      <p class="auto-style4"> </p>
      <p><strong>         This
screen allows you to control the Lounge environment:</strong></p>
      <p class="auto-style4"> </p>
    </div>
  </div>


    <?php

    // Connect to the MySQL Database Environment
    //=========================================
    $con = mysql_connect("192.168.1.176","steve","william");    // This
works on Archimedes

    if (!$con)
    {
      die('Could not connect as: ' . mysql_error());
      echo "<br />";
    }

    // Access the 'system_control' database
    //==================================
    mysql_select_db("system_control", $con);
```

```
// Insert data into the 'house_state' table
//===================================

if ($_GET["watch_tv"] == 1)
{
    mysql_query ("UPDATE house_state SET watch_tv = 1");
}


if ($_GET["go_to_bed"] == 1)
{
    mysql_query ("UPDATE house_state SET go_to_bed = 1");
}


// Insert data into the 'house_code_events' table
//===================================================

// Lounge Wall Light ON
if ($_GET["lounge_wall_light_on"] == 1)
{
    mysql_query ("INSERT INTO house_code_events (house, unit, type,
state, timeout, timestamp) VALUES (8, 1, 1, 1, 777,
'".$_GET["calendar"]."')");
}

// Lounge Wall Light OFF
if ($_GET["lounge_wall_light_off"] == 1)
{
    mysql_query ("INSERT INTO house_code_events (house, unit, type,
state, timeout, timestamp) VALUES (8, 1, 1, 0, 777,
'".$_GET["calendar"]."')");
}


// Lounge Window Light ON
if ($_GET["lounge_window_light_on"] == 1)
{
    mysql_query ("INSERT INTO house_code_events (house, unit, type,
state, timeout, timestamp) VALUES (8, 2, 1, 1, 777,
'".$_GET["calendar"]."')");
}

// Lounge Window Light OFF
if ($_GET["lounge_window_light_off"] == 1)
{
    mysql_query ("INSERT INTO house_code_events (house, unit, type,
state, timeout, timestamp) VALUES (8, 2, 1, 0, 777,
'".$_GET["calendar"]."')");
}
```

```
    // Diningroom Table Lights ON
    if ($_GET["diningroom_table_lights_on"] == 1)
    {
        mysql_query ("INSERT INTO house_code_events (house, unit, type,
state, timeout, timestamp) VALUES (8, 3, 1, 1, 777,
'".$_GET["calendar"]."')");
    }


    // Diningroom Table Lights OFF
    if ($_GET["diningroom_table_lights_off"] == 1)
    {
        mysql_query ("INSERT INTO house_code_events (house, unit, type,
state, timeout, timestamp) VALUES (8, 3, 1, 0, 777,
'".$_GET["calendar"]."')");
    }



    // Fishtank Lights ON
    if ($_GET["fishtank_lights_on"] == 1)
    {
        mysql_query ("INSERT INTO house_code_events (house, unit, type,
state, timeout, timestamp) VALUES (8, 4, 1, 1, 777,
'".$_GET["calendar"]."')");
    }


    // Fishtank Lights OFF
    if ($_GET["fishtank_lights_off"] == 1)
    {
        mysql_query ("INSERT INTO house_code_events (house, unit, type,
state, timeout, timestamp) VALUES (8, 4, 1, 0, 777,
'".$_GET["calendar"]."')");
    }



    // Inside Entrance Light ON
    if ($_GET["inside_entrance_light_on"] == 1)
    {
        mysql_query ("INSERT INTO house_code_events (house, unit, type,
state, timeout, timestamp) VALUES (7, 7, 1, 1, 777,
'".$_GET["calendar"]."')");
    }


    // Inside Entrance Light OFF
    if ($_GET["inside_entrance_light_off"] == 1)
    {
        mysql_query ("INSERT INTO house_code_events (house, unit, type,
state, timeout, timestamp) VALUES (7, 7, 1, 0, 777,
'".$_GET["calendar"]."')");
    }



    // Main Hallway Light ON
```

```
    if ($_GET["main_hallway_lights_on"] == 1)
    {
        mysql_query ("INSERT INTO house_code_events (house, unit, type,
state, timeout, timestamp) VALUES (5, 6, 1, 1, 777,
'".$_GET["calendar"]."')");
    }

    // Main Hallway Light OFF
    if ($_GET["main_hallway_lights_off"] == 1)
    {
        mysql_query ("INSERT INTO house_code_events (house, unit, type,
state, timeout, timestamp) VALUES (5, 6, 1, 0, 777,
'".$_GET["calendar"]."')");
    }


    // Season Front Lights ON
    if ($_GET["season_front_lights_on"] == 1)
    {
        mysql_query ("INSERT INTO house_code_events (house, unit, type,
state, timeout, timestamp) VALUES (16, 2, 1, 1, 777,
'".$_GET["calendar"]."')");
    }

    // Season Front Lights OFF
    if ($_GET["season_front_lights_off"] == 1)
    {
        mysql_query ("INSERT INTO house_code_events (house, unit, type,
state, timeout, timestamp) VALUES (16, 2, 1, 0, 777,
'".$_GET["calendar"]."')");
    }


    // Season Back Lights ON
    if ($_GET["season_back_lights_on"] == 1)
    {
        mysql_query ("INSERT INTO house_code_events (house, unit, type,
state, timeout, timestamp) VALUES (16, 3, 1, 1, 777,
'".$_GET["calendar"]."')");
    }

    // Season Back Lights OFF
    if ($_GET["season_back_lights_off"] == 1)
    {
        mysql_query ("INSERT INTO house_code_events (house, unit, type,
state, timeout, timestamp) VALUES (16, 3, 1, 0, 777,
'".$_GET["calendar"]."')");
    }


    // Close the 'home_control' database
    //===================================
```

79

```
        mysql_close($con);
    ?>
<div id="key_background">
<form action="family.php" method="post">
    <div class="auto-style2">
        <span class="auto-style3">  </span><br class="auto-style3">
        <a id="smc1a" href="lounge.php?lounge_wall_light_on=1">
        <img id="img22" alt="Lounge Wall Light          ON" fp-style="fp-
btn: Embossed Rectangle 6; fp-font-size: 14; fp-img-hover: 0; fp-img-
press: 0; fp-preload: 0; fp-transparent: 1; fp-proportional: 0" fp-
title="Lounge Wall Light          ON" height="45"
src="../images/buttonF0.gif" style="border: 0"
width="275"></a>    
        <a id="smc1b" href="lounge.php?lounge_wall_light_off=1">
        <img id="img23" alt="OFF" fp-style="fp-btn: Embossed Rectangle 6;
fp-font-size: 14; fp-img-hover: 0; fp-img-press: 0; fp-preload: 0; fp-
transparent: 1; fp-proportional: 0" fp-title="OFF" height="45"
src="../images/buttonF4.gif" style="border: 0"
width="100"></a>         &nb
sp;           &nbs
p;     
        <a id="smc5a" href="lounge.php?inside_entrance_light_on=1">
        <img id="img24" alt="Inside Entrance Light     ON" fp-style="fp-
btn: Embossed Rectangle 6; fp-font-size: 14; fp-img-hover: 0; fp-img-
press: 0; fp-preload: 0; fp-transparent: 1; fp-proportional: 0" fp-
title="Inside Entrance Light     ON" height="45"
src="../images/buttonF9.gif" style="border: 0"
width="275"></a>    
        <a id="smc5b" href="lounge.php?inside_entrance_light_off=1">
        <img id="img25" alt="OFF" fp-style="fp-btn: Embossed Rectangle 6;
fp-font-size: 14; fp-img-hover: 0; fp-img-press: 0; fp-preload: 0; fp-
transparent: 1; fp-proportional: 0" fp-title="OFF" height="45"
src="../images/buttonFD.gif" style="border: 0" width="100"></a><br>
        <br><a id="smc2a" href="lounge.php?lounge_window_light_on=1">
        <img id="img26" alt="Lounge Window Light      ON" fp-style="fp-
btn: Embossed Rectangle 6; fp-font-size: 14; fp-img-hover: 0; fp-img-
press: 0; fp-preload: 0; fp-transparent: 1; fp-proportional: 0" fp-
title="Lounge Window Light      ON" height="45"
src="../images/buttonF1.gif" style="border: 0"
width="275"></a>    
        <a id="smc2b" href="lounge.php?lounge_window_light_off=1">
        <img id="img27" alt="OFF" fp-style="fp-btn: Embossed Rectangle 6;
fp-font-size: 14; fp-img-hover: 0; fp-img-press: 0; fp-preload: 0; fp-
transparent: 1; fp-proportional: 0" fp-title="OFF" height="45"
src="../images/buttonF5.gif" style="border: 0"
width="100"></a>         &nb
sp;           &nbs
p;     
        <a id="smc6a" href="lounge.php?main_hallway_lights_on=1">
        <img id="img28" alt="Main Hallway Lights       ON" fp-style="fp-
btn: Embossed Rectangle 6; fp-font-size: 14; fp-img-hover: 0; fp-img-
press: 0; fp-preload: 0; fp-transparent: 1; fp-proportional: 0" fp-
```

```
title="Main Hallway Lights        ON" height="45"
src="../images/buttonFA.gif" style="border: 0"
width="275"></a>    
        <a id="smc6b" href="lounge.php?main_hallway_lights_off=1">
        <img id="img29" alt="OFF" fp-style="fp-btn: Embossed Rectangle 6;
fp-font-size: 14; fp-img-hover: 0; fp-img-press: 0; fp-preload: 0; fp-
transparent: 1; fp-proportional: 0" fp-title="OFF" height="45"
src="../images/buttonFE.gif" style="border: 0" width="100"></a><br>
        <br><a id="smc3a" href="lounge.php?diningroom_table_lights_on=1">
        <img id="img30" alt="Diningroom Table Lights    ON" fp-style="fp-
btn: Embossed Rectangle 6; fp-font-size: 14; fp-img-hover: 0; fp-img-
press: 0; fp-preload: 0; fp-transparent: 1; fp-proportional: 0" fp-
title="Diningroom Table Lights    ON" height="45"
src="../images/buttonF2.gif" style="border: 0"
width="275"></a>    
        <a id="smc3b" href="lounge.php?diningroom_table_lights_off=1">
        <img id="img31" alt="OFF" fp-style="fp-btn: Embossed Rectangle 6;
fp-font-size: 14; fp-img-hover: 0; fp-img-press: 0; fp-preload: 0; fp-
transparent: 1; fp-proportional: 0" fp-title="OFF" height="45"
src="../images/buttonF6.gif" style="border: 0"
width="100"></a>         &nb
sp;           &nbs
p;     
        <a id="smc7a" href="lounge.php?season_front_lights_on=1">
        <img id="img32" alt="Season Front Lights        ON" fp-style="fp-
btn: Embossed Rectangle 6; fp-font-size: 14; fp-img-hover: 0; fp-img-
press: 0; fp-preload: 0; fp-transparent: 1; fp-proportional: 0" fp-
title="Season Front Lights        ON" height="45"
src="../images/buttonFB.gif" style="border: 0"
width="275"></a>    
        <a id="smc7b" href="lounge.php?season_front_lights_off=1">
        <img id="img33" alt="OFF" fp-style="fp-btn: Embossed Rectangle 6;
fp-font-size: 14; fp-img-hover: 0; fp-img-press: 0; fp-preload: 0; fp-
transparent: 1; fp-proportional: 0" fp-title="OFF" height="45"
src="../images/buttonFF.gif" style="border: 0" width="100"></a><br>
        <br><a id="smc4a" href="lounge.php?fishtank_lights_on=1">
        <img id="img34" alt="Fishtank Lights            ON" fp-
style="fp-btn: Embossed Rectangle 6; fp-font-size: 14; fp-img-hover: 0;
fp-img-press: 0; fp-preload: 0; fp-transparent: 1; fp-proportional: 0"
fp-title="Fishtank Lights            ON" height="45"
src="../images/buttonF3.gif" style="border: 0"
width="275"></a>    
        <a id="smc4b" href="lounge.php?fishtank_lights_off=1">
        <img id="img35" alt="OFF" fp-style="fp-btn: Embossed Rectangle 6;
fp-font-size: 14; fp-img-hover: 0; fp-img-press: 0; fp-preload: 0; fp-
transparent: 1; fp-proportional: 0" fp-title="OFF" height="45"
src="../images/buttonF7.gif" style="border: 0"
width="100"></a>         &nb
sp;           &nbs
p;     
        <a id="smc8a" href="lounge.php?season_back_lights_on=1">
```

```
        <img id="img36" alt="Season Back Lights        ON" fp-style="fp-
btn: Embossed Rectangle 6; fp-font-size: 14; fp-img-hover: 0; fp-img-
press: 0; fp-preload: 0; fp-transparent: 1; fp-proportional: 0" fp-
title="Season Back Lights        ON" height="45"
src="../images/buttonFC.gif" style="border: 0"
width="275"></a>    
        <a id="smc8b" href="lounge.php?season_back_lights_off=1">
        <img id="img37" alt="OFF" fp-style="fp-btn: Embossed Rectangle 6;
fp-font-size: 14; fp-img-hover: 0; fp-img-press: 0; fp-preload: 0; fp-
transparent: 1; fp-proportional: 0" fp-title="OFF" height="45"
src="../images/button100.gif" style="border: 0" width="100"></a></div>
    <p> </p>
    <p> </p>

</form>
</div>
</div>
</body>
</html>
```

File: kitchen.php

```
<!DOCTYPE HTML>
<html>
<head>
<title>HC-Kitchen</title>

<!--
File name:
    kitchen.php
Author:
    Steve McClure
Book:
    Designing Embedded Sytems
Description:
    This file is used by the Home Control / Security application
    to build the Kitchen Web page.
 -->

<link href="../css/reset.css" rel="stylesheet" type="text/css"
media="screen">
<link href="../css/styles.css" rel="stylesheet" type="text/css"
media="screen">

<script type="text/javascript" src="../js/kitchen_calendar.js"> </script>

<style type="text/css">
.auto-style1 {
    color: #FFFFFF;
}
.auto-style2 {
    text-align: center;
}
.auto-style3 {
    font-size: small;
}
.auto-style4 {
    font-size: large;
}
</style>

</head>

<body onload=" startTime()">

<div style="width:980px; margin: 0 auto; overflow: hidden;">
<div id="wrapper">
  <div id="navigation">
    <div id="navigation_picture">
      <img src="../images/HouseFront1.jpg" height="200" width="900" />
    </div>
```

```
    <div id="navigation_heading">
      <p><span class="auto-style1">Navigation</span> <span class="auto-
style1">- Kitchen</span></p>
    </div>

    <div id="navigation_time">
      <p>Date and Time</p>
    </div>

   <div id="navigation_links">
      <ul>
         <li><a href="security.php">Security</a></li>
         <li><a href="master.php">Master</a></li>
         <li><a href="lounge.php">Lounge</a></li>
         <li><a href="kitchen">Kitchen</a></li>
         <li><a href="family.php">Family</a></li>
         <li><a href="steve.php">Steve</a></li>
         <li><a href="state.php">State</a></li>
         <li><a href="events.php">Events</a></li>
      </ul>
   </div>
  </div>

  <div id="main_stuff">
    <p class="auto-style3"> </p>
    <p><strong>         This
screen allows you to control the Kitchen environment:</strong></p>
     <p class="auto-style3"> </p>
  </div>
</div>


    <?php

    // Connect to the MySQL Database Environment
    //===========================================
    $con = mysql_connect("192.168.1.176","steve","william");    // This
works on Archimedes

    if (!$con)
    {
      die('Could not connect as: ' . mysql_error());
      echo "<br />";
    }

    // Access the 'system_control' database
    //==================================
     mysql_select_db("system_control", $con);


    // Insert data into the 'house_state' table
```

```
//====================================

if ($_GET["watch_tv"] == 1)
{
    mysql_query ("UPDATE house_state SET watch_tv = 1");
 }


if ($_GET["go_to_bed"] == 1)
 {
    mysql_query ("UPDATE house_state SET go_to_bed = 1");
 }


// Insert data into the 'house_code_events' table
//===================================================

// Kitchen Main Lights ON
if ($_GET["kitchen_main_lights_on"] == 1)
{
    mysql_query ("INSERT INTO house_code_events (house, unit, type,
state, timeout, timestamp) VALUES (4, 3, 1, 1, 777,
'".$_GET["calendar"]."')");
    }

// Kitchen Main Lights OFF
 if ($_GET["kitchen_main_lights_off"] == 1)
{
    mysql_query ("INSERT INTO house_code_events (house, unit, type,
state, timeout, timestamp) VALUES (4, 3, 1, 0, 777,
'".$_GET["calendar"]."')");
    }


// Kitchen Counter Lights ON
 if ($_GET["kitchen_counter_lights_on"] == 1)
{
    mysql_query ("INSERT INTO house_code_events (house, unit, type,
state, timeout, timestamp) VALUES (4, 5, 1, 1, 777,
'".$_GET["calendar"]."')");
    }

// Kitchen Counter Lights OFF
 if ($_GET["kitchen_counter_lights_off"] == 1)
{
    mysql_query ("INSERT INTO house_code_events (house, unit, type,
state, timeout, timestamp) VALUES (4, 5, 1, 0, 777,
'".$_GET["calendar"]."')");
    }


// Kitchen Sink Light ON
```

```
    if ($_GET["kitchen_sink_light_on"] == 1)
    {
        mysql_query ("INSERT INTO house_code_events (house, unit, type,
state, timeout, timestamp) VALUES (4, 6, 1, 1, 777,
'".$_GET["calendar"]."')");
    }


    // Kitchen Sink Light OFF
    if ($_GET["kitchen_sink_light_off"] == 1)
    {
        mysql_query ("INSERT INTO house_code_events (house, unit, type,
state, timeout, timestamp) VALUES (4, 6, 1, 0, 777,
'".$_GET["calendar"]."')");
    }



    // Kitchen Nook Light ON
    if ($_GET["kitchen_nook_light_on"] == 1)
    {
        mysql_query ("INSERT INTO house_code_events (house, unit, type,
state, timeout, timestamp) VALUES (4, 4, 1, 1, 777,
'".$_GET["calendar"]."')");
    }


    // Kitchen Nook Light OFF
    if ($_GET["kitchen_nook_light_off"] == 1)
    {
        mysql_query ("INSERT INTO house_code_events (house, unit, type,
state, timeout, timestamp) VALUES (4, 4, 1, 0, 777,
'".$_GET["calendar"]."')");
    }



    // Diningroom Table Lights ON
    if ($_GET["diningroom_table_lights_on"] == 1)
    {
        mysql_query ("INSERT INTO house_code_events (house, unit, type,
state, timeout, timestamp) VALUES (8, 3, 1, 1, 777,
'".$_GET["calendar"]."')");
    }


    // Diningroom Table Lights OFF
    if ($_GET["diningroom_table_lights_off"] == 1)
    {
        mysql_query ("INSERT INTO house_code_events (house, unit, type,
state, timeout, timestamp) VALUES (8, 3, 1, 0, 777,
'".$_GET["calendar"]."')");
    }



    // Main Hallway Light ON
    if ($_GET["main_hallway_lights_on"] == 1)
```

```
    {
        mysql_query ("INSERT INTO house_code_events (house, unit, type,
state, timeout, timestamp) VALUES (5, 6, 1, 1, 777,
'".$_GET["calendar"]."')");
    }

    // Main Hallway Light OFF
    if ($_GET["main_hallway_lights_off"] == 1)
    {
        mysql_query ("INSERT INTO house_code_events (house, unit, type,
state, timeout, timestamp) VALUES (5, 6, 1, 0, 777,
'".$_GET["calendar"]."')");
    }


    // Pantry Light ON
    if ($_GET["pantry_light_on"] == 1)
    {
        mysql_query ("INSERT INTO house_code_events (house, unit, type,
state, timeout, timestamp) VALUES (7, 8, 1, 1, 777,
'".$_GET["calendar"]."')");
    }

    // Pantry Light OFF
    if ($_GET["pantry_light_off"] == 1)
    {
        mysql_query ("INSERT INTO house_code_events (house, unit, type,
state, timeout, timestamp) VALUES (7, 8, 1, 0, 777,
'".$_GET["calendar"]."')");
    }


    // Laundry Light ON
    if ($_GET["laundry_light_on"] == 1)
    {
        mysql_query ("INSERT INTO house_code_events (house, unit, type,
state, timeout, timestamp) VALUES (7, 10, 1, 1, 777,
'".$_GET["calendar"]."')");
    }

    // Laundry Light OFF
    if ($_GET["laundry_light_off"] == 1)
    {
        mysql_query ("INSERT INTO house_code_events (house, unit, type,
state, timeout, timestamp) VALUES (7, 10, 1, 0, 777,
'".$_GET["calendar"]."')");
    }


    // Close the 'home_control' database
    //================================
    mysql_close($con);
```

```
    ?>
<div id="key_background">
<form action="family.php" method="post">
    <div class="auto-style2">
        <span class="auto-style4"> </span><br>
        <a id="smc1a" href="kitchen.php?kitchen_main_lights_on=1">
        <img id="img38" alt="Kitchen Main Lights        ON" fp-style="fp-
btn: Embossed Rectangle 6; fp-font-size: 14; fp-img-hover: 0; fp-img-
press: 0; fp-preload: 0; fp-transparent: 1; fp-proportional: 0" fp-
title="Kitchen Main Lights        ON" height="45"
src="../images/buttonA9.gif" style="border: 0"
width="270"></a>    
        <a id="smc1b" href="kitchen.php?kitchen_main_lights_off=1">
        <img id="img39" alt="OFF" fp-style="fp-btn: Embossed Rectangle 6;
fp-font-size: 14; fp-img-hover: 0; fp-img-press: 0; fp-preload: 0; fp-
transparent: 1; fp-proportional: 0" fp-title="OFF" height="45"
src="../images/buttonA13.gif" style="border: 0"
width="100"></a>         &nb
sp;           &nbs
p;     
        <a id="smc5a" href="kitchen.php?diningroom_table_lights_on=1">
        <img id="img40" alt="Diningroom Table Lights  ON" fp-style="fp-
btn: Embossed Rectangle 6; fp-font-size: 14; fp-img-hover: 0; fp-img-
press: 0; fp-preload: 0; fp-transparent: 1; fp-proportional: 0" fp-
title="Diningroom Table Lights  ON" height="45"
src="../images/buttonBC.gif" style="border: 0"
width="270"></a>    
        <a id="smc5b" href="kitchen.php?diningroom_table_lights_off=1">
        <img id="img41" alt="OFF" fp-style="fp-btn: Embossed Rectangle 6;
fp-font-size: 14; fp-img-hover: 0; fp-img-press: 0; fp-preload: 0; fp-
transparent: 1; fp-proportional: 0" fp-title="OFF" height="45"
src="../images/buttonC0.gif" style="border: 0" width="100"></a> <br>
        <span class="auto-style3"> </span><br>
        <a id="smc2a" href="kitchen.php?kitchen_counter_lights_on=1">
        <img id="img42" alt="Kitchen Counter Lights    ON" fp-style="fp-
btn: Embossed Rectangle 6; fp-font-size: 14; fp-img-hover: 0; fp-img-
press: 0; fp-preload: 0; fp-transparent: 1; fp-proportional: 0" fp-
title="Kitchen Counter Lights    ON" height="45"
src="../images/buttonA10.gif" style="border: 0"
width="270"></a>    
        <a id="smc2b" href="kitchen.php?kitchen_counter_lights_off=1">
        <img id="img43" alt="OFF" fp-style="fp-btn: Embossed Rectangle 6;
fp-font-size: 14; fp-img-hover: 0; fp-img-press: 0; fp-preload: 0; fp-
transparent: 1; fp-proportional: 0" fp-title="OFF" height="45"
src="../images/buttonAA.gif" style="border: 0"
width="100"></a>         &nb
sp;           &nbs
p;     
        <a id="smc6a" href="kitchen.php?main_hallway_lights_on=1">
        <img id="img44" alt="Main Hallway Lights        ON" fp-style="fp-
btn: Embossed Rectangle 6; fp-font-size: 14; fp-img-hover: 0; fp-img-
press: 0; fp-preload: 0; fp-transparent: 1; fp-proportional: 0" fp-
```

```
title="Main Hallway Lights        ON" height="45"
src="../images/buttonBD.gif" style="border: 0"
width="270"></a>    
        <a id="smc6b" href="kitchen.php?main_hallway_lights_off=1">
        <img id="img45" alt="OFF" fp-style="fp-btn: Embossed Rectangle 6;
fp-font-size: 14; fp-img-hover: 0; fp-img-press: 0; fp-preload: 0; fp-
transparent: 1; fp-proportional: 0" fp-title="OFF" height="45"
src="../images/buttonC1.gif" style="border: 0" width="100"></a> <br>
        <span class="auto-style3"> </span><br class="auto-style3">
        <a id="smc3a" href="kitchen.php?kitchen_sink_light_on=1">
        <img id="img46" alt="Kitchen Sink Light        ON" fp-style="fp-
btn: Embossed Rectangle 6; fp-font-size: 14; fp-img-hover: 0; fp-img-
press: 0; fp-preload: 0; fp-transparent: 1; fp-proportional: 0" fp-
title="Kitchen Sink Light        ON" height="45"
src="../images/buttonA11.gif" style="border: 0"
width="270"></a>    
        <a id="smc3b" href="kitchen.php?kitchen_sink_light_off=1">
        <img id="img47" alt="OFF" fp-style="fp-btn: Embossed Rectangle 6;
fp-font-size: 14; fp-img-hover: 0; fp-img-press: 0; fp-preload: 0; fp-
transparent: 1; fp-proportional: 0" fp-title="OFF" height="45"
src="../images/buttonAB.gif" style="border: 0"
width="100"></a>       
            &
nbsp;      
        <a id="smc7a" href="kitchen.php?pantry_light_on=1">
        <img id="img48" alt="Pantry Light        ON" fp-
style="fp-btn: Embossed Rectangle 6; fp-font-size: 14; fp-img-hover: 0;
fp-img-press: 0; fp-preload: 0; fp-transparent: 1; fp-proportional: 0"
fp-title="Pantry Light        ON" height="45"
src="../images/buttonBE.gif" style="border: 0"
width="270"></a>    
        <a id="smc7b" href="kitchen.php?pantry_light_off=1">
        <img id="img49" alt="OFF" fp-style="fp-btn: Embossed Rectangle 6;
fp-font-size: 14; fp-img-hover: 0; fp-img-press: 0; fp-preload: 0; fp-
transparent: 1; fp-proportional: 0" fp-title="OFF" height="45"
src="../images/buttonC2.gif" style="border: 0" width="100"></a> <br>
        <span class="auto-style3"> <br></span>
        <a id="smc4a" href="kitchen.php?kitchen_nook_light_on=1">
        <img id="img50" alt="Kitchen Nook Light        ON" fp-style="fp-
btn: Embossed Rectangle 6; fp-font-size: 14; fp-img-hover: 0; fp-img-
press: 0; fp-preload: 0; fp-transparent: 1; fp-proportional: 0" fp-
title="Kitchen Nook Light        ON" height="45"
src="../images/buttonA12.gif" style="border: 0"
width="270"></a>    
        <a id="smc4b" href="kitchen.php?kitchen_nook_light_off=1">
        <img id="img51" alt="OFF" fp-style="fp-btn: Embossed Rectangle 6;
fp-font-size: 14; fp-img-hover: 0; fp-img-press: 0; fp-preload: 0; fp-
transparent: 1; fp-proportional: 0" fp-title="OFF" height="45"
src="../images/buttonAC.gif" style="border: 0"
width="100"></a>         &nb
sp;           &nbs
p;     
```

89

```
        <a id="smc8a" href="kitchen.php?laundry_light_on=1">
        <img id="img52" alt="Laundry Light                  ON" fp-
style="fp-btn: Embossed Rectangle 6; fp-font-size: 14; fp-img-hover: 0;
fp-img-press: 0; fp-preload: 0; fp-transparent: 1; fp-proportional: 0"
fp-title="Laundry Light                  ON" height="45"
src="../images/buttonBF.gif" style="border: 0"
width="270"></a>    
        <a id="smc8b" href="kitchen.php?laundry_light_off=1">
        <img id="img53" alt="OFF" fp-style="fp-btn: Embossed Rectangle 6;
fp-font-size: 14; fp-img-hover: 0; fp-img-press: 0; fp-preload: 0; fp-
transparent: 1; fp-proportional: 0" fp-title="OFF" height="45"
src="../images/buttonC3.gif" style="border: 0"
width="100"></a> <br></div>

    <p> </p>
    <p> </p>

</form>
</div>
</div>
</body>
</html>
```

File: family.php

```
<!DOCTYPE HTML>
<html>
<head>
<title>HC-Family</title>

<!--
File name:
    family.php
Author:
    Steve McClure
Book:
    Designing Embedded Sytems
Description:
    This file is used by the Home Control / Security application
    to build the Family Web page.
-->

<link href="../css/reset.css" rel="stylesheet" type="text/css"
media="screen">
<link href="../css/styles.css" rel="stylesheet" type="text/css"
media="screen">

<script type="text/javascript" src="../js/family_calendar.js"> </script>

<style type="text/css">
.auto-style1 {
    color: #FFFFFF;
}
.auto-style2 {
    text-align: center;
}
.auto-style3 {
    vertical-align: middle;
    text-align: center;
}
.auto-style4 {
    vertical-align: middle;
    text-align: center;
    font-size: xx-small;
}
.auto-style5 {
    font-size: xx-small;
}
.auto-style6 {
    font-size: small;
}

</style>
```

```
</head>
<body onload=" startTime()">

<div style="width:980px; margin: 0 auto; overflow: hidden;">
<div id="wrapper">
  <div id="navigation">
    <div id="navigation_picture">
      <img src="../images/HouseFront1.jpg" height="200" width="900" />
    </div>

    <div id="navigation_heading">
      <p><span class="auto-style1">Navigation</span> <span class="auto-
style1">- Family Room</span></p>
    </div>

    <div id="navigation_time">
      <p>Date and Time</p>
    </div>

  <div id="navigation_links">
      <ul>
          <li><a href="security.php">Security</a></li>
          <li><a href="master.php">Master</a></li>
          <li><a href="lounge.php">Lounge</a></li>
          <li><a href="kitchen">Kitchen</a></li>
          <li><a href="family.php">Family</a></li>
          <li><a href="steve.php">Steve</a></li>
          <li><a href="state.php">State</a></li>
          <li><a href="events.php">Events</a></li>
      </ul>
  </div>
  </div>
</div>

  <div id="main_stuff">
    <?php

    // Connect to the MySQL Database Environment
    //=========================================
    $con = mysql_connect("192.168.1.176","steve","william");    // This
works on Archimedes

    if (!$con)
    {
       die('Could not connect as: ' . mysql_error());
       echo "<br />";
    }

    // Access the 'system_control' database
    //=================================
    mysql_select_db("system_control", $con);
```

```php
// Insert data into the 'house_code_events' table
//=================================================

// Track Lights - TV ON
if ($_GET["track_lights_tv_on"] == 1)
{
    mysql_query ("INSERT INTO house_code_events (house, unit, type,
state, timeout, timestamp) VALUES (12, 3, 1, 1, 777,
'".$_GET["calendar"]."')");
}


// Track Lights - TV OFF
if ($_GET["track_lights_tv_off"] == 1)
{
    mysql_query ("INSERT INTO house_code_events (house, unit, type,
state, timeout, timestamp) VALUES (12, 3, 1, 0, 777,
'".$_GET["calendar"]."')");
}



// Track Lights - Reading ON
if ($_GET["track_lights_reading_on"] == 1)
{
    mysql_query ("INSERT INTO house_code_events (house, unit, type,
state, timeout, timestamp) VALUES (12, 4, 1, 1, 777,
'".$_GET["calendar"]."')");
}

// Track Lights - Reading OFF
if ($_GET["track_lights_reading_off"] == 1)
{
    mysql_query ("INSERT INTO house_code_events (house, unit, type,
state, timeout, timestamp) VALUES (12, 4, 1, 0, 777,
'".$_GET["calendar"]."')");
}



// TV Wall Unit Lights ON
if ($_GET["tv_wall_unit_lights_on"] == 1)
{
    mysql_query ("INSERT INTO house_code_events (house, unit, type,
state, timeout, timestamp) VALUES (12, 5, 1, 1, 777,
'".$_GET["calendar"]."')");
}

// TV Wall Unit Lights OFF
if ($_GET["tv_wall_unit_lights_off"] == 1)
{
    mysql_query ("INSERT INTO house_code_events (house, unit, type,
state, timeout, timestamp) VALUES (12, 5, 1, 0, 777,
'".$_GET["calendar"]."')");
}
```

```php
    // TV Wall Unit Spotlights ON
    if ($_GET["tv_wall_unit_spots_on"] == 1)
    {
        mysql_query ("INSERT INTO house_code_events (house, unit, type,
state, timeout, timestamp) VALUES (12, 6, 1, 1, 777,
'".$_GET["calendar"]."')");
    }

    // TV Wall Unit Spotlights OFF
    if ($_GET["tv_wall_unit_spots_off"] == 1)
    {
        mysql_query ("INSERT INTO house_code_events (house, unit, type,
state, timeout, timestamp) VALUES (12, 6, 1, 0, 777,
'".$_GET["calendar"]."')");
    }



    // Family Window Light ON
    if ($_GET["window_light_on"] == 1)
    {
        mysql_query ("INSERT INTO house_code_events (house, unit, type,
state, timeout, timestamp) VALUES (12, 1, 1, 1, 777,
'".$_GET["calendar"]."')");
    }

    // Family Window Light OFF
    if ($_GET["window_light_off"] == 1)
    {
        mysql_query ("INSERT INTO house_code_events (house, unit, type,
state, timeout, timestamp) VALUES (12, 1, 1, 0, 777,
'".$_GET["calendar"]."')");
    }



    // Family Wall Light ON
    if ($_GET["wall_light_on"] == 1)
    {
        mysql_query ("INSERT INTO house_code_events (house, unit, type,
state, timeout, timestamp) VALUES (12, 2, 1, 1, 777,
'".$_GET["calendar"]."')");
    }

    // Family Wall Light OFF
    if ($_GET["wall_light_off"] == 1)
    {
        mysql_query ("INSERT INTO house_code_events (house, unit, type,
state, timeout, timestamp) VALUES (12, 2, 1, 0, 777,
'".$_GET["calendar"]."')");
    }
```

```php
$HS_NORMAL_MODE          = 0;
$HS_NORMAL_MODE_TRIGGER = 1;
$HS_TV_MODE              = 2;
$HS_TV_MODE_TRIGGER      = 3;


$result = mysql_query("SELECT * FROM house_state");
$row = mysql_fetch_array($result);

// Was the Watch TV button pressed?
if ($_GET["watch_tv"] == 1)
{
    // Set TV Mode
    mysql_query ("UPDATE house_state SET family_lights =
$HS_TV_MODE");
    mysql_query ("INSERT INTO house_code_events (house, unit, type,
state, timeout, timestamp) VALUES (12, 5, 1, 1, 1,
'".$_GET["calendar"]."')");  // TV Wall Unit Lights ON
    mysql_query ("INSERT INTO house_code_events (house, unit, type,
state, timeout, timestamp) VALUES (12, 6, 1, 0, 2,
'".$_GET["calendar"]."')");  // TV Wall Unit Spots OFF
    mysql_query ("INSERT INTO house_code_events (house, unit, type,
state, timeout, timestamp) VALUES (12, 2, 1, 1, 3,
'".$_GET["calendar"]."')");  // Set Wall Light ON
    mysql_query ("INSERT INTO house_code_events (house, unit, type,
state, timeout, timestamp) VALUES (12, 1, 1, 0, 4,
'".$_GET["calendar"]."')");  // Set Window Light OFF

    mysql_query ("INSERT INTO house_code_events (house, unit, type,
state, timeout, timestamp) VALUES ( 4, 3, 1, 0, 5,
'".$_GET["calendar"]."')");  // Kitchen light OFF
    mysql_query ("INSERT INTO house_code_events (house, unit, type,
state, timeout, timestamp) VALUES ( 4, 4, 1, 0, 6,
'".$_GET["calendar"]."')");  // Kitchen Nook OFF
    mysql_query ("INSERT INTO house_code_events (house, unit, type,
state, timeout, timestamp) VALUES ( 5, 6, 1, 0, 7,
'".$_GET["calendar"]."')");  // Main Hallway Light OFF

    mysql_query ("INSERT INTO house_code_events (house, unit, type,
state, timeout, timestamp) VALUES (12, 3, 1, 0, 8,
'".$_GET["calendar"]."')");  // Track TV OFF
    mysql_query ("INSERT INTO house_code_events (house, unit, type,
state, timeout, timestamp) VALUES (12, 4, 1, 0, 9,
'".$_GET["calendar"]."')");  // Track Reading OFF
}

// Was the Normal Lights button pressed?
if ($_GET["normal_lights"] == 1)
{
    // Set Normal Mode
    mysql_query ("UPDATE house_state SET family_lights =
$HS_NORMAL_MODE");
```

```php
        mysql_query ("INSERT INTO house_code_events (house, unit, type,
state, timeout, timestamp) VALUES (12, 5, 1, 1, 1,
'".$_GET["calendar"]."')");  // TV Wall Unit Lights ON
        mysql_query ("INSERT INTO house_code_events (house, unit, type,
state, timeout, timestamp) VALUES (12, 6, 1, 1, 2,
'".$_GET["calendar"]."')");  // TV Wall Unit Spots ON
        mysql_query ("INSERT INTO house_code_events (house, unit, type,
state, timeout, timestamp) VALUES (12, 2, 1, 1, 3,
'".$_GET["calendar"]."')");  // Set Wall Light ON
        mysql_query ("INSERT INTO house_code_events (house, unit, type,
state, timeout, timestamp) VALUES (12, 1, 1, 1, 4,
'".$_GET["calendar"]."')");  // Set Window Light OFF
        mysql_query ("INSERT INTO house_code_events (house, unit, type,
state, timeout, timestamp) VALUES (12, 3, 1, 0, 5,
'".$_GET["calendar"]."')");  // Track TV OFF
        mysql_query ("INSERT INTO house_code_events (house, unit, type,
state, timeout, timestamp) VALUES (12, 4, 1, 0, 6,
'".$_GET["calendar"]."')");  // Track Reading OFF
        mysql_query ("INSERT INTO house_code_events (house, unit, type,
state, timeout, timestamp) VALUES ( 4, 3, 1, 0, 7,
'".$_GET["calendar"]."')");  // Kitchen light OFF
      mysql_query ("INSERT INTO house_code_events (house, unit, type,
state, timeout, timestamp) VALUES ( 4, 4, 1, 0, 8,
'".$_GET["calendar"]."')");  // Kitchen Nook OFF
        mysql_query ("INSERT INTO house_code_events (house, unit, type,
state, timeout, timestamp) VALUES ( 5, 6, 1, 0, 9,
'".$_GET["calendar"]."')");  // Main Hallway Light OFF
    }

    $result = mysql_query("SELECT * FROM house_state");

    $row = mysql_fetch_array($result);
     ?>

    <p class="auto-style6">  </p>
     <?php
     echo "         ";
     echo "This screen allows you to control the Family Room
environment:";
     echo "   ";

     if ($row['family_lights'] == $HS_NORMAL_MODE)
     {
       echo "Normal Lights";
      }
     else
     {
       echo "Watch TV";
     }
     ?>

    <p class="auto-style6">  </p>
```

```php
    <?php

    // Close the 'home_control' database
    //================================
      mysql_close($con);

    ?>
  </div>
</div>
```

```html
<div id="key_background">
<form action="family.php" method="post">
    <span class="auto-style5"> </span><br>
          <table style="width: 967px; height: 30px" align="center">
              <tr>
                    <td class="auto-style3" style="width: 482px; height:
55px">

                    <a id="smc1a" href="family.php?track_lights_tv_on=1">
                    <img id="img44" alt="Track Lights - TV           ON"
fp-style="fp-btn: Embossed Rectangle 6; fp-font-size: 14; fp-img-hover:
0; fp-img-press: 0; fp-preload: 0; fp-transparent: 1; fp-proportional: 0"
fp-title="Track Lights - TV           ON" height="45"
src="../images/button119.gif" style="border: 0"
width="272"></a>    
                    <a id="smc1b" href="family.php?track_lights_tv_off=1">
                    <img id="img45" alt="OFF" fp-style="fp-btn: Embossed
Rectangle 6; fp-font-size: 14; fp-img-hover: 0; fp-img-press: 0; fp-
preload: 0; fp-transparent: 1; fp-proportional: 0" fp-title="OFF"
height="45" src="../images/button11D.gif" style="border: 0"
width="100"></a>
                    </td>
                    <td class="auto-style3" style="width: 48px; height:
55px">

                     </td>
                    <td class="auto-style3" style="height: 55px">
                    <a id="smc5a" href="family.php?window_light_on=1">
                    <img id="img52" alt="Window Light           ON" fp-
style="fp-btn: Embossed Rectangle 6; fp-font-size: 14; fp-img-hover: 0;
fp-img-press: 0; fp-preload: 0; fp-transparent: 1; fp-proportional: 0"
fp-title="Window Light           ON" height="45"
src="../images/button121.gif" style="border: 0"
width="272"></a>    
                    <a id="smc5b" href="family.php?window_light_off=1">
                    <img id="img53" alt="OFF" fp-style="fp-btn: Embossed
Rectangle 6; fp-font-size: 14; fp-img-hover: 0; fp-img-press: 0; fp-
preload: 0; fp-transparent: 1; fp-proportional: 0" fp-title="OFF"
height="45" src="../images/button123.gif" style="border: 0"
width="100"></a></td>
                    <td class="auto-style2"> </td>
                    <td class="auto-style2"> </td>
              </tr>
```

```
                <tr>
                        <td class="auto-style3" style="width: 482px; height:
55px">
                        <a id="smc2a"
href="family.php?track_lights_reading_on=1">
                                <img id="img46" alt="Track Lights - Reading      ON" fp-
style="fp-btn: Embossed Rectangle 6; fp-font-size: 14; fp-img-hover: 0;
fp-img-press: 0; fp-preload: 0; fp-transparent: 1; fp-proportional: 0"
fp-title="Track Lights - Reading      ON" height="45"
src="../images/button11A.gif" style="border: 0"
width="272"></a>    
                        <a id="smc2b"
href="family.php?track_lights_reading_off=1">
                                <img id="img47" alt="OFF" fp-style="fp-btn: Embossed
Rectangle 6; fp-font-size: 14; fp-img-hover: 0; fp-img-press: 0; fp-
preload: 0; fp-transparent: 1; fp-proportional: 0" fp-title="OFF"
height="45" src="../images/button11E.gif" style="border: 0"
width="100"></a></td>
                        <td class="auto-style3" style="width: 48px; height:
55px">
                         </td>
                        <td class="auto-style3" style="height: 55px">
                        <a id="smc6a" href="family.php?wall_light_on=1">
                                <img id="img54" alt="Wall Light                 ON"
fp-style="fp-btn: Embossed Rectangle 6; fp-font-size: 14; fp-img-hover:
0; fp-img-press: 0; fp-preload: 0; fp-transparent: 1; fp-proportional: 0"
fp-title="Wall Light                 ON" height="45"
src="../images/button122.gif" style="border: 0"
width="272"></a>    
                        <a id="smc6b" href="family.php?wall_light_off=1">
                                <img id="img55" alt="OFF" fp-style="fp-btn: Embossed
Rectangle 6; fp-font-size: 14; fp-img-hover: 0; fp-img-press: 0; fp-
preload: 0; fp-transparent: 1; fp-proportional: 0" fp-title="OFF"
height="45" src="../images/button124.gif" style="border: 0"
width="100"></a></td>
                </tr>
                <tr>
                        <td class="auto-style4" style="height: 3px; width:
482px;">
                        <br></td>
                        <td class="auto-style3" style="height: 3px; width:
48px;"></td>
                        <td class="auto-style3" style="height: 3px"></td>
                </tr>
                <tr>
                        <td class="auto-style3" style="width: 482px; height:
55px">
                        <a id="smc3a"
href="family.php?tv_wall_unit_lights_on=1">
                                <img id="img50" alt="TV Wall Unit Lights          ON" fp-
style="fp-btn: Embossed Rectangle 6; fp-font-size: 14; fp-img-hover: 0;
fp-img-press: 0; fp-preload: 0; fp-transparent: 1; fp-proportional: 0"
```

```
fp-title="TV Wall Unit Lights          ON" height="45"
src="../images/button11B.gif" style="border: 0"
width="272"></a>    
                <a id="smc3b"
href="family.php?tv_wall_unit_lights_off=1">
                <img id="img51" alt="OFF" fp-style="fp-btn: Embossed
Rectangle 6; fp-font-size: 14; fp-img-hover: 0; fp-img-press: 0; fp-
preload: 0; fp-transparent: 1; fp-proportional: 0" fp-title="OFF"
height="45" src="../images/button11F.gif" style="border: 0"
width="100"></a></td>
                <td class="auto-style3" style="width: 48px; height:
55px">
                 </td>
                <td class="auto-style3" rowspan="2">
                <br><a id="smc7" href="family.php?watch_tv=1">
                <img id="img56" alt="Watch TV" fp-style="fp-btn:
Embossed Rectangle 9; fp-font-size: 14; fp-img-hover: 0; fp-img-press: 0;
fp-preload: 0; fp-transparent: 1; fp-proportional: 0" fp-title="Watch TV"
height="80" src="../images/button125.gif" style="border: 0"
width="160"></a>        
                <a id="smc8" href="family.php?normal_lights=1">
                <img id="img57" alt="Normal Lights" fp-style="fp-btn:
Embossed Rectangle 4; fp-font-size: 14; fp-img-hover: 0; fp-img-press: 0;
fp-preload: 0; fp-transparent: 1; fp-proportional: 0" fp-title="Normal
Lights" height="80" src="../images/button126.gif" style="border: 0"
width="160"></a><br></td>
            </tr>
            <tr>
                <td class="auto-style3" style="width: 482px; height:
55px">
                <a id="smc4a" href="family.php?tv_wall_unit_spots_on=1">
                <img id="img48" alt="TV Wall Unit Spots          ON" fp-
style="fp-btn: Embossed Rectangle 6; fp-font-size: 14; fp-img-hover: 0;
fp-img-press: 0; fp-preload: 0; fp-transparent: 1; fp-proportional: 0"
fp-title="TV Wall Unit Spots          ON" height="45"
src="../images/button11C.gif" style="border: 0"
width="272"></a>    
                <a id="smc4b"
href="family.php?tv_wall_unit_spots_off=1">
                <img id="img49" alt="OFF" fp-style="fp-btn: Embossed
Rectangle 6; fp-font-size: 14; fp-img-hover: 0; fp-img-press: 0; fp-
preload: 0; fp-transparent: 1; fp-proportional: 0" fp-title="OFF"
height="45" src="../images/button120.gif" style="border: 0"
width="100"></a></td>
                <td class="auto-style3" style="width: 48px; height:
55px">
                 </td>
            </tr>
        </table>
    <p> </p>
    <p> </p>
```

```
</form>
</div>
</div>
</body>
</html>
```

File: steve.php

```
<!DOCTYPE HTML>
<html>
<head>
<title>HC-Steve</title>

<!--
File name:
    steve.php
Author:
    Steve McClure
Book:
    Designing Embedded Sytems
Description:
    This file is used by the Home Control / Security application
    to build the Steve Web page.
-->

<link href="../css/reset.css" rel="stylesheet" type="text/css"
media="screen">
<link href="../css/styles.css" rel="stylesheet" type="text/css"
media="screen">

<script type="text/javascript" src="../js/steve_calendar.js"></script>

<style type="text/css">
.auto-style1 {
    color:#FFFFFF;
}
.auto-style2 {
    text-align: center;
}
.auto-style3 {
    text-align: center;
    vertical-align: middle;
}
.auto-style4 {
    font-size: large;
}
.auto-style6 {
    font-size: small;
}

</style>
<script type="text/javascript">
<!--
function FP_preloadImgs() {//v1.0
 var d=document,a=arguments; if(!d.FP_imgs) d.FP_imgs=new Array();
 for(var i=0; i<a.length; i++) { d.FP_imgs[i]=new Image;
d.FP_imgs[i].src=a[i]; }
```

```
}
// -->
</script>
</head>
<body
onload="FP_preloadImgs(/*url*/'button22.jpg',/*url*/'button23.jpg',/*url*
/'button58.jpg',/*url*/'button59.jpg'); startTime()">
<div style="width:980px; margin: 0 auto; overflow: hidden;">
<div id="wrapper">

  <div id="navigation">
    <div id="navigation_picture">
      <img src="../images/HouseFront1.jpg" height="200" width="900" />
    </div>

    <div id="navigation_heading">
      <p><span class="auto-style1">Navigation</span> <span class="auto-
style1">- Steve's Bedroom, Bathroom &amp; Study</span></p>
    </div>

    <div id="navigation_time">
      <p>Date and Time</p>
    </div>


    <div id="navigation_links">
      <ul>
        <li><a href="security.php">Security</a></li>
        <li><a href="master.php">Master</a></li>
        <li><a href="lounge.php">Lounge</a></li>
        <li><a href="kitchen">Kitchen</a></li>
        <li><a href="family.php">Family</a></li>
        <li><a href="steve.php">Steve</a></li>
        <li><a href="state.php">State</a></li>
        <li><a href="events.php">Events</a></li>
      </ul>
    </div>
  </div>


  <div id="main_stuff">
    <?php

    // Connect to the MySQL Database Environment
    //=========================================
    $con = mysql_connect("192.168.1.176","steve","william");

    if (!$con)
    {
      die('Could not connect as: ' . mysql_error());
      echo "<br />";
```

```
    }

    // Access the 'system_control' database
    //=================================
      mysql_select_db("system_control", $con);


    // Insert data into the 'house_code_events' table
    //===============================================

    // Bedroom Wall Lights ON
    if ($_GET["bedroom_wall_light_on"] == 1)
    {
       mysql_query ("INSERT INTO house_code_events (house, unit, type,
state, timeout, timestamp) VALUES (5, 2, 1, 1, 777,
'".$_GET["calendar"]."')");        // Window light
       mysql_query ("INSERT INTO house_code_events (house, unit, type,
state, timeout, timestamp) VALUES (5, 3, 1, 1, 777,
'".$_GET["calendar"]."')");     // Wall lights
    }

    // Bedroom Wall Lights OFF
    if ($_GET["bedroom_wall_light_off"] == 1)
    {
       mysql_query ("INSERT INTO house_code_events (house, unit, type,
state, timeout, timestamp) VALUES (5, 2, 1, 0, 777,
'".$_GET["calendar"]."')");        // Window light
       mysql_query ("INSERT INTO house_code_events (house, unit, type,
state, timeout, timestamp) VALUES (5, 3, 1, 0, 777,
'".$_GET["calendar"]."')");     // Wall lights
    }


    // Bedroom Main Lights ON
    if ($_GET["bedroom_main_light_on"] == 1)
    {
       mysql_query ("INSERT INTO house_code_events (house, unit, type,
state, timeout, timestamp) VALUES (5, 4, 1, 1, 777,
'".$_GET["calendar"]."')");
    }

    // Bedroom Main Lights OFF
    if ($_GET["bedroom_main_light_off"] == 1)
    {
       mysql_query ("INSERT INTO house_code_events (house, unit, type,
state, timeout, timestamp) VALUES (5, 4, 1, 0, 777,
'".$_GET["calendar"]."')");
    }


    // Reading Light ON
    if ($_GET["reading_light_on"] == 1)
```

```
    {
        mysql_query ("INSERT INTO house_code_events (house, unit, type,
state, timeout, timestamp) VALUES (5, 1, 1, 1, 777,
'".$_GET["calendar"]."')");
     }

    // Reading Light OFF
    if ($_GET["reading_light_off"] == 1)
    {
        mysql_query ("INSERT INTO house_code_events (house, unit, type,
state, timeout, timestamp) VALUES (5, 1, 1, 0, 777,
'".$_GET["calendar"]."')");
     }


    // Study Main Lights ON
    if ($_GET["study_main_light_on"] == 1)
    {
        mysql_query ("INSERT INTO house_code_events (house, unit, type,
state, timeout, timestamp) VALUES (8, 5, 1, 1, 777,
'".$_GET["calendar"]."')");
     }

    // Study Main Lights OFF
    if ($_GET["study_main_light_off"] == 1)
    {
        mysql_query ("INSERT INTO house_code_events (house, unit, type,
state, timeout, timestamp) VALUES (8, 5, 1, 0, 777,
'".$_GET["calendar"]."')");
     }


    // Washroom Vanity Wall Lights ON
    if ($_GET["washroom_light_on"] == 1)
    {
        mysql_query ("INSERT INTO house_code_events (house, unit, type,
state, timeout, timestamp) VALUES (5, 7, 1, 1, 777,
'".$_GET["calendar"]."')");
     }

    // Washroom Vanity Wall Lights OFF
    if ($_GET["washroom_light_off"] == 1)
    {
        mysql_query ("INSERT INTO house_code_events (house, unit, type,
state, timeout, timestamp) VALUES (5, 7, 1, 0, 777,
'".$_GET["calendar"]."')");      // Vanity lights
        mysql_query ("INSERT INTO house_code_events (house, unit, type,
state, timeout, timestamp) VALUES (5, 8, 1, 0, 777,
'".$_GET["calendar"]."')");      // Flourescent light
     }
```

```
    // Bathroom Light ON
    if ($_GET["bathroom_light_on"] == 1)
    {
        mysql_query ("INSERT INTO house_code_events (house, unit, type,
state, timeout, timestamp) VALUES (8, 8, 1, 1, 777,
'".$_GET["calendar"]."')");
    }

    // Bathroom Light OFF
    if ($_GET["bathroom_light_off"] == 1)
    {
        mysql_query ("INSERT INTO house_code_events (house, unit, type,
state, timeout, timestamp) VALUES (8, 8, 1, 0, 777,
'".$_GET["calendar"]."')");
    }


    $HS_NORMAL_MODE         = 0;
    $HS_NORMAL_MODE_TRIGGER = 1;
    $HS_TV_MODE             = 2;
    $HS_TV_MODE_TRIGGER     = 3;

    $result = mysql_query("SELECT * FROM house_state");
    $row = mysql_fetch_array($result);

    // Is sleep mode off?
    if ($row['sleep'] == 0)
    {
      // Was the Watch TV button pressed?
      if ($_GET["watch_tv"] == 1)
      {
          // Set TV Mode
          mysql_query ("UPDATE house_state SET steve_lights =
$HS_TV_MODE");

          mysql_query ("INSERT INTO house_code_events (house, unit, type,
state, timeout, timestamp) VALUES (5, 3, 1, 1, 0,
'".$_GET["calendar"]."')");        // Bedroom Wall Lights ON
          mysql_query ("INSERT INTO house_code_events (house, unit, type,
state, timeout, timestamp) VALUES (5, 2, 1, 0, 0,
'".$_GET["calendar"]."')");        // Bedroom Window Light OFF

          mysql_query ("INSERT INTO house_code_events (house, unit,
type, state, timeout, timestamp) VALUES (8, 5, 1, 0, 2,
'".$_GET["calendar"]."')");        // Study Main Lights OFF
          mysql_query ("INSERT INTO house_code_events (house, unit,
type, state, timeout, timestamp) VALUES (5, 4, 1, 0, 3,
'".$_GET["calendar"]."')");        // Bedroom Main Lights OFF
          mysql_query ("INSERT INTO house_code_events (house, unit,
type, state, timeout, timestamp) VALUES (5, 3, 1, 1, 4,
'".$_GET["calendar"]."')");        // Bedroom Wall Lights ON
```

```
        mysql_query ("INSERT INTO house_code_events (house, unit,
type, state, timeout, timestamp) VALUES (5, 2, 1, 0, 5,
'".$_GET["calendar"]."')");        // Bedroom Window Light OFF
        mysql_query ("INSERT INTO house_code_events (house, unit,
type, state, timeout, timestamp) VALUES (5, 1, 1, 0, 6,
'".$_GET["calendar"]."')");        // Bedroom Reading Light OFF
        mysql_query ("INSERT INTO house_code_events (house, unit,
type, state, timeout, timestamp) VALUES (5, 8, 1, 0, 7,
'".$_GET["calendar"]."')");        // Washroom Flourescent Light OFF
        mysql_query ("INSERT INTO house_code_events (house, unit,
type, state, timeout, timestamp) VALUES (5, 7, 1, 0, 8,
'".$_GET["calendar"]."')");        // Washroom Lights OFF
        mysql_query ("INSERT INTO house_code_events (house, unit,
type, state, timeout, timestamp) VALUES (8, 8, 1, 0, 9,
'".$_GET["calendar"]."')");        // Bathroom Light OFF
    }

    // Was the Normal Lights button pressed?
    if ($_GET["normal_lights"] == 1)
    {
        // Set Normal Mode
        mysql_query ("UPDATE house_state SET steve_lights =
$HS_NORMAL_MODE");

        mysql_query ("INSERT INTO house_code_events (house, unit, type,
state, timeout, timestamp) VALUES (5, 3, 1, 1, 0,
'".$_GET["calendar"]."')");        // Bedroom Wall Lights ON
        mysql_query ("INSERT INTO house_code_events (house, unit, type,
state, timeout, timestamp) VALUES (5, 2, 1, 1, 0,
'".$_GET["calendar"]."')");        // Bedroom Window Light ON

        mysql_query ("INSERT INTO house_code_events (house, unit, type,
state, timeout, timestamp) VALUES (8, 5, 1, 0, 2,
'".$_GET["calendar"]."')");        // Study Main Lights OFF
        mysql_query ("INSERT INTO house_code_events (house, unit, type,
state, timeout, timestamp) VALUES (5, 4, 1, 0, 3,
'".$_GET["calendar"]."')");        // Bedroom Main Lights OFF
        mysql_query ("INSERT INTO house_code_events (house, unit, type,
state, timeout, timestamp) VALUES (5, 3, 1, 1, 4,
'".$_GET["calendar"]."')");        // Bedroom Wall Lights ON
        mysql_query ("INSERT INTO house_code_events (house, unit, type,
state, timeout, timestamp) VALUES (5, 2, 1, 1, 5,
'".$_GET["calendar"]."')");        // Bedroom Window Light ON
        mysql_query ("INSERT INTO house_code_events (house, unit, type,
state, timeout, timestamp) VALUES (5, 1, 1, 0, 6,
'".$_GET["calendar"]."')");        // Bedroom Reading Light OFF
        mysql_query ("INSERT INTO house_code_events (house, unit, type,
state, timeout, timestamp) VALUES (5, 8, 1, 0, 7,
'".$_GET["calendar"]."')");        // Washroom Flourescent Light OFF
        mysql_query ("INSERT INTO house_code_events (house, unit, type,
state, timeout, timestamp) VALUES (5, 7, 1, 0, 8,
'".$_GET["calendar"]."')");        // Washroom Lights OFF
```

```php
        mysql_query ("INSERT INTO house_code_events (house, unit, type,
state, timeout, timestamp) VALUES (8, 8, 1, 0, 9,
'".$_GET["calendar"]."')");         // Bathroom Light OFF
        }
    }

    $result = mysql_query("SELECT * FROM house_state");

    $row = mysql_fetch_array($result);

    ?><p class="auto-style6">  </p><?php
    echo "         ";
    echo "This screen allows you to control the Bedroom, Bathroom and
Study environments:";
    echo "   ";

    if ($row['sleep'] == 0)
    {
        if ($row['steve_lights'] == $HS_NORMAL_MODE)
        {
          echo "Normal Lights";
        }
        else
        {
          echo "Watch TV";
        }
    }
    else
    {
        echo "SLEEP ACTIVE";
    }

    ?><p class="auto-style6">  </p><?php

    // Close the 'home_control' database
    //================================
    mysql_close($con);

    ?>
    </div>
</div>


<div id="key_background">
<p>      
       
 
<span class="auto-style4"> </span></p>
    <table align="center" cellpadding="5" cellspacing="5" style="width:
970px">
        <tr>
```

```
        <td style="height: 55px; width: 459px;" class="auto-style2">
                
            <a id="smc1a" href="steve.php?bedroom_wall_light_on=1">
            <img id="img1014" alt="Bedroom Wall Light      ON" fp-
style="fp-btn: Embossed Rectangle 6; fp-font-size: 14; fp-img-hover: 0;
fp-img-press: 0; fp-preload: 0; fp-transparent: 1; fp-proportional: 0"
fp-title="Bedroom Wall Light      ON" height="45"
src="../images/button15A.gif" style="border: 0"
width="272"></a>    
            <a id="smc1b" href="steve.php?bedroom_wall_light_off=1">
            <img id="img1015" alt="OFF" fp-style="fp-btn: Embossed
Rectangle 6; fp-font-size: 14; fp-img-hover: 0; fp-img-press: 0; fp-
preload: 0; fp-transparent: 1; fp-proportional: 0" fp-title="OFF"
height="45" src="../images/button15E.gif" style="border: 0"
width="100"></a></td>
        <td style="height: 21px; width: 59px;"></td>
        <td style="height: 21px" class="auto-style2">
            <a id="smc5a" href="steve.php?washroom_light_on=1">
            <img id="img1016" alt="Washroom Light          ON" fp-
style="fp-btn: Embossed Rectangle 6; fp-font-size: 14; fp-img-hover: 0;
fp-img-press: 0; fp-preload: 0; fp-transparent: 1; fp-proportional: 0"
fp-title="Washroom Light          ON" height="45"
src="../images/button162.gif" style="border: 0"
width="272"></a>    
            <a id="smc5b" href="steve.php?washroom_light_off=1">
            <img id="img1017" alt="OFF" fp-style="fp-btn: Embossed
Rectangle 6; fp-font-size: 14; fp-img-hover: 0; fp-img-press: 0; fp-
preload: 0; fp-transparent: 1; fp-proportional: 0" fp-title="OFF"
height="45" src="../images/button164.gif" style="border: 0"
width="100"></a></td>
    </tr>
    <tr>
        <td class="auto-style2" style="width: 459px; height: 55px">
                
            <a id="smc2a" href="steve.php?bedroom_main_light_on=1">
            <img id="img1018" alt="Bedroom Main Light     ON" fp-
style="fp-btn: Embossed Rectangle 6; fp-font-size: 14; fp-img-hover: 0;
fp-img-press: 0; fp-preload: 0; fp-transparent: 1; fp-proportional: 0"
fp-title="Bedroom Main Light     ON" height="45"
src="../images/button15B.gif" style="border: 0"
width="272"></a>    
            <a id="smc2b" href="steve.php?bedroom_main_light_off=1">
            <img id="img1019" alt="OFF" fp-style="fp-btn: Embossed
Rectangle 6; fp-font-size: 14; fp-img-hover: 0; fp-img-press: 0; fp-
preload: 0; fp-transparent: 1; fp-proportional: 0" fp-title="OFF"
height="45" src="../images/button15F.gif" style="border: 0"
width="100"></a></td>
        <td style="width: 59px; height: 55px"></td>
        <td class="auto-style2" style="height: 55px">
            <a id="smc6a" href="steve.php?bathroom_light_on=1">
            <img id="img1020" alt="Bathroom Light          ON" fp-
style="fp-btn: Embossed Rectangle 6; fp-font-size: 14; fp-img-hover: 0;
```

```
fp-img-press: 0; fp-preload: 0; fp-transparent: 1; fp-proportional: 0"
fp-title="Bathroom Light           ON" height="45"
src="../images/button163.gif" style="border: 0"
width="272"></a>    
                <a id="smc6b" href="steve.php?bathroom_light_off=1">
                <img id="img1021" alt="OFF" fp-style="fp-btn: Embossed
Rectangle 6; fp-font-size: 14; fp-img-hover: 0; fp-img-press: 0; fp-
preload: 0; fp-transparent: 1; fp-proportional: 0" fp-title="OFF"
height="45" src="../images/button165.gif" style="border: 0"
width="100"></a></td>
        </tr>
        <tr>
            <td class="auto-style2" style="width: 459px; height: 8px">
                </td>
            <td style="width: 59px; height: 8px"></td>
            <td class="auto-style2" style="height: 8px">
                </td>
        </tr>
        <tr>
            <td class="auto-style2" style="width: 459px; height: 55px">
                    
                <a id="smc3a" href="steve.php?reading_light_on=1">
                <img id="img1022" alt="Reading Light           ON"
fp-style="fp-btn: Embossed Rectangle 6; fp-font-size: 14; fp-img-hover:
0; fp-img-press: 0; fp-preload: 0; fp-transparent: 1; fp-proportional: 0"
fp-title="Reading Light           ON" height="45"
src="../images/button15C.gif" style="border: 0"
width="272"></a>    
                <a id="smc3b" href="steve.php?reading_light_off=1">
                <img id="img1023" alt="OFF" fp-style="fp-btn: Embossed
Rectangle 6; fp-font-size: 14; fp-img-hover: 0; fp-img-press: 0; fp-
preload: 0; fp-transparent: 1; fp-proportional: 0" fp-title="OFF"
height="45" src="../images/button160.gif" style="border: 0"
width="100"></a></td>
            <td style="width: 59px"> </td>
            <td class="auto-style3" rowspan="2"><br>
                <a id="smc7" href="steve.php?watch_tv=1">
                <img id="img1026" alt="Watch TV" fp-style="fp-btn:
Embossed Rectangle 9; fp-font-size: 14; fp-img-hover: 0; fp-img-press: 0;
fp-preload: 0; fp-transparent: 1; fp-proportional: 0" fp-title="Watch TV"
height="80" src="../images/button166.gif" style="border: 0"
width="160"></a>        
                <a id="smc8" href="steve.php?normal_lights=1">
                <img id="img1027" alt="Normal Lights" fp-style="fp-btn:
Embossed Rectangle 4; fp-font-size: 14; fp-img-hover: 0; fp-img-press: 0;
fp-preload: 0; fp-transparent: 1; fp-proportional: 0" fp-title="Normal
Lights" height="80" src="../images/button167.gif" style="border: 0"
width="160"></a><br><br></td>
        </tr>
        <tr>
            <td class="auto-style2" style="width: 459px; height: 55px">
                    
```

```
            <a id="smc4a" href="steve.php?study_main_light_on=1">
               <img id="img1024" alt="Study Main Light        ON" fp-
style="fp-btn: Embossed Rectangle 6; fp-font-size: 14; fp-img-hover: 0;
fp-img-press: 0; fp-preload: 0; fp-transparent: 1; fp-proportional: 0"
fp-title="Study Main Light         ON" height="45"
src="../images/button15D.gif" style="border: 0"
width="272"></a>    
            <a id="smc4b" href="steve.php?study_main_light_off=1">
               <img id="img1025" alt="OFF" fp-style="fp-btn: Embossed
Rectangle 6; fp-font-size: 14; fp-img-hover: 0; fp-img-press: 0; fp-
preload: 0; fp-transparent: 1; fp-proportional: 0" fp-title="OFF"
height="45" src="../images/button161.gif" style="border: 0"
width="100"></a></td>
         <td style="width: 59px"> </td>
      </tr>
   </table>
   <p> </p>
   <p> </p>
</div>
</div>
</body>
</html>
```

File: state.php

```
<!DOCTYPE HTML>
<html>
<head>
<title>HC-State</title>

<!--
File name:
    state.php
Author:
    Steve McClure
Book:
    Designing Embedded Sytems
Description:
    This file is used by the Home Control / Security application
    to build the State Web page.
 -->

<link href="../css/reset.css" media="screen" rel="stylesheet"
type="text/css">
<link href="../css/styles.css" media="screen" rel="stylesheet"
type="text/css">

<script type="text/javascript" src="../js/calendar2.js"> </script>

<style type="text/css">
.auto-style1 {
    color: #FFFFFF;
}
.auto-style2 {
    text-align: center;
}
.auto-style3 {
    font-size: small;
}
</style>
</head>

<body onload="startTime()">
<div style="width:980px; margin: 0 auto; overflow: hidden;">
<div id="wrapper" class="auto-style2">
    <div id="navigation">
        <div id="navigation_picture">
            <img alt="images/HouseFront1.jpg" height="200"
src="../images/HouseFront1.jpg" width="900">
        </div>
        <div id="navigation_time">
            <p>Date and Time</p>
        </div>
        <div id="navigation_heading">
```

```
        <p><span class="auto-style1">Navigation</span>
        <span class="auto-style1">- State</span></p>
    </div>

    <div id="navigation_links">
      <ul>
        <li><a href="security.php">Security</a></li>
        <li><a href="master.php">Master</a></li>
        <li><a href="lounge.php">Lounge</a></li>
        <li><a href="kitchen">Kitchen</a></li>
        <li><a href="family.php">Family</a></li>
        <li><a href="steve.php">Steve</a></li>
        <li><a href="state.php">State</a></li>
        <li><a href="events.php">Events</a></li>

      </ul>
    </div>
  </div>

<div id="state_stuff">
<p class="auto-style3">    </p>

<form action="state.php" method="post">

<button name="house_code_selection" value=1>HOUSE:  A</button>
      
<button name="house_code_selection" value=2>B</button>
      
<button name="house_code_selection" value=3>C</button>
      
<button name="house_code_selection" value=4>D</button>
      
<button name="house_code_selection" value=5>E</button>
      
<button name="house_code_selection" value=6>F</button>
      
<button name="house_code_selection" value=7>G</button>
      
<button name="house_code_selection" value=8>H</button>
      
<button name="house_code_selection" value=9>I</button>
      
<button name="house_code_selection" value=10>J</button>
      
<button name="house_code_selection" value=11>K</button>
      
<button name="house_code_selection" value=12>L</button>
      
<button name="house_code_selection" value=13>M</button>
      
<button name="house_code_selection" value=14>N</button>
      
```

```
<button name="house_code_selection" value=15>O</button>
      
<button name="house_code_selection" value=16>P</button>
</form>
<p class="auto-style3"> </p>
</div>

    <div id="general_text">
     <?php

    // Connect to the MySQL Database Environment
    //========================================
     $con = mysql_connect("192.168.1.176","steve","william");    // This
works on Archimedes

      if (!$con)
      {
        die('Could not connect as: ' . mysql_error());
        echo "<br />";
      }



    // Access the 'system_control' database
    //===================================
      mysql_select_db("system_control", $con);

     ?>

    </div>
</div>

<div id="state_list">
    <?php
     $selection = $_POST["house_code_selection"];

    if ($selection == 0)
      $selection = 1;

    $result = mysql_query("SELECT * FROM house_code_states");

    while($row = mysql_fetch_array($result))
      {
        if ($selection== $row['house'])
        {
          if ($row['description'] == "No Description")
            continue;

          echo "<br />";
          echo " ";

          if ($row['timestamp'] == "No Time")
```

```
        echo "----/--/-- --:--:-- ";
    else
        echo $row['timestamp'] . " ";

    if ($row['type'] == 0)
        echo " Sensor ";
    elseif ($row['type'] == 1)
        echo " Device ";
    else
        echo " ------ ";

    switch ($row['house'])
    {
      case  1: echo "A"; break;
      case  2: echo "B"; break;
      case  3: echo "C"; break;
      case  4: echo "D"; break;
      case  5: echo "E"; break;
      case  6: echo "F"; break;
      case  7: echo "G"; break;
      case  8: echo "H"; break;
      case  9: echo "I"; break;
      case 10: echo "J"; break;
      case 11: echo "K"; break;
      case 12: echo "L"; break;
      case 13: echo "M"; break;
      case 14: echo "N"; break;
      case 15: echo "O"; break;
      case 16: echo "P"; break;
      default: echo "Invalid";
    }

    if ($row['unit'] < 10)
      echo "0" . $row['unit'];
     else
      echo $row['unit'];

    if ($row['state'] == 0)
        echo " OFF ";
    elseif ($row['state'] == 1)
    {
        echo " ON ";
          echo " ";
    }
    else
        echo " --- ";

    echo $row['description'];
  }
}
```

```php
        for ($index = 0; $index < 16; $index++)
        {
            echo "<br />";
        }

    // Close the 'home_control' database
    //=================================
     mysql_close($con);

     ?>
</div>
</div>
</body>

</html>
```

File: events.php

```
<!DOCTYPE HTML>
<html>
<head>
<meta http-equiv="refresh" content="60">
<title>HC-Events</title>

<!--
File name:
    events.php
Author:
    Steve McClure
Book:
    Designing Embedded Sytems
Description:
    This file is used by the Home Control / Security application
    to build the Events Web page.  This page is automatically
    refreshed every 60 seconds.
 -->

<link href="../css/reset.css" media="screen" rel="stylesheet"
type="text/css">
<link href="../css/styles.css" media="screen" rel="stylesheet"
type="text/css">

<script type="text/javascript" src="../js/calendar2.js"> </script>

<style type="text/css">
.auto-style1 {
    color: #FFFFFF;
}
.auto-style6 {
    font-size: small;
}

</style>
</head>

<body onload="startTime()">
<div style="width:980px; margin: 0 auto; overflow: hidden;">
<div id="wrapper">
    <div id="navigation">
        <div id="navigation_picture">
            <img alt="images/HouseFront1.jpg" height="200"
src="../images/HouseFront1.jpg" width="900">
        </div>
        <div id="navigation_time">
            <p>Date and Time</p>
        </div>
        <div id="navigation_heading">
```

```
        <p><span class="auto-style1">Navigation</span>
        <span class="auto-style1">- Events</span></p>
    </div>

    <div id="navigation_links">
      <ul>
        <li><a href="security.php">Security</a></li>
        <li><a href="master.php">Master</a></li>
        <li><a href="lounge.php">Lounge</a></li>
        <li><a href="kitchen">Kitchen</a></li>
        <li><a href="family.php">Family</a></li>
        <li><a href="steve.php">Steve</a></li>
        <li><a href="state.php">State</a></li>
        <li><a href="events.php">Events</a></li>
      </ul>
    </div>
  </div>

  <div id="main_stuff">
    <p class="auto-style6"> </p>
    <p><strong>         This
screen displays the current events list:</strong></p>
      <p class="auto-style6"> </p>
  </div>
</div>

<div id="event_list">
    <?php

    // Connect to the MySQL Database Environment
    //=========================================
    $con = mysql_connect("192.168.1.176","steve","william");    // This
works on Archimedes

    if (!$con)
    {
      die('Could not connect as: ' . mysql_error());
      echo "<br />";
    }


    // Access the 'system_control' database
    //====================================
    mysql_select_db("system_control", $con);

    $result = mysql_query("SELECT * FROM house_code_events ORDER BY
timestamp, description ASC");

    while($row = mysql_fetch_array($result))
      {

        echo "<br />";
```

```php
echo " ";
echo $row['timestamp'];
echo " ";


if ($row['type'] == 0)
   echo " Sensor ";
elseif ($row['type'] == 1)
   echo " Device ";
else
   echo " ------ ";


switch ($row['house'])
   {
      case  1: echo "A"; break;
      case  2: echo "B"; break;
      case  3: echo "C"; break;
      case  4: echo "D"; break;
      case  5: echo "E"; break;
      case  6: echo "F"; break;
      case  7: echo "G"; break;
      case  8: echo "H"; break;
      case  9: echo "I"; break;
      case 10: echo "J"; break;
      case 11: echo "K"; break;
      case 12: echo "L"; break;
      case 13: echo "M"; break;
      case 14: echo "N"; break;
      case 15: echo "O"; break;
      case 16: echo "P"; break;
      default: echo "Invalid";
   }

if ($row['unit'] < 10)
   echo "0" . $row['unit'];
 else
   echo $row['unit'];

if ($row['state'] == 0)
   echo " OFF ";
elseif ($row['state'] == 1)
   {
      echo " ON ";
       echo " ";
   }
else
   echo " --- ";

echo $row['description'];
}
```

```php
        for ($index = 0; $index < 16; $index++)
        {
            echo "<br />";
        }

    // Close the 'home_control' database
    //=================================
      mysql_close($con);

    ?>

</div>
</div>
</body>

</html>
```

File: system.php

```
<!DOCTYPE HTML>
<html>
<head>
<meta http-equiv="refresh" content="60; url=security.php">

<!--
File name:
    system.php
Author:
    Steve McClure
Book:
    Designing Embedded Sytems
Description:
    This file is used by the Home Control / Security application
    to build the System Web page.
 -->

<title>HC-System</title>
<link href="../css/reset.css" rel="stylesheet" type="text/css"
media="screen">
<link href="../css/styles.css" rel="stylesheet" type="text/css"
media="screen">

<script type="text/javascript" src="../js/calendar2.js"> </script>

<style type="text/css">
.auto-style1 {
    color:#FFFFFF;
}
.auto-style2 {
    text-align: center;
}
.auto-style3 {
    font-size: large;
}
.auto-style6 {
    font-size: small;
}
</style>

<script type="text/javascript">
<!--
function FP_preloadImgs() {//v1.0
 var d=document,a=arguments; if(!d.FP_imgs) d.FP_imgs=new Array();
 for(var i=0; i<a.length; i++) { d.FP_imgs[i]=new Image;
d.FP_imgs[i].src=a[i]; }
}
// -->
</script>
```

```
</head>

<body
onload="FP_preloadImgs(/*url*/'button22.jpg',/*url*/'button23.jpg',/*url*
/'button58.jpg',/*url*/'button59.jpg'); startTime()">
<div style="width:980px; margin: 0 auto; overflow: hidden;">
<div id="wrapper">

  <div id="navigation">
    <div id="navigation_picture">
      <img src="../images/HouseFront1.jpg" height="200" width="900" />
    </div>

    <div id="navigation_heading">
      <p><span class="auto-style1">Navigation</span> <span class="auto-
style1">- System</span></p>
    </div>

    <div id="navigation_time">
      <p>Date and Time</p>
    </div>


    <div id="navigation_links">
      <ul>
        <li><a href="security.php">Security</a></li>
        <li><a href="master.php">Master</a></li>
        <li><a href="lounge.php">Lounge</a></li>
        <li><a href="kitchen">Kitchen</a></li>
        <li><a href="family.php">Family</a></li>
        <li><a href="steve.php">Steve</a></li>
        <li><a href="state.php">State</a></li>
        <li><a href="events.php">Events</a></li>
      </ul>
    </div>
  </div>

  <?php

  // Connect to the MySQL Database Environment
  //==========================================
   $con = mysql_connect("192.168.1.176","steve","william");

   if (!$con)
   {
     die('Could not connect as: ' . mysql_error());
     echo "<br />";
   }


  // Access the 'system_control' database
  //====================================
```

```
    mysql_select_db("system_control", $con);

  // Insert data into the 'house_state' table
  //=========================================

  if ($_GET["security_off"] == 1)
  {
      mysql_query ("UPDATE house_state SET security = 0, security_delay
= 0");
    }


  if ($_GET["security_on"] == 1)
  {
      $result = mysql_query("SELECT * FROM house_state");

      $row = mysql_fetch_array($result);

      // Enter SECURITY mode ONLY if we are currently in SECURITY OFF
mode
      if ($row['security'] == 0)
      {
        // Force sleep mode off
        mysql_query ("UPDATE house_state SET sleep = 0, sleep_delay = 0,
security = 1, security_delay = 0");
      }
    }



  // Insert data into the 'house_state' table
  //=========================================

  if ($_GET["sleep_off"] == 1)
  {
      mysql_query ("UPDATE house_state SET sleep = 0, sleep_delay = 0");
    }


  if ($_GET["sleep_on"] == 1)
  {
      $result = mysql_query("SELECT * FROM house_state");

      $row = mysql_fetch_array($result);

      // Enter SLEEP mode ONLY if we are currently in SECURITY OFF mode
      if ($row['security'] == 0)
      {
        // Initiate sleep
        mysql_query ("UPDATE house_state SET sleep = 1, sleep_delay =
0");
      }
```

```
    }


    // Insert data into the 'house_code_events' table
    //================================================

    // If Garage Front Light ON button pressed
    if ($_GET["garage_front_light_on"] == 1)
    {
       mysql_query ("INSERT INTO house_code_events (house, unit, state,
    timeout) VALUES (7, 5, 1, 777)");
    }

    // If Garage Front Light OFF button pressed
    if ($_GET["garage_front_light_off"] == 1)
    {
       mysql_query ("INSERT INTO house_code_events (house, unit, state,
    timeout) VALUES (7, 5, 0, 777)");
    }


    // If Garage Back Light ON button pressed
    if ($_GET["garage_back_light_on"] == 1)
    {
       mysql_query ("INSERT INTO house_code_events (house, unit, state,
    timeout) VALUES (7, 1, 1, 777)");
    }

    // If Garage Back Light OFF button pressed
    if ($_GET["garage_back_light_off"] == 1)
    {
       mysql_query ("INSERT INTO house_code_events (house, unit, state,
    timeout) VALUES (7, 1, 0, 777)");
    }


    // If Porch Light ON button pressed
    if ($_GET["porch_light_on"] == 1)
    {
       mysql_query ("INSERT INTO house_code_events (house, unit, state,
    timeout) VALUES (7, 6, 1, 777)");
    }

    // If Porch Light OFF button pressed
    if ($_GET["porch_light_off"] == 1)
    {
       mysql_query ("INSERT INTO house_code_events (house, unit, state,
    timeout) VALUES (7, 6, 0, 777)");
    }
```

```php
    // If Varanda Light ON button pressed
    if ($_GET["varanda_light_on"] == 1)
    {
        mysql_query ("INSERT INTO house_code_events (house, unit, state,
timeout) VALUES (7, 2, 1, 777)");
    }


    // If Varanda Light OFF button pressed
    if ($_GET["varanda_light_off"] == 1)
    {
        mysql_query ("INSERT INTO house_code_events (house, unit, state,
timeout) VALUES (7, 2, 0, 777)");
    }


    // If Master Bedroom Outside Light ON button pressed
    if ($_GET["master_outside_light_on"] == 1)
    {
        mysql_query ("INSERT INTO house_code_events (house, unit, state,
timeout) VALUES (7, 4, 1, 777)");
    }

    // If Master Bedroom Outside Light OFF button pressed
    if ($_GET["master_outside_light_off"] == 1)
    {
        mysql_query ("INSERT INTO house_code_events (house, unit, state,
timeout) VALUES (7, 4, 0, 777)");
    }


    // If Dining Room Outside Light ON button pressed
    if ($_GET["dining_outside_light_on"] == 1)
    {
        mysql_query ("INSERT INTO house_code_events (house, unit, state,
timeout) VALUES (7, 3, 1, 777)");
    }

    // If Dining Room Outside Light OFF button pressed
    if ($_GET["dining_outside_light_off"] == 1)
    {
        mysql_query ("INSERT INTO house_code_events (house, unit, state,
timeout) VALUES (7, 3, 0, 777)");
    }

    ?>


  <div id="main_stuff">
    <?php
    $result = mysql_query("SELECT * FROM house_state");
```

```php
    $row = mysql_fetch_array($result);

     ?><p class="auto-style6">  </p><?php
    echo "         ";
    echo "This screen allows you to control the System Parameters:";
    echo "   ";

    if ($row['security'] == 0)
    {
      echo "SECURITY OFF - ";
    }
    else
    {
      echo "SECURITY ACTIVE - ";
    }


    if ($row['sleep'] == 0)
    {
      echo "SLEEP OFF";
     }
    else
    {
      echo "SLEEP ACTIVE";
    }

     ?><p class="auto-style6">  </p><?php

   // Close the 'home_control' database
   //==================================
    mysql_close($con);

    ?>
  </div>
</div>



<div id="key_background">
<!-- Control the buttons -->
   <p>  <span class="auto-style3"> </span></p>
   <p class="auto-style2"> <a
href="system.php?garage_front_light_on=1"><img id="img20" alt="Garage
Front Light    ON" fp-style="fp-btn: Embossed Rectangle 6; fp-font-size:
14; fp-img-hover: 0; fp-img-press: 0; fp-preload: 0; fp-transparent: 1;
fp-proportional: 0" fp-title="Garage Front Light     ON" height="45"
src="../images/button17C.gif" style="border: 0"
width="244"></a>       
   <a href="system.php?garage_front_light_off=1">
   <img id="img21" alt="OFF" fp-style="fp-btn: Embossed Rectangle 6; fp-
font-size: 14; fp-img-hover: 0; fp-img-press: 0; fp-preload: 0; fp-
transparent: 1; fp-proportional: 0" fp-title="OFF" height="45"
```

```
src="../images/button17F.gif" style="border: 0"
width="100"></a>         &nb
sp;           &nbs
p;    
    <a href="system.php?garage_back_light_on=1">
    <img id="img22" alt="Garage Back Light      ON" fp-style="fp-btn:
Embossed Rectangle 6; fp-font-size: 14; fp-img-hover: 0; fp-img-press: 0;
fp-preload: 0; fp-transparent: 1; fp-proportional: 0" fp-title="Garage
Back Light      ON" height="45" src="../images/button184.gif"
style="border: 0"
width="244"></a>       
    <a href="system.php?garage_back_light_off=1">
    <img id="img23" alt="OFF" fp-style="fp-btn: Embossed Rectangle 6; fp-
font-size: 14; fp-img-hover: 0; fp-img-press: 0; fp-preload: 0; fp-
transparent: 1; fp-proportional: 0" fp-title="OFF" height="45"
src="../images/button187.gif" style="border: 0" width="100"></a> 
</p>
    <p> </p>
    <p class="auto-style2"> <a
href="system.php?porch_light_on=1"><img id="img24" alt="Porch Light
ON" fp-style="fp-btn: Embossed Rectangle 6; fp-font-size: 14; fp-img-
hover: 0; fp-img-press: 0; fp-preload: 0; fp-transparent: 1; fp-
proportional: 0" fp-title="Porch Light           ON" height="45"
src="../images/button17D.gif" style="border: 0"
width="244"></a>       
    <a href="system.php?porch_light_off=1">
    <img id="img25" alt="OFF" fp-style="fp-btn: Embossed Rectangle 6; fp-
font-size: 14; fp-img-hover: 0; fp-img-press: 0; fp-preload: 0; fp-
transparent: 1; fp-proportional: 0" fp-title="OFF" height="45"
src="../images/button180.gif" style="border: 0"
width="100"></a>         &nb
sp;           &nbs
p;    
    <a href="system.php?varanda_light_on=1">
    <img id="img26" alt="Varanda Light          ON" fp-style="fp-btn:
Embossed Rectangle 6; fp-font-size: 14; fp-img-hover: 0; fp-img-press: 0;
fp-preload: 0; fp-transparent: 1; fp-proportional: 0" fp-title="Varanda
Light           ON" height="45" src="../images/button185.gif"
style="border: 0"
width="244"></a>       
    <a href="system.php?varanda_light_off=1">
    <img id="img27" alt="OFF" fp-style="fp-btn: Embossed Rectangle 6; fp-
font-size: 14; fp-img-hover: 0; fp-img-press: 0; fp-preload: 0; fp-
transparent: 1; fp-proportional: 0" fp-title="OFF" height="45"
src="../images/button188.gif" style="border: 0" width="100"></a> 
</p>
    <p> </p>
    <p class="auto-style2"> <a
href="system.php?master_outside_light_on=1"><img id="img28" alt="Master
Outside Light   ON" fp-style="fp-btn: Embossed Rectangle 6; fp-font-size:
14; fp-img-hover: 0; fp-img-press: 0; fp-preload: 0; fp-transparent: 1;
fp-proportional: 0" fp-title="Master Outside Light   ON" height="45"
```

```
src="../images/button17E.gif" style="border: 0"
width="244"></a>       
    <a href="system.php?master_outside_light_off=1">
    <img id="img29" alt="OFF" fp-style="fp-btn: Embossed Rectangle 6; fp-
font-size: 14; fp-img-hover: 0; fp-img-press: 0; fp-preload: 0; fp-
transparent: 1; fp-proportional: 0" fp-title="OFF" height="45"
src="../images/button181.gif" style="border: 0"
width="100"></a>         &nb
sp;           &nbs
p;    
    <a href="system.php?dining_outside_light_on=1">
    <img id="img30" alt="Dining Outside Light    ON" fp-style="fp-btn:
Embossed Rectangle 6; fp-font-size: 14; fp-img-hover: 0; fp-img-press: 0;
fp-preload: 0; fp-transparent: 1; fp-proportional: 0" fp-title="Dining
Outside Light    ON" height="45" src="../images/button186.gif"
style="border: 0"
width="244"></a>       
    <a href="system.php?dining_outside_light_off=1">
    <img id="img31" alt="OFF" fp-style="fp-btn: Embossed Rectangle 6; fp-
font-size: 14; fp-img-hover: 0; fp-img-press: 0; fp-preload: 0; fp-
transparent: 1; fp-proportional: 0" fp-title="OFF" height="45"
src="../images/button189.gif" style="border: 0" width="100"></a> 
</p>
    <p><span class="auto-style3"> </span></p>
    <p class="auto-style2">  <a
href="system.php?security_on=1"><img id="img33" alt="SECURITY    ON" fp-
style="fp-btn: Embossed Rectangle 8; fp-font-size: 14; fp-img-hover: 0;
fp-img-press: 0; fp-preload: 0; fp-transparent: 1; fp-proportional: 0"
fp-title="SECURITY    ON" height="45" src="../images/button182.gif"
style="border: 0"
width="151"></a>        
    <a href="system.php?security_off=1">
    <img id="img32" alt="SECURITY    OFF" fp-style="fp-btn: Embossed
Rectangle 2; fp-font-size: 14; fp-img-hover: 0; fp-img-press: 0; fp-
preload: 0; fp-transparent: 1; fp-proportional: 0" fp-title="SECURITY
OFF" height="45" src="../images/button183.gif" style="border: 0"
width="177"></a>      
            &
nbsp;         
    <a href="system.php?sleep_on=1">
    <img id="img34" alt="SLEEP    ON" fp-style="fp-btn: Embossed Rectangle
1; fp-font-size: 14; fp-img-hover: 0; fp-img-press: 0; fp-preload: 0; fp-
transparent: 1; fp-proportional: 0" fp-title="SLEEP    ON" height="45"
src="../images/button18A.gif" style="border: 0"
width="163"></a>       
    <a href="system.php?sleep_off=1">
    <img id="img35" alt="SLEEP    OFF" fp-style="fp-btn: Embossed Rectangle
4; fp-font-size: 14; fp-img-hover: 0; fp-img-press: 0; fp-preload: 0; fp-
transparent: 1; fp-proportional: 0" fp-title="SLEEP    OFF" height="45"
src="../images/button18B.gif" style="border: 0"
width="163"></a>   </p>
    <p> </p>
```

```
    <p> </p>
</div>
</div>

</body>
</html>
```

C Source Code

File: hc_literals.h

```
//**************************************************************************
//   Author: Stephen W. McClure
//     Date: March 2014
// Project: Designing Embedded Systems [Book]
//
//**************************************************************************
// Purpose:
//
// This program provides a home control application.
//
//**************************************************************************
//
// File Name: hc_literals.c
//
// This file includes all the common literal definitions.
//**************************************************************************

#ifndef HC_LITERALS
#define HC_LITERALS

// Serial Interface
//#define BAUDRATE B9600
#define   SERIAL_PORT_0     "/dev/ttyS0"
#define   SERIAL_PORT_1     "/dev/ttyS1"
#define   _POSIX_SOURCE     1 /* POSIX compliant source */

#define   BAUDRATE          B4800


// Literal Definitions
#define   Uint8     unsigned char
#define   Uint16    unsigned int

#define   INVALID       0
#define   VALID         1

#define   FAILURE       0
#define   SUCCESS       1

#define   X10_OFF       0
#define   X10_ON        1


// Day Name Literals
#define   SUNDAY        0
#define   MONDAY        1
#define   TUESDAY       2
#define   WEDNESDAY     3
#define   THURSDAY      4
#define   FRIDAY        5
#define   SATURDAY      6
```

```
// Calender Month Literals
#define  JANUARY      1
#define  FEBRUARY     2
#define  MARCH        3
#define  APRIL        4
#define  MAY          5
#define  JUNE         6
#define  JULY         7
#define  AUGUST       8
#define  SEPTEMBER    9
#define  OCTOBER     10
#define  NOVEMBER    11
#define  DECEMBER    12


// Days in year
#define  DAYS_IN_STANDARD_YEAR      365
#define  DAYS_IN_LEAP_YEAR          366


// Sensor/Device Literals
#define  SENSOR       0
#define  DEVICE       1

#define  OFF          0
#define  ON           1


// Main Loop Execution Periodic Sleep
#define  EXECUTION_SLEEP_MS       333   // Execute loop delay in milliseconds


#define  HS_NORMAL_MODE           0
#define  HS_NORMAL_MODE_TRIGGER   1
#define  HS_TV_MODE               2
#define  HS_TV_MODE_TRIGGER       3

#define  HS_SECURITY              0
#define  HS_SECURITY_DELAY        1
#define  HS_SLEEP                 2
#define  HS_SLEEP_DELAY           3
#define  HS_FAMILY_LIGHTS         4
#define  HS_STEVE_LIGHTS          5
#define  HS_GO_TO_BED             6
#define  HS_MASTER_WATCH_TV       7

#define  HCE_HOUSE                0
#define  HCE_UNIT                 1
#define  HCE_TYPE                 2
#define  HCE_STATE                3
#define  HCE_TIMESTAMP            4
#define  HCE_TIMEOUT              5
#define  HCE_DESCRIPTION          6
```

```
// Security Mode Literals
#define   SECURITY_MODE_INACTIVE        0
#define   SECURITY_MODE_INITIATED       1
#define   SECURITY_MODE_DELAY           2
#define   SECURITY_MODE_ACTIVE          3


// Sleep Mode Literals
#define   SLEEP_MODE_INACTIVE           0
#define   SLEEP_MODE_INITIATED          1
#define   SLEEP_MODE_DELAY              2
#define   SLEEP_MODE_ACTIVE             3


// Time Offsets
#define   ZERO_PRESENCE_TIMEOUT      ((long int) 0)
#define   MAX_PRESENCE        1800    //  30 minutes (in seconds)

#define   DELAY_EXPIRED          0
#define   ACTIVATE_NOW          0    //     0 seconds
#define   OFFSET_ZERO           0    //     0 seconds

#define   OFFSET_3SEC              3    //     3 seconds
#define   OFFSET_5SEC              5    //     5 seconds
#define   OFFSET_7SEC              7    //     7 seconds
#define   OFFSET_10SEC            10    //    10 seconds
#define   OFFSET_13SEC            13    //    13 seconds
#define   OFFSET_15SEC            15    //    15 seconds
#define   OFFSET_20SEC            20    //    20 seconds
#define   OFFSET_30SEC            30    //    30 seconds
#define   OFFSET_40SEC            40    //    40 seconds
#define   OFFSET_1MIN      ( 1 * 60)    //    60 seconds
#define   OFFSET_1MIN30SEC    (90)    //    90 seconds
#define   OFFSET_2MIN      ( 2 * 60)    //   120 seconds
#define   OFFSET_3MIN      ( 3 * 60)    //   180 seconds
#define   OFFSET_5MIN      ( 5 * 60)    //   300 seconds
#define   OFFSET_10MIN     (10 * 60)    //   600 seconds
#define   OFFSET_13MIN     (13 * 60)    //   780 seconds
#define   OFFSET_15MIN     (15 * 60)    //   900 seconds
#define   OFFSET_20MIN     (20 * 60)    //  1200 seconds
#define   OFFSET_30MIN     (30 * 60)    //  1800 seconds
#define   OFFSET_35MIN     (35 * 60)    //  1800 seconds
#define   OFFSET_40MIN     (40 * 60)    //  2400 seconds
#define   OFFSET_45MIN     (45 * 60)    //  2700 seconds
#define   OFFSET_55MIN     (55 * 60)    //  3000 seconds
#define   OFFSET_59MIN     (59 * 60)    //  3540 seconds
#define   OFFSET_60MIN     (60 * 60)    //  3600 seconds

#define   OFFSET_1HR              ( 1 * 60 * 60)
#define   OFFSET_2HRS             ( 2 * 60 * 60)
#define   OFFSET_3HRS             ( 3 * 60 * 60)
#define   OFFSET_4HRS             ( 4 * 60 * 60)
#define   OFFSET_9HRS             ( 9 * 60 * 60)
#define   OFFSET_12HRS            (12 * 60 * 60)
```

```
#define   OFFSET_21HRS            (21 * 60 * 60)
#define   OFFSET_22HRS            (22 * 60 * 60)
#define   OFFSET_23HRS            (23 * 60 * 60)
#define   OFFSET_23HRS_20MIN     ((23 * 60 * 60) + (20 * 60))
#define   OFFSET_23HRS_40MIN     ((23 * 60 * 60) + (40 * 60))
#define   OFFSET_23HRS_45MIN     ((23 * 60 * 60) + (45 * 60))
#define   OFFSET_23HRS_30MIN     ((23 * 60 * 60) + (30 * 60))
#define   OFFSET_23HRS_58MIN     ((23 * 60 * 60) + (58 * 60))
#define   OFFSET_23HRS_59MIN     ((23 * 60 * 60) + (59 * 60))
#define   OFFSET_24HRS            (24 * 60 * 60)


// EMAIL Definitions
#define   EMAIL_ACTIVE        // Comment definition to disable email feature

#define   MAX_EMAIL_HEADER_SIZE      100
#define   MAX_EMAIL_MESSAGE_SIZE     800

#define   EMAIL_SENDER_ADDRESS       "smc_security@cox.net"
#define   EMAIL_RECEIVER_ADDRESS     "smc_security@cox.net"
#define   EMAIL_CC_ADDRESS       ""

#define   SERVICE_PROVIDER_SMTP      "smtp.cox.net"

// Picture file locations
#define   STUDY_PICTURE_FILE         "/home/orion/Projects/Execs/study.jpg"

// General Definitions
#define   ACTIVE_MODE                (sleep_mode == FALSE)


#endif
```

File: hc_typedefs.h

```
//**************************************************************************
//   Author: Stephen W. McClure
//     Date: March 2014
// Project: Designing Embedded Systems [Book]
//
//**************************************************************************
// Purpose:
//
// This program provides a home control application.
//
//**************************************************************************
//
// File Name: hc_typedefs.c
//
// This file includes all the common typedef definitions.
//**************************************************************************

#ifndef HC_TYPEDEFS
#define HC_TYPEDEFS

typedef struct
{
    Uint16  hour;
    Uint16  minute;
}
TIME_OF_DAY;


typedef struct
{
    char    name[255];
    Uint16 index;
}
    HOUSE_STATE_PARAMETER;


typedef struct
{
    Uint8   house_code;
    Uint8   unit_code;
}
    X10_CODE;


typedef struct
{
    X10_CODE   x10;
    Uint8      type;
    Uint8      state;
    char       description[255];
}
    X10_DEVICE;

#endif
```

File: hc_publics.h

```
//***************************************************************************
//   Author: Stephen W. McClure
//     Date: March 2014
// Project: Designing Embedded Systems [Book]
//
//***************************************************************************
// Purpose:
//
// This program provides a home control application.
//
//
//***************************************************************************
//
// File Name: hc_publics.h
//
// This file includes all the common variable definitions.
//***************************************************************************

#ifndef HC_PUBLICS
#define HC_PUBLICS


// InterruptControl exit flag
static int exit_flag = 0;

// Device reset startup condition
Uint8   device_reset = FALSE;


// MySQL Database Variables
MYSQL   *conn1;
MYSQL   *conn2;


// Global variables
int fd; /* File descriptor for the port */


// Setup serial interface
struct termios new_options;
struct termios old_options;


// House State Table Parameter Names
HOUSE_STATE_PARAMETER  house_state_parameter [ ] =
        { { "security",            0 },
          { "security_delay",      1 },
          { "sleep",               2 },
          { "sleep_delay",         3 },
          { "family_lights",       4 },
          { "steve_lights",        5 },
          { "go_to_bed",           6 },
          { "master_watch_tv",     7 } };
```

```
// Common Devices                              X10        Sensor/
//                                             Home, Unit  Device   State
Description
X10_DEVICE  steve_bedroom_sensor       = {{ 1,     2},  SENSOR,  OFF,
"Steve Room"};
X10_DEVICE  garage_z71_sensor          = {{ 1,     3},  SENSOR,  OFF,
"Garage (Z71)"};
X10_DEVICE  mini_hallway_sensor        = {{ 1,     5},  SENSOR,  OFF,
"Mini Hallway"};
X10_DEVICE  study_sensor               = {{ 1,     7},  SENSOR,  OFF,
"Study"};
X10_DEVICE  master_bedroom_sensor      = {{ 1,     9},  SENSOR,  OFF,
"Master Bedroom"};
X10_DEVICE  familyroom_sensor          = {{ 1,    11},  SENSOR,  OFF,
"Family Room"};
X10_DEVICE  inside_front_door_sensor   = {{ 1,    13},  SENSOR,  OFF,
"Inside Front Door"};
X10_DEVICE  guest_shower_sensor        = {{ 1,    15},  SENSOR,  OFF,
"Guest Shower"};

X10_DEVICE  garage_bike_sensor         = {{ 2,     3},  SENSOR,  OFF,
"Garage (Bike)"};
X10_DEVICE  main_hallway_sensor        = {{ 2,     5},  SENSOR,  OFF,
"Main Hallway"};
X10_DEVICE  lounge_hallway_sensor      = {{ 2,     7},  SENSOR,  OFF,
"Lounge Hallway"};
X10_DEVICE  master_hallway_sensor      = {{ 2,     9},  SENSOR,  OFF,
"Master Hallway"};
X10_DEVICE  pantry_sensor              = {{ 2,    11},  SENSOR,  OFF,
"Pantry"};
X10_DEVICE  cloakroom_sensor           = {{ 2,    13},  SENSOR,  OFF,
"Cloakroom"};

X10_DEVICE  kitchen_sensor             = {{ 3,     3},  SENSOR,  OFF,
"Kitchen"};
X10_DEVICE  counter_fridge_sensor      = {{ 3,     5},  SENSOR,  OFF,
"Counter Fridge"};
X10_DEVICE  counter_cooktop_left_sensor = {{ 3,    7},  SENSOR,  OFF,
"Counter Cooktop Left"};
X10_DEVICE  counter_cooktop_right_sensor = {{ 3,  9},  SENSOR,  OFF,
"Counter Cooktop Right"};
X10_DEVICE  kitchen_nook_sensor        = {{ 3,    11},  SENSOR,  OFF,
"Kitchen Nook"};
X10_DEVICE  master_bedroom_closet_sensor = {{ 3, 13},  SENSOR,  OFF,
"Master Bedroom Closet"};
X10_DEVICE  garage_fridge_sensor       = {{ 3,    15},  SENSOR,  OFF,
"Garage (Fridge)"};

X10_DEVICE  light_sensor               = {{ 4,     1},  SENSOR,  OFF,
"Light Detector"};
X10_DEVICE  kitchen_light              = {{ 4,     3},  DEVICE,  OFF,
"Kitchen Lights"};
X10_DEVICE  kitchen_nook_light         = {{ 4,     4},  DEVICE,  OFF,
"Kitchen Nook Table light"};
X10_DEVICE  kitchen_counter_light      = {{ 4,     5},  DEVICE,  OFF,
"Kitchen Counter Lights"};
X10_DEVICE  kitchen_sink_light         = {{ 4,     6},  DEVICE,  OFF,
"Kitchen Sink Light"};
```

```
X10_DEVICE  garage_light              = {{ 4,    7},   DEVICE,   OFF,
"Garage Lights"};
X10_DEVICE  guest_bathroom_light      = {{ 4,    8},   DEVICE,   OFF,
"Guest Bathroom Light"};
X10_DEVICE  security_alarm_siren      = {{ 4,    9},   DEVICE,   OFF,
"Security Alarm Siren"};
X10_DEVICE  laundry_sensor            = {{ 4,   11},   SENSOR,   OFF,
"Laundry"};
X10_DEVICE  common_washroom_sensor    = {{ 4,   13},   SENSOR,   OFF,
"Common Washroom"};
X10_DEVICE  front_porch_sensor        = {{ 4,   15},   SENSOR,   OFF,
"Front Porch"};


X10_DEVICE  steve_bedroom_reading_light = {{ 5,  1},   DEVICE,   OFF,
"Steve Bedroom Reading Light"};
X10_DEVICE  steve_bedroom_window_light  = {{ 5,  2},   DEVICE,   OFF,
"Steve Bedroom Window Light"};
X10_DEVICE  steve_bedroom_wall_light    = {{ 5,  3},   DEVICE,   OFF,
"Steve Bedroom Wall lights"};
X10_DEVICE  steve_bedroom_ceiling_light = {{ 5,  4},   DEVICE,   OFF,
"Steve Bedroom Ceiling Lights"};
X10_DEVICE  mini_hallway_light        = {{ 5,    5},   DEVICE,   OFF,
"Mini-Hall Light"};
X10_DEVICE  main_hallway_light        = {{ 5,    6},   DEVICE,   OFF,
"Main-Hall Lights"};
X10_DEVICE  common_washroom_light     = {{ 5,    7},   DEVICE,   OFF,
"Washroom Vanity Lights"};
X10_DEVICE  common_washroom_flight    = {{ 5,    8},   DEVICE,   OFF,
"Washroom Flourescent Light"};
X10_DEVICE  common_bathroom_sensor    = {{ 5,    9},   SENSOR,   OFF,
"Common Bathroom"};
X10_DEVICE  guest_bathroom_sensor     = {{ 5,   11},   SENSOR,   OFF,
"Guest Bathroom"};
X10_DEVICE  guest_bedroom_door_sensor = {{ 5,   13},   SENSOR,   OFF,
"Guest Bedroom Door"};
X10_DEVICE  guest_bedroom_window_sensor = {{ 5, 15},   SENSOR,   OFF,
"Guest Bedroom Window"};


X10_DEVICE  garage_back_outside_light = {{ 7,    1},   DEVICE,   OFF,
"Outside Garage Back Door Light"};
X10_DEVICE  familyroom_outside_light  = {{ 7,    2},   DEVICE,   OFF,
"Outside Family Door Light"};
X10_DEVICE  diningroom_outside_light  = {{ 7,    3},   DEVICE,   OFF,
"Outside Dining Room Door Light"};
X10_DEVICE  master_bedroom_outside_light = {{ 7, 4},   DEVICE,   OFF,
"Outside Master Bedroom Door Light"};
X10_DEVICE  garage_front_outside_light = {{ 7,   5},   DEVICE,   OFF,
"Outside Garage Front Door Lights"};
X10_DEVICE  porch_outside_light       = {{ 7,    6},   DEVICE,   OFF,
"Outside Front Porch Door Light"};
X10_DEVICE  inside_entrance_light     = {{ 7,    7},   DEVICE,   OFF,
"Front Door Inside Entrance Light"};
X10_DEVICE  pantry_light              = {{ 7,    8},   DEVICE,   OFF,
"Pantry Light"};
X10_DEVICE  laundry_fan               = {{ 7,    9},   DEVICE,   OFF,
"Laundry Fan"};
```

```
X10_DEVICE  laundry_light            = {{ 7,     10},   DEVICE,  OFF,
"Laundry Light"};
X10_DEVICE  guest_bathroom_flight    = {{ 7,     11},   DEVICE,  OFF,
"Guest Bathroom Flourescent Light"};
X10_DEVICE  guest_bathroom_fan       = {{ 7,     12},   DEVICE,  OFF,
"Guest Bathroom Fan"};
X10_DEVICE  cloakroom_light          = {{ 7,     13},   DEVICE,  OFF,
"Cloakroom Light"};

X10_DEVICE  lounge_wall_light        = {{ 8,      1},   DEVICE,  OFF,
"Lounge Wall Light"};
X10_DEVICE  lounge_window_light      = {{ 8,      2},   DEVICE,  OFF,
"Lounge Window Light"};
X10_DEVICE  diningroom_table_light   = {{ 8,      3},   DEVICE,  OFF,
"Dining Room Table Light"};
X10_DEVICE  fishtank_light           = {{ 8,      4},   DEVICE,  OFF,
"Lounge Fishtank Lights"};
X10_DEVICE  study_ceiling_light      = {{ 8,      5},   DEVICE,  OFF,
"Study Ceiling Lights"};
X10_DEVICE  common_bathroom_light    = {{ 8,      8},   DEVICE,  OFF,
"Common Bathroom Light"};
X10_DEVICE  master_bathroom_sensor   = {{ 8,      9},   SENSOR,  OFF,
"Master Bathroom"};
X10_DEVICE  master_toilet_sensor     = {{ 8,     11},   SENSOR,  OFF,
"Master Toilet"};

X10_DEVICE  barking_doggy            = {{ 9,      1},   DEVICE,  OFF,
"Barking Doggy"};

X10_DEVICE  guest_main_light         = {{11,      1},   DEVICE,  OFF,
"Guest Bedroom Main Light"};
X10_DEVICE  guest_bed_light          = {{11,      2},   DEVICE,  OFF,
"Guest Bedroom Bed Light"};

X10_DEVICE  familyroom_window_light  = {{12,      1},   DEVICE,  OFF,
"Familyroom Window Light"};
X10_DEVICE  familyroom_wall_light    = {{12,      2},   DEVICE,  OFF,
"Familyroom Wall Light"};
X10_DEVICE  familyroom_track_tv_light = {{12,     3},   DEVICE,  OFF,
"Familyroom Track TV Light"};
X10_DEVICE  familyroom_track_reading_light = {{12,  4},   DEVICE,  OFF,
"Familyroom Track Reading Light"};
X10_DEVICE  familyroom_wall_unit_light = {{12,     5},   DEVICE,  OFF,
"Familyroom Wall Unit Light"};
X10_DEVICE  familyroom_wall_unit_spotlight = {{12,  6},   DEVICE,  OFF,
"Familyroom Wall Unit Spotlight"};
X10_DEVICE  familyroom_radio         = {{12,     16},   DEVICE,  OFF,
"Familyroom Radio"};

X10_DEVICE  master_bedroom_light     = {{15,      1},   DEVICE,  OFF,
"Master Bedroom Light"};
X10_DEVICE  master_bedroom_mum_light = {{15,      2},   DEVICE,  OFF,
"Master Bedroom Mum Light"};
X10_DEVICE  master_bedroom_closet_light = {{15,   3},   DEVICE,  OFF,
"Master Bedroom Closet Light"};
X10_DEVICE  master_bedroom_dad_light = {{15,      4},   DEVICE,  OFF,
"Master Bedroom Dad Light"};
```

```
X10_DEVICE  season_front_light            = {{16,    2},   DEVICE,  OFF,
"Season Front Lights"};     // Hanging icicles
X10_DEVICE  season_back_light             = {{16,    3},   DEVICE,  OFF,
"Season Back Lights"};      // Hanging icicles


// Sunrise/Sunset Times
TIME_OF_DAY  sunrise;
TIME_OF_DAY  sunset;


// Common Timeout variables
long int    sunrise_timeout  = 0;
long int    sunset_timeout   = 0;
long int    midday_timeout   = 0;
long int    midnight_timeout = 0;
long int    dusk_timeout     = 0;
long int    dawn_timeout     = 0;


// Time flags
Uint8  daytime  = FALSE;
Uint8  midday   = FALSE;
Uint8  nightime = FALSE;

Uint8  between_dawn_and_dusk  = FALSE;
Uint8  between_dusk_and_dawn  = FALSE;

Uint8  small_hours_of_the_morning = FALSE;


// Reset day/night start flags
Uint8  midnight_start = FALSE;
Uint8  day_start      = FALSE;
Uint8  dawn_start     = FALSE;
Uint8  midday_start   = FALSE;
Uint8  dusk_start     = FALSE;
Uint8  night_start    = FALSE;


// Setup home/security default states
Uint8  security_mode         = FALSE;
Uint8  security_mode_started = FALSE;
Uint8  security_mode_stopped = FALSE;

// Setup active/sleep default states
Uint8  sleep_mode  = FALSE;
Uint8  sleep_mode_pending = FALSE;

Uint8  sleep_mode_start = FALSE;


// Security flags
Uint8  steve_bedroom_sensor_security              = FALSE;
Uint8  common_washroom_sensor_security            = FALSE;
Uint8  common_bathroom_sensor_security            = FALSE;
Uint8  mini_hallway_sensor_security               = FALSE;
Uint8  study_sensor_security                      = FALSE;
```

```
Uint8    familyroom_sensor_security               = FALSE;
Uint8    inside_front_door_sensor_security        = FALSE;
Uint8    main_hallway_sensor_security             = FALSE;
Uint8    lounge_hallway_sensor_security           = FALSE;
Uint8    master_hallway_sensor_security           = FALSE;
Uint8    kitchen_sensor_security                  = FALSE;
Uint8    kitchen_nook_sensor_security             = FALSE;
Uint8    master_bedroom_sensor_security           = FALSE;
Uint8    master_bathroom_sensor_security          = FALSE;
Uint8    master_closet_sensor_security            = FALSE;
Uint8    garage_sensor_security                   = FALSE;
Uint8    master_bedroom_closet_sensor_security    = FALSE;
Uint8    pantry_sensor_security                   = FALSE;
Uint8    laundry_sensor_security                  = FALSE;
Uint8    guest_bathroom_sensor_security           = FALSE;
Uint8    guest_bedroom_door_sensor_security       = FALSE;

// Security timer
long int    front_porch_sensor_security_timer = DELAY_EXPIRED;


// Detailed time
struct timeval start, end;


// Fast Transition Events
long int   study_event;
long int   common_washroom_event;
long int   common_bathroom_event;
long int   steve_bedroom_event;


// Constants for Sunrise / Sunset time calculations
const   float zenith  = -0.01454;
const   float radians = (3.141592654 / 180.0);
const   float degrees = (180.0 / 3.141592654);

#endif
```

File: hc_common.c

```
//**********************************************************************
//   Author: Stephen W. McClure
//     Date: March 2014
// Project: Designing Embedded Systems [Book]
//
//**********************************************************************
// Purpose:
//
// This program provides a home control application.
//
//
//**********************************************************************
//
// File Name: hc_common.h
//
// This file includes all the common functions that are being used by both
// hc_main.c and hc_ti103.c modules.
//**********************************************************************

#ifndef HC_COMMON
#define HC_COMMON


//**********************************************************************
// Catch Signal Interrupts
//
// This function catches the user termination signal.
// When the main control loop detects exit_flag set to 1 it terminated.
//
//**********************************************************************

static void catch_signal_interrupts (int signo)
{
    exit_flag = 1;
}
```

```
//****************************************************************************
// Install Signal Interrupt Handler
//
// This function installs the signal interrupt handler.
//
// SIGTERM - Catches Kill
// SIGINT  - Catches ctrl-c            To shut-down in a nice manner...
//****************************************************************************

void install_signal_interrupt_handler (void)
{
    struct sigaction action;

    memset (&action, '\0', sizeof(action));
    action.sa_handler = catch_signal_interrupts;


    if (sigaction(SIGINT, &action, NULL) < 0)
    {
        perror ("sigaction");
        exit(1);
    }

}
```

```
//**************************************************************************
// Julian Day Of Year
//
// The Julian day of the year is the day number for that year.
// This is a number in the range [1..365] (depending upon leay year).
//
// As we know the old rythme...
// Thirty days has September, April, June and November, all the rest have 31
// except February which has 28 days (and 29 on leap years).
// A leap year is defined as a year that is cleanly divisible by
// (cleanly divisible means that no remainder is left behind).
//
// Now this method might not be as 'elegant' as others but I can assure you
// it is very easy to understand and check for its accuracy of operation.
//**************************************************************************

int julian_day_of_year (int day, int month, int year)
{
    int  julian_day_count = 0;

    // Add the days IN the month
    if (month > JANUARY)   julian_day_count += 31;    // Add in days for January
    if (month > FEBRUARY)  julian_day_count +=         // Add in days for February
        ((year % 4) == 0) ? 29 : 28;
    if (month > MARCH)     julian_day_count += 31;    // Add in days for March
    if (month > APRIL)     julian_day_count += 30;    // Add in days for April
    if (month > MAY)       julian_day_count += 31;    // Add in days for May
    if (month > JUNE)      julian_day_count += 30;    // Add in days for June
    if (month > JULY)      julian_day_count += 31;    // Add in days for July
    if (month > AUGUST)    julian_day_count += 31;    // Add in days for August
    if (month > SEPTEMBER) julian_day_count += 30;    // Add in days for September
    if (month > OCTOBER)   julian_day_count += 31;    // Add in days for October
    if (month > NOVEMBER)  julian_day_count += 30;    // Add in days for November

    // Add the remaining days OF the month
    julian_day_count += day;                          // Add in days for current
month

    // Return the Julian day for this year
    return (julian_day_count);
}
```

```
//**************************************************************************
// Determine Julian Date
//
// The Julian day of the year is the day number for that year.
//
// As we know the old rythme...
// Thirty days has September, April, June and November, all the rest have 31
// except February which has 28 days (and 29 on leap years).
// A leap year is defined as a year that is cleanly divisible by 4
// (cleanly divisible means that no remainder is left behind).
//
// Now this method might not be as 'elegant' as others but I can assure you
// it is very easy to understand and check for its accuracy of operation.
// Since this calculation will be performed infrequently it does not require
// to be very fast and efficient (and inherently difficult to understand)...
//**************************************************************************

double   determine_julian_date (int day, int month,  int year,
                                int hour, int minute, int second)
{
    int year_index;
    double julian_date = 2451544.0;  // For the date Jan 1st 2000 at time 00:00:00


    // Add in days up till year before this one
    for (year_index = 2000; year_index < year; year_index++)
    {
        // Was this a leap year?
        if ((year_index % 4) == 0)
        {
            // Yes - Add in julian days for a leap year
            julian_date += DAYS_IN_LEAP_YEAR;
        }
        else
        {
            // No - Add in julian days for a standard year
            julian_date += DAYS_IN_STANDARD_YEAR;
        }
    }

    // Add in the days up till the current month
    julian_date += julian_day_of_year (day, month, year);

    // Now add in the offset for the hours, minutes and seconds
    julian_date += ((hour - 12.0) / 24.0) + (minute / 1440.0) + (second /
86400.0);

    // Return the Julian day for this year
    return (julian_date);
}
```

```
//**************************************************************************
// Determine Sunrise Sunset Times
//
// This function computes the sunrise and sunset times for today at the
// specified location.
//
//**************************************************************************
double   determine_sunrise_sunset_times (void)
{
    int day, month, year;
    int hour, minute, second;
    int daylight_savings_time_in_effect;
    int n, elevation;
    int set_hour, set_minute, set_second;
    int rise_hour, rise_minute, rise_second;
    double  Jstar;
    double  M, C, lambda, Jtransit;
    double  delta, elevation_adjustment, OmegaZero;
    double  set, rise, Jset, Jrise;
    double  set2, rise2;
    double  latitude, longitude;
    double  Jdate, n_star;
    double  remainder;
    double  julian_date_fraction;

    time_t  td;
    struct tm   *dcp;


#if 0  // Test example
        // Enter your location and elevation
        latitude  = 33.0417111;        // North is positive
        longitude = 116.868082;        // West  is positive
        elevation = 1440;      // Elevation in feet
#endif

        // Enter your location and elevation (from GPS)
        latitude  = 33.02415;          // North is positive
        longitude = 116.8708;          // West  is positive
        elevation = 1426;      // Elevation in feet


    // Get the system time and date (and DST (Daylight Savings Time))
    time(&td);
    dcp = localtime(&td);

    // Determine current day, month, year, etc...
    day     = dcp->tm_mday;
    month   = dcp->tm_mon  + 1;
    year    = dcp->tm_year + 1900;
    hour    = dcp->tm_hour;
    minute = dcp->tm_min;
    second = dcp->tm_sec;
    daylight_savings_time_in_effect = dcp->tm_isdst;


    // Determine the Julian Date
```

```
    Jdate = determine_julian_date (day, month, year, hour, minute, second);

    // Calculate Julian Cycle (2451545.0009 = Saturday 1st Jan 2000 at 12:01:18)
    n_star = Jdate - 2451545.0009 - (longitude / 360.0);
    n = (int)(n_star + 0.5);

    // Approximate solar noon
    Jstar = 2451545.0009 + (longitude / 360.0) + n;

    // Solar mean anomaly
    M = fmod((357.5291 + 0.98560028 * (Jstar - 2451545)), 360.0);

    // Equation of center
    C = (1.9148 * sin(M * radians)) + (0.0200 * sin (2 * M * radians)) + (0.0003 *
sin (3 * M * radians));

    // Ecliptic Longitude
    lambda = fmod ((M + 102.9372 + C + 180), 360.0);

    // Solar transit
    Jtransit = Jstar + (0.0053 * sin (M * radians)) - (0.0069 * sin (2 * lambda *
radians));

    // Declination of the sun
    delta = asin (sin (lambda * radians) * sin(23.45 * radians)) * degrees;

    // Hour angle
    elevation_adjustment = (-1.15 * sqrt(elevation)) / 60.0;

    OmegaZero = acos ((sin ((-0.83 + elevation_adjustment) * radians) - (sin
(latitude * radians) * sin (delta * radians))) / (cos (latitude * radians) * cos
(delta * radians))) * degrees;

    // Calculate Julian date for Sunset
    Jset = 2451545.0009 + ((OmegaZero + longitude) / 360.0) + n + (0.0053 * sin (M
* radians)) - (0.0069 * sin (2 * lambda * radians));

    // Calculate Julian date for Sunrise
    Jrise = Jtransit - (Jset - Jtransit);

    // Convert the Sunrise Julian Date to hours, minutes and seconds
    // First determine the fractional part of the julian date
    julian_date_fraction = Jrise - (int)(Jrise);

    rise_hour   = (julian_date_fraction * 24);
    remainder   = (julian_date_fraction * 24) - rise_hour;
    rise_minute = (remainder * 60);
    remainder   = (remainder * 60) - rise_minute;
    rise_second = (remainder * 60);

    if (julian_date_fraction < 0.5)
        rise_hour += 12;
    else
        rise_hour -= 12;


    // Convert the Sunset Juliam Date to hours, minutes and seconds
    // First determine the fractional part of the julian date
```

```
julian_date_fraction = Jset - (int)(Jset);

set_hour   = (julian_date_fraction * 24);
remainder  = (julian_date_fraction * 24) - set_hour;
set_minute = (remainder * 60);
remainder  = (remainder * 60) - set_minute;
set_second = (remainder * 60);

if (julian_date_fraction < 0.5)
    set_hour += 12;
else
    set_hour -= 12;


// Information regarding the Daylight Savings Rules
// http://www.nist.gov/pml/div688/dst.cfm
//
// Daylight Saving Time in the United States
// begins at 2:00 a.m. on the second Sunday of March and
// ends at 2:00 a.m. on the first Sunday of November
//
// Note that this is taken care of by the Operating System
// so all the user need do is to determine if the DST
// parameter is set and add in another hour.

// Also adjust for longitude
//   rise_hour = fmod ((rise_hour += 16), 24);
//   set_hour  = fmod ((set_hour  += 16), 24);

// Convert UT time into local San Diego, California USA time.
// San Diego, California, USA is 8 hours behind UK time.
// So add on 16 hours and use fmod to take care of 24hrs clock.
// (If it is Daylight Savings Time then add 17 hours.

if (daylight_savings_time_in_effect == 1)
{
    rise_hour = fmod ((rise_hour += 17), 24);   // DST (Add one hour)
    set_hour  = fmod ((set_hour  += 17), 24);   // DST (Add one hour)
}
else
{
    rise_hour = fmod ((rise_hour += 16), 24);   // DST is NOT in effect
    set_hour  = fmod ((set_hour  += 16), 24);   // DST is NOT in effect
}

// Setup final sunrise time
sunrise.hour   = rise_hour;
sunrise.minute = rise_minute + EASTERN_ESCARPMENT_ADJUSTMENT;
sunrise.second = rise_second;

// Did the minutes proceed into the next hour?
if (sunrise.minute > 59)
{
    // Yes - Adjust the minutes and increment the hour
    sunrise.minute -= 60;
    sunrise.hour++;
}
```

```
    // Setup final sunset time
    sunset.hour   = set_hour;
    sunset.minute = set_minute - WESTERN_ESCARPMENT_ADJUSTMENT;
    sunset.second = set_second;

    // Did the minutes step into the previous hour?
    if (sunset.minute < 0)
    {
        // Yes - Adjust the minutes and decrement the hour
        sunset,minute += 60;
        sunset.hour--;
    }


    // Print out computed and expected values
//  printf ("Computed values are: Sunrise = %02d:%02d     and   Sunset =
%02d:%02d\n",
//          sunrise.hour, sunrise.minute, sunset.hour, sunset.minute);

}
```

```
//****************************************************************************
// Determine System Timestamp
//
// This function determines the current system timestamp.
//
//****************************************************************************

void  determine_system_timestamp (char *  timestamp_buffer)
{

    time_t  td;
    struct tm   *dcp;


    // Get system date and time
    time(&td);
    dcp = localtime(&td);

    // Create time stamp
    sprintf (timestamp_buffer, "%04d/%02d/%02d %02d:%02d:%02d",
            dcp->tm_year + 1900,
            dcp->tm_mon + 1,
            dcp->tm_mday,
            dcp->tm_hour,
            dcp->tm_min,
            dcp->tm_sec);

}
```

```
//****************************************************************************
// Print Log
//
// This function prints the timestamped log message.
//
//****************************************************************************

void  print_log (char *  message)
{
    char    timestamp[255];


    // Is a blank line to be printed?
    if (strlen(message) == 0x00)
    {
        // Yes - Print a blank line
        printf ("\n");
        return;
    }


    // Determine current timestamp
    determine_system_timestamp (timestamp);

    // Display timestamped log message
    printf ("%s %s\n", timestamp, message);
}
```

```
//***********************************************************************
// msleep
//
// This function sleeps for the specified number of milliseconds.
//
//***********************************************************************

int msleep (unsigned long    milliseconds)
{
    struct timespec req={0},rem={0};
    time_t seconds;

    seconds = (int)(milliseconds / 1000);
    milliseconds = milliseconds - (seconds * 1000);
    req.tv_sec  = seconds;
    req.tv_nsec = milliseconds * 1000000L;

    // Sleep for nanoseconds
    nanosleep (&req, &rem);
    return 1;
}
```

```
//**************************************************************************
// Get Raw Time
//
// This function gets the elapsed time (in seconds) since start of 1970.
//
//**************************************************************************

ulonglong  get_raw_time (void)
{
    struct tm   *tm_ptr;
    time_t  raw_time;

    raw_time = time ((time_t *) 0x0);
    return (raw_time);

}
```

```
//****************************************************************************
// Determine Days In Month
//
// This function determines the number of days in the month based on the
// specified date.
//
//****************************************************************************
Uint16  determine_days_in_month (Uint16 day, Uint16 month, Uint16 year)
{
    Uint8    leap_year;
    Uint8    days_in_month = 0;


    // Determine if this is a leap year
    leap_year = (((year % 4) == 0) && ((year % 100) == 0) && ((year % 400) != 0));

    // Determine days in month
    switch (month)
    {
    case JANUARY   : days_in_month = 31;  break;
    case FEBRUARY  : if (leap_year)
                          days_in_month = 29;
                      else
                          days_in_month = 28;
                      break;
    case MARCH     : days_in_month = 31;  break;
    case APRIL     : days_in_month = 30;  break;
    case MAY       : days_in_month = 31;  break;
    case JUNE      : days_in_month = 30;  break;
    case JULY      : days_in_month = 31;  break;
    case AUGUST    : days_in_month = 31;  break;
    case SEPTEMBER : days_in_month = 30;  break;
    case OCTOBER   : days_in_month = 31;  break;
    case NOVEMBER  : days_in_month = 30;  break;
    case DECEMBER  : days_in_month = 31;  break;
    default:
        print_log ("determine_days_in_month() failed - Invalid month!");
        break;
    }

    // Return days in the month
    return (days_in_month);
}
```

```
//***************************************************************************
// Determine Next Date
//
// This function increments the date by one day.
//
//***************************************************************************
void  determine_next_date (Uint16 *  day, Uint16 *  month, Uint16 *  year)
{
    Uint16  number_days_in_this_month;


    // Determine days in the current month date
    number_days_in_this_month = determine_days_in_month (*day, *month, *year);


    // Determine next date
    *day = *day + 1;

    // Have we exceeded the number of days in this month
    if (*day > number_days_in_this_month)
    {
        // Yes - Reset the day count to 1 and jump to next month
        *day = 1;
        *month = *month + 1;

        // Have we passed december?
        if (*month > DECEMBER)
        {
            // Yes - Reset the month count to January and jump to next year
            *month = JANUARY;
            *year = *year + 1;
        }
    }


}
```

```
//**************************************************************************
// Determine Standard Time
//
// This function determines the standard time in hours:minutes:seconds
// for the current time (seconds since midnight).
//
//**************************************************************************
void  determine_standard_time (long int  time_in_seconds, char *  buffer)
{
    Uint16      hours;
    Uint16      minutes;
    Uint16      seconds;
    Uint16      remaining_seconds;
    Uint16      seconds_since_midnight;
    Uint16      day, month, year, hour, minute, second;;
    long int    current_time;
    long int    midnight_offset;


    // Date and time variables
    time_t  td;
    struct tm    *dcp;


    // Get system date and time
    time(&td);
    dcp = localtime(&td);

    // Initialize calandar variables
    day     = dcp->tm_mday;
    month   = dcp->tm_mon + 1;
    year    = dcp->tm_year + 1900;
    hour    = dcp->tm_hour;
    minute = dcp->tm_min;
    second = dcp->tm_sec;


    // Get current time in seconds
    current_time = get_raw_time();

    // Determine current time offset from midnight
    midnight_offset = (hour * 3600) + (minute * 60) + second;

    // Current time for today at first midnight
    midnight_timeout = current_time - midnight_offset;

    // Determine seconds since midnight
    seconds_since_midnight = time_in_seconds - midnight_timeout;

    // Convert to hours:minutes:seconds
    hours = (seconds_since_midnight / 3600);
    remaining_seconds = seconds_since_midnight - (hours * 3600);

    minutes = (remaining_seconds / 60);
    seconds = remaining_seconds - (minutes * 60);
```

```
    // Does the event occur today?
    if (hours < 24)
    {
        // Yes - Use today's date
        sprintf (buffer, "%04d/%02d/%02d %02d:%02d:%02d", year, month, day, hours,
minutes, seconds);
    }
    else
    {
        // Determine tomorrow's date
        hours -= 24;
        determine_next_date (&day, &month, &year);

        sprintf (buffer, "%04d/%02d/%02d %02d:%02d:%02d", year, month, day, hours,
minutes, seconds);
    }

}
```

```
//***********************************************************************
// Determine Periodic Transition Times
//
// This function determines the raw seconds count for the sunrise/sunset
// for the current day.  It also determines the dawn/dusk and day/night periods.
//
//***********************************************************************
void  determine_periodic_transition_times (void)
{
    long int    current_time;
    long int    midnight_offset;
    char        time_buffer[255];
    char        message[255];
    Uint16      day, month, year, hour, minute, second;


    // Date and time variables
    time_t   td;
    struct tm    *dcp;


    // Get system date and time
    time(&td);
    dcp = localtime(&td);

    // Print out the current time
    sprintf (time_buffer, "%04d/%02d/%02d %02d:%02d:%02d",
        dcp->tm_year + 1900,
        dcp->tm_mon + 1,
        dcp->tm_mday,
        dcp->tm_hour,
        dcp->tm_min,
        dcp->tm_sec);

    // Initialize calandar variables
    day     = dcp->tm_mday;
    month   = dcp->tm_mon + 1;
    year    = dcp->tm_year + 1900;
    hour    = dcp->tm_hour;
    minute = dcp->tm_min;
    second = dcp->tm_sec;


    // Get current time in seconds
    current_time = get_raw_time();

    // Determine current time offset from midnight
    midnight_offset = (hour * 3600) + (minute * 60) + second;

    // Current time for today at first midnight
    midnight_timeout = current_time - midnight_offset;

    // Current time for midday
    midday_timeout = midnight_timeout + OFFSET_12HRS;

    // Is this the next day?
    // The next day is defined when the next midnight timeout
```

```
// event is calculated to be AFTER (ie. greater than)
// the sunrise timeout event of the previous day.
if (midnight_timeout > sunrise_timeout)
{
    // Yes - Compute sunrise, sunset, dawn and dusk timeout event times
    //       for this specific day of the month.
    determine_sunrise_sunset_times();

    sunrise_timeout =  midnight_timeout +
            (sunrise.hour   * 3600) +
            (sunrise.minute * 60);

    sunset_timeout  =  midnight_timeout +
            (sunset.hour    * 3600) +
            (sunset.minute * 60);

    dawn_timeout = sunrise_timeout + OFFSET_20MIN;    // ie. Just after sunrise
    dusk_timeout = sunset_timeout  - OFFSET_15MIN;    // ie. Just before sunset


    // Print out these event times
    determine_standard_time (sunrise_timeout, time_buffer);

    print_log ("");
    sprintf (message, "Sunrise at %s", time_buffer);
    print_log (message);

    determine_standard_time (dawn_timeout, time_buffer);
    sprintf (message, "   Dawn at %s", time_buffer);
    print_log (message);

    determine_standard_time (dusk_timeout, time_buffer);
    sprintf (message, "   Dusk at %s", time_buffer);
    print_log (message);

    determine_standard_time (sunset_timeout, time_buffer);
    sprintf (message, " Sunset at %s", time_buffer);
    print_log (message);
    print_log ("");

    // Indicate that the midnight event has started.
    // This is used to configure specific event times
    // that are only setup once each day at midnight.
    midnight_start = TRUE;
}



// Is it daytime?
if ((sunrise_timeout < current_time) && (current_time < sunset_timeout))
{
    // Yes - Did the day just start?
    if (daytime == FALSE)
    {
        // Yes - Set flag for processing specific day start events
        day_start = TRUE;
    }
```

```
    // It is day time
    daytime  = TRUE;
    nightime = FALSE;
}
else
{
    // It is night time - Did the night just start?
    if (nightime == FALSE)
    {
        // Yes - Set flag for processing specific night start events
        night_start = TRUE;
    }

    // It is night time
    daytime  = FALSE;
    nightime = TRUE;
}


// Is it after the dawn but before the dusk)?
if ((dawn_timeout < current_time) && (current_time < dusk_timeout))
{
    // Has the dawn just started?
    if (between_dawn_and_dusk == FALSE)
    {
        // Yes - Set flag for processing specific dawn start events
        dawn_start = TRUE;
    }

    // We are in the [Dawn..Dusk] range
    between_dawn_and_dusk = TRUE;
    between_dusk_and_dawn = FALSE;
}
else
{
    // Has the dusk just started?
    if (between_dusk_and_dawn == FALSE)
    {
        // Yes - Set flag for processing specific dawn start events
        dusk_start = TRUE;
    }

    // We are in the [Dusk..Dawn] range
    between_dawn_and_dusk = FALSE;
    between_dusk_and_dawn = TRUE;
}


// Have we passed midday?
if ((midday_timeout <= current_time) && (current_time < sunset_timeout))
{
    // Yes - Did it just start?
    if (midday == FALSE)
    {
        // Yes - Set flag for processing specific midday events
        midday_start = TRUE;
    }
```

```
        midday = TRUE;
    }
    else
    {
        // No - We have not reached midday
        midday = FALSE;
    }


    // Are we in the wee small hours of the morning?
    if ((midnight_timeout <= current_time) && (current_time < sunrise_timeout))
    {
        // Yes we are...
        small_hours_of_the_morning = TRUE;
    }
    else
    {
        // No we are not...
        small_hours_of_the_morning = FALSE;
    }

}
```

```
//*************************************************************************
// Activate Device
//
// This function places a device command into the house_code_events table.
// The retries are to ensure device operation in locations where there is a
// large amount of electrical noise on the mains line (eg. generated by
// CFL lamps).
//
//*************************************************************************

void  activate_device (X10_DEVICE     device,
                       Uint8          device_state,
                       long int       timeout)
{
    Uint8        index;
    Uint8        number_of_tries;
    long int     time_offset = 0;
    char         buffer[255];
    char         time_buffer[255];


    // Are we setting this device?
    if (device_state == ON)
    {
        // Yes - Perform more retries to ensure device is on
        //       Adjust to suit the electrical environment...

        number_of_tries = 1; // Increase for noisy environments;
    }
    else
    {
        // No - Perform more retries to ensure device is off
        //       Adjust to suit the electrical environment...
        number_of_tries = 1; // Increase for noisy environments;
    }


    // Configure device
    device.state = device_state;


    // Issue the device command with retries
    for (index = 0; index < number_of_tries; index++)
    {
        // Determine time in HH:MM:SS format
        determine_standard_time ((timeout + time_offset), time_buffer);

        // Build the event command and enter into the database table
        sprintf (buffer, "INSERT INTO house_code_events VALUES(%d, %d, %d, %d,
'%s', %ld, '%s')",
                 device.x10.house_code,
                 device.x10.unit_code,
                 device.type,
                 device.state,
                 time_buffer,
                 (timeout + time_offset),
                 device.description);
```

160

```
//       printf ("%s\n", buffer);
mysql_query(conn1, buffer);

// Is the device being switched ON
if (device_state == ON)
{
    // Yes - Increment time offset (sequence = 0, 1, 3, 6, 10, 15, etc.)
    //        Insert the commands in close proximity
    //            time_offset += index + 1;
    time_offset += 2;
}
else
{
    // No - Increment time offset (sequence = 0, 7, 14, 21, etc.)
    //        Insert the commands further paced apart to allow other
    //        commands the chance to execute (ie. speeds up process).
    time_offset += 7;
}
}
}
```

```
//***************************************************************************
// get_house_state_security
//
// This function access the house_state database table and returns the security
// parameter that lets us know if the SECURITY button has been pressed.
//
//***************************************************************************

int  get_house_state_security (int *  new_house_state_security)
{
    char            message [255];
    int             house_state_security;
    MYSQL_RES       *mysqlResult;
    MYSQL_ROW        mysqlRow;
    MYSQL_FIELD     *mysqlFields;
    my_ulonglong     numRows;
    unsigned int     numFields;


    // Determine if we are engaging security mode (ask for only the security
parameter)
    if (mysql_query(conn1, "SELECT security FROM house_state"))
    {
        // Error detected - Print error message
        sprintf (message, "Error_G0 %u: %s\n", mysql_errno(conn1),
mysql_error(conn1));
        print_log (message);
        return (FAILURE);
    }
    else
    {
        // Determine the number of event entries
        mysqlResult = mysql_store_result (conn1);

        // Are there any entries?
        if (mysqlResult)
        {
            // Yes - Get the number of database table rows and fields
            numRows  = mysql_num_rows (mysqlResult);
            numFields = mysql_num_fields (mysqlResult);

            // Print these out when testing
            // printf ("Number of Rows = %lld,  Number of Fields = %d \n", numRows,
numFields);
        }
        else
        {
            // Print these out when testing
            print_log ("Result set is empty\n");
            return (FAILURE);
        }


        // Get the first row in the table
        mysqlRow = mysql_fetch_row(mysqlResult);

        // Does it exist?
        if (mysqlRow)
```

```
        {
            // Yes - Get the house state security parameter from the MySQL table
            house_state_security = (int) (atoi (mysqlRow[0]));
        }

        // Was a MySQL result pointer returned?
        if (mysqlResult)
        {
            // Yes - Free the pointer
            mysql_free_result(mysqlResult);
            mysqlResult = NULL;
        }
    }

    // Return parameter
    *new_house_state_security = house_state_security;
    return (SUCCESS);
}
```

```
//***********************************************************************
// get_house_state_sleep
//
// This function access the house_state database table and returns the sleep
// parameter that lets us know if the SLEEP button has been pressed.
//
//***********************************************************************

int  get_house_state_sleep (int *  new_house_state_sleep)
{
    char            message [255];
    int             house_state_sleep;
    MYSQL_RES       *mysqlResult;
    MYSQL_ROW       mysqlRow;
    MYSQL_FIELD     *mysqlFields;
    my_ulonglong    numRows;
    unsigned int    numFields;


    // Determine if we are engaging sleep mode (ask for only the security
parameter)
    if (mysql_query(conn1, "SELECT sleep FROM house_state"))
    {
        // Error detected - Print error message
        sprintf (message, "Error_GO %u: %s", mysql_errno(conn1),
mysql_error(conn1));
        print_log (message);
        return (FAILURE);
    }
    else
    {
        // Determine the number of event entries
        mysqlResult = mysql_store_result (conn1);

        // Are there any entries?
        if (mysqlResult)
        {
            // Yes - Get the number of database table rows and fields
            numRows  = mysql_num_rows (mysqlResult);
            numFields = mysql_num_fields (mysqlResult);

            // Print these out when testing
            // printf ("Number of Rows = %lld,  Number of Fields = %d \n", numRows,
numFields);
        }
        else
        {
            // Print these out when testing
            print_log ("Result set is empty");
            return (FAILURE);
        }


        // Get the first row in the table
        mysqlRow = mysql_fetch_row (mysqlResult);

        // Does it exist?
        if (mysqlRow)
```

```
        {
            // Yes - Get the house state sleep parameter from the MySQL table
            house_state_sleep = (int) (atoi (mysqlRow[0]));
        }

        // Was a MySQL result pointer returned?
        if (mysqlResult)
        {
            // Yes - Free the pointer
            mysql_free_result(mysqlResult);
            mysqlResult = NULL;
        }
    }

    // Return parameter
    *new_house_state_sleep = house_state_sleep;
    return (SUCCESS);
}
```

```
//***********************************************************************
// get_house_state_watch_tv
//
// This function access the house_state database table and returns the watch tv
// parameter that lets us know if the 'Watch TV' button has been pressed.
//
//***********************************************************************

int  get_house_state_watch_tv (int *  new_house_state_watch_tv)
{
    char            message [255];
    int             house_state_watch_tv;
    MYSQL_RES       *mysqlResult;
    MYSQL_ROW        mysqlRow;
    MYSQL_FIELD     *mysqlFields;
    my_ulonglong     numRows;
    unsigned int     numFields;


    // Determine if the watch tv parameter has been pressed
    if (mysql_query(conn1, "SELECT watch_tv FROM house_state"))
    {
        // Error detected - Print error message
        sprintf (message, "Error_G0 %u: %s", mysql_errno(conn1),
mysql_error(conn1));
        print_log (message);
        return (FAILURE);
    }
    else
    {
        // Determine the number of event entries
        mysqlResult = mysql_store_result (conn1);

        // Are there any entries?
        if (mysqlResult)
        {
            // Yes - Get the number of database table rows and fields
            numRows   = mysql_num_rows (mysqlResult);
            numFields = mysql_num_fields (mysqlResult);

            // Print these out when testing
            // printf ("Number of Rows = %lld,  Number of Fields = %d \n", numRows,
numFields);
        }
        else
        {
            // Print these out when testing
            print_log ("Result set is empty");
            return (FAILURE);
        }


        // Get the first row in the table
        mysqlRow = mysql_fetch_row (mysqlResult);

        // Does it exist?
        if (mysqlRow)
        {
```

```
            // Yes - Get the house state 'watch_tv' parameter from the MySQL table
            house_state_watch_tv = (int) (atoi (mysqlRow[0]));
        }

        // Was a MySQL result pointer returned?
        if (mysqlResult)
        {
            // Yes - Free the pointer
            mysql_free_result(mysqlResult);
            mysqlResult = NULL;
        }
    }

    // Return parameter
    *new_house_state_watch_tv = house_state_watch_tv;
    return (SUCCESS);
}
```

```
//************************************************************************
// get_house_state_parameter
//
// This function access the house_state database table for a specific parameter.
//
//************************************************************************

int  get_house_state_parameter (int  hs_index, int *  new_parameter_value)
{
    int             parameter_value;
    MYSQL_RES       *mysqlResult;
    MYSQL_ROW       mysqlRow;
    MYSQL_FIELD     *mysqlFields;
    my_ulonglong    numRows;
    unsigned int    numFields;
    char            buffer[255];
    char            message [255];


    // Determine if the watch tv parameter has been pressed
    sprintf (buffer, "SELECT %s FROM house_state",
house_state_parameter[hs_index].name);

    if (mysql_query(conn1, buffer))
    {
        // Error detected - Print error message
        sprintf (message, "Error_GA0 %u: %s", mysql_errno(conn1),
mysql_error(conn1));
        print_log (message);
        return (FAILURE);
    }
    else
    {
        // Determine the number of event entries
        mysqlResult = mysql_store_result (conn1);

        // Are there any entries?
        if (mysqlResult)
        {
            // Yes - Get the number of database table rows and fields
            numRows   = mysql_num_rows (mysqlResult);
            numFields = mysql_num_fields (mysqlResult);

            // Print these out when testing
            // printf ("Number of Rows = %lld,  Number of Fields = %d \n", numRows,
numFields);
        }
        else
        {
            // Print these out when testing
            print_log ("Result set is empty");
            return (FAILURE);
        }


        // Get the first row in the table
        mysqlRow = mysql_fetch_row (mysqlResult);
```

```
        // Does it exist?
        if (mysqlRow)
        {
            // Yes - Get the parameter value from the MySQL table
            parameter_value = (int) (atoi (mysqlRow[0]));          // We
have only requested one parameter
            // printf ("Parameter = %d\n", parameter_value);
        }

        // Was a MySQL result pointer returned?
        if (mysqlResult)
        {
            // Yes - Free the pointer
            mysql_free_result(mysqlResult);
            mysqlResult = NULL;
        }
    }

    //  Return the parameter value);
    *new_parameter_value = parameter_value;
    return (SUCCESS);
}
```

```
//********************************************************************************
// get_house_state_go_to_bed
//
// This function access the house_state database table and returns the go to bed
// parameter that lets us know if the 'Go To Bed' button has been pressed.
//
//********************************************************************************

int  get_house_state_go_to_bed (int *  new_house_state_go_to_bed)
{
    int            house_state_go_to_bed;
    MYSQL_RES      *mysqlResult;
    MYSQL_ROW       mysqlRow;
    MYSQL_FIELD    *mysqlFields;
    my_ulonglong    numRows;
    unsigned int    numFields;
    char            message [255];


    // Determine if the 'go_to_bed' parameter has been pressed
    if (mysql_query(conn1, "SELECT go_to_bed FROM house_state"))
    {
        // Error detected - Print error message
        sprintf (message, "Error_GO %u: %s", mysql_errno(conn1),
mysql_error(conn1));
        print_log (message);
        return (FAILURE);
    }
    else
    {
        // Determine the number of event entries
        mysqlResult = mysql_store_result (conn1);

        // Are there any entries?
        if (mysqlResult)
        {
            // Yes - Get the number of database table rows and fields
            numRows   = mysql_num_rows (mysqlResult);
            numFields = mysql_num_fields (mysqlResult);

            // Print these out when testing
            // printf ("Number of Rows = %lld,  Number of Fields = %d \n", numRows,
numFields);
        }
        else
        {
            // Print these out when testing
            print_log ("Result set is empty");
            return (FAILURE);
        }


        // Get the first row in the table
        mysqlRow = mysql_fetch_row (mysqlResult);

        // Does it exist?
        if (mysqlRow)
        {
```

```
            // Yes - Get the house state 'go_to_bed' parameter from the MySQL table
            house_state_go_to_bed = (int) (atoi (mysqlRow[0]));
        }

        // Was a MySQL result pointer returned?
        if (mysqlResult)
        {
            // Yes - Free the pointer
            mysql_free_result(mysqlResult);
            mysqlResult = NULL;
        }
    }

    // Return parameter
    *new_house_state_go_to_bed = house_state_go_to_bed;
    return (SUCCESS);
}




//***************************************************************************
// Delete House Code Events
//
// This function deletes all the house code events for a specific device.
// This includes both ON and OFF events.
//
//***************************************************************************

void  delete_house_code_events (X10_DEVICE  device)
{
    char    buffer[255];


    sprintf (buffer, "DELETE FROM house_code_events WHERE house=%d AND unit=%d",
            device.x10.house_code,
            device.x10.unit_code);

    //  printf ("%s \n", buffer);
    mysql_query(conn1, buffer);
}
```

```
//****************************************************************************
// Delete House Code OFF Events
//
// This function deletes all the house code OFF events for a specific device.
//
//****************************************************************************

void  delete_house_code_off_events (X10_DEVICE  device)
{
    char    buffer[255];


    sprintf (buffer, "DELETE FROM house_code_events WHERE house=%d AND unit=%d AND
state=0",
             device.x10.house_code,
             device.x10.unit_code);

    //  printf ("%s \n", buffer);
    mysql_query(conn1, buffer);
}




//****************************************************************************
// Delete House Code ON Events
//
// This function deletes all the house code ON events for a specific device.
//
//****************************************************************************

void  delete_house_code_on_events (X10_DEVICE  device)
{
    char    buffer[255];


    sprintf (buffer, "DELETE FROM house_code_events WHERE house=%d AND unit=%d AND
state=1",
             device.x10.house_code,
             device.x10.unit_code);

    //  printf ("%s \n", buffer);
    mysql_query(conn1, buffer);
}
```

```
//****************************************************************************
// Delete House Code OFF Events Before Dusk
//
// This function deletes all the house code OFF events for a specific device
// with a specific timeout value.
//
//****************************************************************************

void  delete_house_code_off_events_at_timeout (X10_DEVICE  device, long int
turn_off_time)
{
    char     buffer[255];


    sprintf (buffer, "DELETE FROM house_code_events WHERE house=%d AND unit=%d AND
state=0 AND timeout=%ld",
            device.x10.house_code,
            device.x10.unit_code,
            turn_off_time);

    //  printf ("%s \n", buffer);
    mysql_query(conn1, buffer);
}




//****************************************************************************
// Delete House Code OFF Events Before Dusk
//
// This function deletes all the house code OFF events for a specific device
// prior to dusk.
//
//****************************************************************************

void  delete_house_code_off_events_before_dusk (X10_DEVICE  device)
{
    char     buffer[255];


    sprintf (buffer, "DELETE FROM house_code_events WHERE house=%d AND unit=%d AND
state=0 AND timeout<%ld",
            device.x10.house_code,
            device.x10.unit_code,
            dusk_timeout);

    //  printf ("%s \n", buffer);
    mysql_query(conn1, buffer);
}
```

```c
//************************************************************************
// Delete House Code Events After Dusk
//
// This function deletes all the house code events for a specific device
// after dusk.
//
//************************************************************************

void  delete_house_code_events_after_dusk (X10_DEVICE  device)
{
    char   buffer[255];


    sprintf (buffer, "DELETE FROM house_code_events WHERE house=%d AND unit=%d AND
timeout>%ld",
            device.x10.house_code,
            device.x10.unit_code,
            dusk_timeout);

    //  printf ("%s \n", buffer);
    mysql_query(conn1, buffer);
}




//************************************************************************
// Delete House Code Events After Sunset
//
// This function deletes all the house code events for a specific device
// after sunset.
//
//************************************************************************

void  delete_house_code_events_after_sunset (X10_DEVICE  device)
{
    char   buffer[255];


    sprintf (buffer, "DELETE FROM house_code_events WHERE house=%d AND unit=%d AND
timeout>%ld",
            device.x10.house_code,
            device.x10.unit_code,
            sunset_timeout);

    //  printf ("%s \n", buffer);
    mysql_query(conn1, buffer);
}
```

```
//**************************************************************************
// Delete All House Code Events
//
// This function deletes all the house code events from the table.
//
//**************************************************************************

void  delete_all_house_code_events (void)
{
    Uint8   house_code;
    Uint8   unit_code;
    char    buffer[255];


    // Delete all house code events
    print_log ("*** Delete ALL house code events...");

    // Delete all the events for each house code
    for (house_code = 1; house_code < 17; house_code++)
    {
        sprintf (buffer, "DELETE FROM house_code_events WHERE house=%d",
house_code);
        mysql_query(conn1, buffer);
    }

}




//**************************************************************************
// Turn Alarm Siren On
//
// This function places required alarm siren on event into the
// house_code_events table.
//
//**************************************************************************

void  turn_alarm_siren_on (void)
{
    long int    current_time;
    long int    turn_off_time;


    // Get current system time
    current_time = get_raw_time ();

    turn_off_time = current_time + OFFSET_5MIN;

    // Delete any existing alarm siren events
    delete_house_code_events (security_alarm_siren);

    // Turn alarm siren ON
    activate_device (security_alarm_siren, ON, current_time);

    // Turn alarm siren OFF after delay
    activate_device (security_alarm_siren, OFF, turn_off_time);
}
```

```
//****************************************************************************
// Turn Alarm Siren Off
//
// This function places required alarm siren off event into the
// house_code_events table.
//
//****************************************************************************

void  turn_alarm_siren_off (void)
{
    long int    current_time;


    // Get current system time
    current_time = get_raw_time();

    // Delete any existing alarm siren events
    delete_house_code_events (security_alarm_siren);

    // Turn alarm siren OFF
    activate_device (security_alarm_siren, OFF, current_time);
}




//****************************************************************************
// Kick The Dog
//
// This function gets the dog to start barking.
//
//****************************************************************************

void  kick_the_dog (void)
{
    long int    current_time;

    // Get current system time
    current_time = get_raw_time();

    // Delete any existing alarm siren events
    delete_house_code_events (barking_doggy);

    // Turn alarm siren ON
    activate_device (barking_doggy, ON, current_time);

}
```

```
//**************************************************************************
// Tell The Dog To Be Quiet
//
// This function forces the dog to stop barking.
//
//**************************************************************************

void  tell_the_dog_to_be_quiet (void)
{
    long int    current_time;


    // Get current system time
    current_time = get_raw_time();

    // Delete any existing alarm siren events
    delete_house_code_events (barking_doggy);

    // Turn alarm siren OFF
    activate_device (barking_doggy, OFF, current_time);
}
```

```
//**********************************************************************
// Send Security Email
//
// This function builds and then sends the security email message.
// If we do not limit the buffer sizes then we run the risk of memory
// corruption and the generation of a system page fault.
//
//**********************************************************************

void  send_security_email (char * header, char * message)
{

    char    buffer[1024];


#ifdef EMAIL_ACTIVE

    // Is the header too big?
    if (strlen(header) > MAX_EMAIL_HEADER_SIZE)
    {
        // Yes - limit the header size
        header[MAX_EMAIL_HEADER_SIZE] = 0x00;
    }


    // Is the message too big?
    if (strlen(message) > MAX_EMAIL_MESSAGE_SIZE)
    {
        // Yes - limit the message size
        message[MAX_EMAIL_MESSAGE_SIZE] = 0x00;
    }


    // Build email command
    sprintf (buffer, "sendemail -f %s -t %s -cc %s -s %s -u \"%s\" -m \"%s\" ",
             EMAIL_SENDER_ADDRESS,
             EMAIL_RECEIVER_ADDRESS,
             EMAIL_CC_ADDRESS,
             SERVICE_PROVIDER_SMTP,
             header,
             message);

    // Send email
    system (buffer);

#endif
}
```

```
//****************************************************************************
// Send Security Email
//
// This function builds and then sends the security email message.
// If we do not limit the buffer sizes then we run the risk of memory
// corruption and the generation of a system page fault.
//
//****************************************************************************

void  send_security_email_with_attachment (char * header, char * message, char *
attachment)
{

    char    buffer[1024];

#ifdef EMAIL_ACTIVE

    // Is the header too big?
    if (strlen(header) > MAX_EMAIL_HEADER_SIZE)
    {
        // Yes - limit the header size
        header[MAX_EMAIL_HEADER_SIZE] = 0x00;
    }


    // Is the message too big?
    if (strlen(message) > MAX_EMAIL_MESSAGE_SIZE)
    {
        // Yes - limit the message size
        message[MAX_EMAIL_MESSAGE_SIZE] = 0x00;
    }


    // Build email command
    sprintf (buffer, "sendemail -f %s -t %s -cc %s -s %s -u \"%s\" -m \"%s\" -a
\"%s\"",
            EMAIL_SENDER_ADDRESS,
            EMAIL_RECEIVER_ADDRESS,
            EMAIL_CC_ADDRESS,
            SERVICE_PROVIDER_SMTP,
            header,
            message,
            attachment);

    // Send email
    system (buffer);

#endif
}
```

```
//****************************************************************************
// Determine Current Day Name
//
// This function determines the current day name.
//
//****************************************************************************

void  determine_current_day_name (char *  day_name)
{
    // Date and time variables
    time_t  td;
    struct tm    *dcp;
    Uint16  day_of_week;


    // Get system date and time
    time(&td);
    dcp = localtime(&td);

    // Initialize calandar variables
    day_of_week = dcp->tm_wday;

    // Determine day of week name
    switch (day_of_week)
    {
        case  SUNDAY:     strcpy (day_name, "Sunday");        break;
        case  MONDAY:     strcpy (day_name, "Monday");        break;
        case  TUESDAY:    strcpy (day_name, "Tuesday");       break;
        case  WEDNESDAY:  strcpy (day_name, "Wednesday");     break;
        case  THURSDAY:   strcpy (day_name, "Thursday");      break;
        case  FRIDAY:     strcpy (day_name, "Friday");        break;
        case  SATURDAY:   strcpy (day_name, "Saturday");      break;
    }


}
```

```
//***********************************************************************
// Determine Current Month
//
// This function determines the current month.
//
//***********************************************************************
void  determine_current_month (Uint16 *  month_index)
{
    // Date and time variables
    time_t  td;
    struct tm    *dcp;
    Uint16  day, month, year, hour, minute, second;


    // Get system date and time
    time(&td);
    dcp = localtime(&td);

    // Initialize calandar variables
    day    = dcp->tm_mday;
    month  = dcp->tm_mon + 1;
    year   = dcp->tm_year + 1900;
    hour   = dcp->tm_hour;
    minute = dcp->tm_min;
    second = dcp->tm_sec;

    // Return the current month
    *month_index = month;
}
```

```
//**************************************************************************
// Determine Current Month Name
//
// This function determines the current month name.
//
//**************************************************************************

void  determine_current_month_name (char *  month_name)
{
    // Date and time variables
    Uint16  month_index;


    determine_current_month (&month_index);

    switch (month_index)
    {
        case  JANUARY:    strcpy (month_name, "January");    break;
        case  FEBRUARY:   strcpy (month_name, "February");   break;
        case  MARCH:      strcpy (month_name, "March");      break;
        case  APRIL:      strcpy (month_name, "April");      break;
        case  MAY:        strcpy (month_name, "May");        break;
        case  JUNE:       strcpy (month_name, "June");       break;
        case  JULY:       strcpy (month_name, "July");       break;
        case  AUGUST:     strcpy (month_name, "August");     break;
        case  SEPTEMBER:  strcpy (month_name, "September");  break;
        case  OCTOBER:    strcpy (month_name, "October");    break;
        case  NOVEMBER:   strcpy (month_name, "November");   break;
        case  DECEMBER:   strcpy (month_name, "December");   break;
        default:
            strcpy (month_name, "");
            break;
    }

}
```

```
//****************************************************************************
// Speak
//
// This function builds and speak command for the passed text message.
// The festival utility is used to generate the speech sounds.
//
// Basic command to say 'good morning': echo "Good morning."  | festival --tts
//
//****************************************************************************

void  speak (char * message)
{

    char    buffer[1024];

    // Build the speech command
    sprintf (buffer, "echo \"%s\" | festival --tts", message);

    // Speak the words
    system (buffer);

}
```

```
//*************************************************************************
// Speak Time And Date
//
// This function determines the current time and date and then speaks it out.
//
// The format is as shown in the following example:
// It is 26 minutes past 2 in the afternoon, on Saturday the 29th of March 2014
//
//*************************************************************************

void  speak_time_and_date (void)
{

    time_t   td;
    struct tm     *dcp;
    Uint16  day, month, year, hour, minute, second;

    char     message[255]         = "Not defined";
    char     old_time[255]        = "Not defined";
    char     day_name[24]         = "Not defined";
    char     month_name[24]       = "Not defined";
    char     part_of_day[48]      = "Not defined";
    char     day_number_suffix[16] = "Not defined";


    // Get system date and time
    time(&td);
    dcp = localtime(&td);

    // Initialize calandar variables
    day     = dcp->tm_mday;
    month   = dcp->tm_mon + 1;
    year    = dcp->tm_year + 1900;
    hour    = dcp->tm_hour;
    minute = dcp->tm_min;
    second = dcp->tm_sec;


    // Determine the part of day
    if (hour < 12)
    {
        // It is morning - which part?
        if (hour < 4)
        {
            // It is the wee hours of the morning
            strcpy (part_of_day, "in the early hours of the morning");
        }
        else
        {
            // It is later on in the morning
            strcpy (part_of_day, "in the morning");
        }
    }
    else
    {
        // Is it the afternoon [24 hour clock]?
        if (hour < 18)
        {
```

184

```
            // Yes - It is the afternoon
            strcpy (part_of_day, "in the afternoon");
        }
        // Is this the evening?
        else if (hour < 20)
        {
            // Yes - It is the evening
            strcpy (part_of_day, "in the evening");
        }
        else
        {
            // Yes - It is the evening
            strcpy (part_of_day, "at night");
        }
    }


    // Determine the day index
    switch (day)
    {
        case 1:
        case 21:
        case 31:    strcpy (day_number_suffix, "st");
                    break;

        case 2:
        case 22:    strcpy (day_number_suffix, "nd");
                    break;

        case 3:
        case 23:    strcpy (day_number_suffix, "rd");
                    break;

        default :   strcpy (day_number_suffix, "th");
                    break;
    }


    // Determine the 'old time' description
    if ((hour == 0) && (minute == 0))
    {
        sprintf (old_time, "midnight");
        strcpy (part_of_day, "");               // Erase part of day description
    }
    else if ((hour == 12) && (minute == 0))
    {
        sprintf (old_time, "midday");
        strcpy (part_of_day, "");               // Erase part of day description
    }
    else
    {
        // Is this the midnight hour?
        if (hour == 0)
        {
            // Yes - make it now 12 "am"
            hour = 12;
        }
```

```
        if (minute == 0)
            sprintf (old_time, "%d o'clock", (hour <= 12) ? hour : (hour - 12));
        else if (minute == 15)
            sprintf (old_time, "quarter past %d", (hour <= 12) ? hour : (hour -
12));
        else if (minute == 30)
            sprintf (old_time, "half past %d", (hour <= 12) ? hour : (hour - 12));
        else if (minute == 45)
            sprintf (old_time, "quarter to %d", (hour <= 12) ? hour : (hour - 12));
        else if (minute < 2)
            sprintf (old_time, "one minute after %d", (hour <= 12) ? hour : (hour -
12));
        else if (minute < 30)
            sprintf (old_time, "%d minutes after %d", minute, (hour <= 12) ? hour :
(hour - 12));
        else if (minute < 59)
            sprintf (old_time, "%d minutes before %d", (60 - minute), (++hour <=
12) ? hour : (hour - 12));
        else
            sprintf (old_time, "one minute to %d", (++hour <= 12) ? hour : (hour -
12));
    }

    // Determine the day and month names
    determine_current_day_name (day_name);
    determine_current_month_name (month_name);

    // Say the time and date.  It should have the following format...
    // It is 26 minutes past 2 in the afternoon, on Saturday the 29th of March
2014
    sprintf (message, "It is %s %s on %s the %d%s of %s %d %d",
            old_time,
            part_of_day,
            day_name,
            day,
            day_number_suffix,
            month_name,
            (year / 100) * 100,
            year % 100);

    print_log (message);

    speak(message);

}
```

```
//*************************************************************************
// Snap Picture
//
// This function builds and then executes the security email message.
// If we do not limit the buffer sizes then we run the risk of memory
// corruption and the generation of a system page fault.
//
// Different command line examples:
// fswebcam -save /home/orion/Projects/Execs/steve.jpg
// fswebcam -save /home/orion/Projects/Execs/steve.jpg -r 960x720 -s
brightness=150
// fswebcam -save /home/orion/Projects/Execs/steve.jpg -r 1920x1080 -s
brightness=150
//*************************************************************************

void  snap_picture (char * file_name)
{

    char    buffer[1024];


    // Build command
    sprintf (buffer, "fswebcam -r 1920x1080 -s brightness=150 -save \"%s\"",
file_name);

    // Execute the command
    system (buffer);

}
```

```
//****************************************************************************
// Reset Security Detection Flags
//
// This function resets all the security flags.
//
//****************************************************************************

void  reset_security_detection_flags (void)
{

    // Reset all security detection flags
    steve_bedroom_sensor_security            = FALSE;
    common_washroom_sensor_security          = FALSE;
    common_bathroom_sensor_security          = FALSE;
    mini_hallway_sensor_security             = FALSE;
    study_sensor_security                    = FALSE;
    familyroom_sensor_security               = FALSE;
    inside_front_door_sensor_security        = FALSE;
    main_hallway_sensor_security             = FALSE;
    lounge_hallway_sensor_security           = FALSE;
    master_hallway_sensor_security           = FALSE;
    kitchen_sensor_security                  = FALSE;
    kitchen_nook_sensor_security             = FALSE;
    master_bedroom_sensor_security           = FALSE;
    master_bathroom_sensor_security          = FALSE;
    master_closet_sensor_security            = FALSE;
    garage_sensor_security                   = FALSE;
    master_bedroom_closet_sensor_security    = FALSE;
    pantry_sensor_security                   = FALSE;
    laundry_sensor_security                  = FALSE;
    guest_bathroom_sensor_security           = FALSE;
    guest_bedroom_door_sensor_security       = FALSE;
}




//****************************************************************************
// Limit Turn Off Time To Just After Dusk
//
// This function ensures that if the lamp turn off time is at or past the dusk
// time then it will be adjusted to just after the dusk timeout period.
// This will then permit the IR sensor some time in triggering and by
// such extending the turn off time without switching off the light.
//
//****************************************************************************

void  limit_turn_off_time_to_just_after_dusk (long int *  time)
{

    if (*time > dusk_timeout)
    {
        // Force turn off time to just after dusk
        *time = dusk_timeout + OFFSET_1MIN30SEC;
    }
}
```

188

```
//*************************************************************************
// Get High Resolution Timer
//
// This function obtains a system timer count with milliseconds resolution.
//
//*************************************************************************
long int  get_high_resolution_timer (void)
{
    long int    milliseconds;
    struct      timeval timer;


    // Get the current timer count
    gettimeofday(&timer, NULL);

    // Convert it into milliseconds
    milliseconds = (timer.tv_sec * 1000) + (timer.tv_usec / 1000.0) + 0.5;

    return (milliseconds);

}



#endif
```

File: hc_main.c

```
//**********************************************************************
//   Author: Stephen W. McClure
//     Date: March 2014
// Project: Designing Embedded Systems [Book]
//
//**********************************************************************
// Purpose:
//
// This program is part of the X10 Home Control Project.
//
// InfraRed RF Sensors are used to detect the presence of a person in a
// specific room or area of the home.  When a presence is detected, the
// InfraRed Sensor transmits an RF code.  Each InfraRed Sensor my be
// programmed with its own user assigned RF code.  This code consists of a
// House / Unit set of values.  For example [A,1] for house code 'A' and
// unit code '1'.
//
// A device called the WF800 RF32A Receiver is used to pick up the InfraRed
// RF transmissions and provide them to the Linux Computer system as an RS232
// serial transmission over a serial port.  Each of these serial
// transmissions are decoded and the contained house / unit codes extracted
// and stored in a MySQL Database.
//
// These sensors are easily purchased from Home Control supply stores.
//
// When this program is started, the MySQL databases will be created if they
// do not currently exist. Device codes and descriptions are also placed into
// the databases tables.
//
//**********************************************************************
//
// File Name: hc_main.c
//
// Build command
// gcc hc_main.c -o hc_main `mysql_config --cflags --libs`
//
// Execution Command
// ./hc_main > hc_main.log &
//
//
// But first don't forget to sign in as SU and give the appropriate serial
// ports the access right permissions (eg.: chmod a+rw /dev/ttyS1) and to
// also use the static ip address: 192.168.1.176 (set by using wired network
// connection icon in the bottom right of the Mint 13 GUI)
//
// For example:
// $ su
// Password: enter super user password
// # chmod a+rw  /dev/ttyS0
// # chmod a+rw  /dev/ttyS1
// # exit
//
// chmod a+r  /dev/ttyS0  Set ttyS0 for Input Only  [ORION-ITX TOP    Port]
// chmod a+rw /dev/ttyS1  Set ttyS1 for I/O         [ORION-ITX BOTTOM Port]
//
```

```
// ttyS0  -  Top Port    = RF X10 Commands
// ttyS1  -  Bottom Port = TI-103
//
// Or make the user 'orion' part of the "dialout" group
// which will give it RW permission to the ttys0 and ttys1 serial ports
// by issuing the following instruction: sudo adduser orion dialout
// (will need to provide the su password).
//
// When using autostart a delay is required at the start of this program's
// execution in order to allow the MySQL system to be initialized prior to it
// being accessed.
//***************************************************************************


// Include Files
#include <sys/types.h>
#include <sys/stat.h>
#include <fcntl.h>
#include <termios.h>
#include <stdio.h>
#include <my_global.h>
#include <mysql.h>
#include <sys/time.h>
#include <unistd.h>
#include <signal.h>
#include <string.h>
#include <time.h>


// Include local header Files
#include "hc_literals.h"
#include "hc_typedefs.h"
#include "hc_publics.h"

// Include local modules
#include "hc_common.c"


// X10 Validity
Uint8  x10_rf_code = INVALID;


// Bytes received from W800RF32A:
Uint8  byte_1;
Uint8  byte_2;
Uint8  byte_3;
Uint8  byte_4;

// Translation into House and Unit Codes:
Uint8  house_code;
Uint8  unit_code;
Uint8  command;
Uint8  x10_rf_code;
```

```c
//***********************************************************************
// Initialize Serial Port for WF800
//
// This function opens the serial port for reading the WF800 32A RF
// X10 Control Codes from the InfraRed Sensors.
//
//***********************************************************************
void  initialize_serial_port_for_wf800 (void)
{

    // Open the Serial Port [TOP PORT ON ORION-ITX, Read Only]
    fd = open(SERIAL_PORT_0, O_RDWR | O_NOCTTY );

    // Error detected in opening port?
    if (fd < 0)
    {
        // Yes - Display error message
        perror(SERIAL_PORT_1);
        exit(-1);    // Exit application with Error
    }


    // Save current serial port settings
    tcgetattr(fd, &old_options);

    // Setup the Serial Port Configuration
    new_options.c_cflag = BAUDRATE | CRTSCTS | CS8 | CLOCAL | CREAD;
    new_options.c_iflag = IGNPAR;
    new_options.c_oflag = 0;


    // Set input mode (non-canonical, no echo,...)
    new_options.c_lflag = 0;

    // Wait until either 4 characters have been received;
    // OR the time interval between characters exceeds 100ms
    new_options.c_cc[VTIME] = 10;     /* inter-character timer used */
    new_options.c_cc[VMIN]  = 4;      /* blocking read until 4 chars received */

    // Flush the input buffer
    tcflush(fd, TCIFLUSH);

    // Configure the Serial Port
    tcsetattr(fd, TCSANOW, &new_options);


}
```

```
//*************************************************************************
// Process Events That Occur At Midnight              UNIQUE TO HC_MAIN
//
// This function handles events that occur at midnight.
//
//*************************************************************************

void  process_events_that_occur_at_midnight (void)
{

    // Has midnight just started?
    if (midnight_start == TRUE)
    {
        // Place all midnight start events here...
        // =====================================
        reset_security_detection_flags();

        // Reset event flag
        midnight_start = FALSE;
    }

}




//*************************************************************************
// Process Events That Occur At Sunrise               UNIQUE TO HC_MAIN
//
// This function handles events that occur as night transitions into day.
//
//*************************************************************************

void  process_events_that_occur_at_sunrise (void)
{

    // Has the day just started?
    if (day_start == TRUE)
    {
        // Place all day start events here...
        // ==================================


        // Reset event flag
        day_start = FALSE;
    }

}
```

```
//****************************************************************************
// Process Events That Occur At Sunset                    UNIQUE TO HC_MAIN
//
// This function handles events that occur as day transitions into night.
//
//****************************************************************************

void  process_events_that_occur_at_sunset (void)
{
    // Has the night just started?
    if (night_start == TRUE)
    {
        // Place all night start events here...
        // ===================================


        // Reset event flag
        night_start = FALSE;
    }

}
```

```
//****************************************************************************
// Initialize House Code States Table
//
// This function places default data into the MySQL 'house_code_state' table.
// This sets all table entries to 'No Time' and 'No Description'.
//
// Translation from W800RF32A to House/Unit Codes:
//
// Provides the following:
// =======================
//
// house_code  in range [1..16]
// unit_code   in range [1..16]
// command     in range [X10_OFF, X10_ON]
// x10_rf_code in range [INVALID, VALID]
//
//****************************************************************************

#define NO_PRESENCE 0
#define NO_TIMEOUT  0
#define NO_TYPE     0

void  initialize_house_code_states_table (void)
{
    char    buffer [255];
    char    message [255];


    for (house_code = 1; house_code <= 16; house_code++)
    {
        for (unit_code = 1; unit_code <= 16; unit_code++)
        {
            sprintf (buffer, "INSERT INTO house_code_states VALUES(%d, %d, 2, 2,
'No Time', %d, %d, 'No Description')",
                     house_code, unit_code, NO_TIMEOUT, NO_PRESENCE);

            if (mysql_query(conn2, buffer))
            {
                sprintf (message, "Error_Init %u: %s\n", mysql_errno(conn2),
mysql_error(conn2));
                print_log (message);
            }
        }
    }

}
```

```
//***************************************************************************
// Update House Code States
//
// This function updates the house code states description for a specific device.
//
//***************************************************************************

void  update_house_code_states (X10_DEVICE  device)
{
    char    buffer[255];


    sprintf (buffer, "UPDATE house_code_states SET description='%s', type=%d WHERE
house=%d AND unit=%d",
            device.description,
            device.type,
            device.x10.house_code,
            device.x10.unit_code);

    //  printf ("%s \n", buffer);
    mysql_query(conn2, buffer);
}
```

```
//**********************************************************************
// Initialize States Table Descriptions
//
// This function places description data into the MySQL 'house_code_state_table'
// for specific House and Unit codes.
//
//**********************************************************************
void  initialize_states_table_descriptions (void)
{
    // Add in State Descriptions

    // General Descriptions
    update_house_code_states (light_sensor);

    // Porch Descriptions
    update_house_code_states (front_porch_sensor);
    update_house_code_states (porch_outside_light);

    // Inside Front Door Descriptions
    update_house_code_states (inside_front_door_sensor);

    update_house_code_states (inside_entrance_light);

    // Hallway Descriptions
    update_house_code_states (main_hallway_sensor);
    update_house_code_states (mini_hallway_sensor);
    update_house_code_states (lounge_hallway_sensor);
    update_house_code_states (master_hallway_sensor);
    update_house_code_states (mini_hallway_light);
    update_house_code_states (main_hallway_light);

    // Laundry Descriptions
    update_house_code_states (laundry_sensor);
    update_house_code_states (laundry_fan);
    update_house_code_states (laundry_light);

    // Pantry Descriptions
    update_house_code_states (pantry_sensor);
    update_house_code_states (pantry_light);

    // Kitchen Descriptions
    update_house_code_states (kitchen_sensor);
    update_house_code_states (counter_fridge_sensor);
    update_house_code_states (counter_cooktop_left_sensor);
    update_house_code_states (counter_cooktop_right_sensor);
    update_house_code_states (kitchen_nook_sensor);
    update_house_code_states (kitchen_light);
    update_house_code_states (kitchen_nook_light);
    update_house_code_states (kitchen_counter_light);
    update_house_code_states (kitchen_sink_light);

    // Lounge Area Descriptions
    update_house_code_states (lounge_wall_light);
    update_house_code_states (lounge_window_light);
    update_house_code_states (fishtank_light);
```

```
// Dining Room Descriptions
update_house_code_states (diningroom_outside_light);
update_house_code_states (diningroom_table_light);

// Family Room Descriptions
update_house_code_states (familyroom_sensor);
update_house_code_states (familyroom_window_light);
update_house_code_states (familyroom_wall_light);
update_house_code_states (familyroom_track_tv_light);
update_house_code_states (familyroom_track_reading_light);
update_house_code_states (familyroom_radio);
update_house_code_states (familyroom_outside_light);

// Cloakroom Descriptions
update_house_code_states (cloakroom_sensor);
update_house_code_states (cloakroom_light);

// Guest Bathroom Descriptions
update_house_code_states (guest_shower_sensor);
update_house_code_states (guest_bathroom_sensor);
update_house_code_states (guest_bathroom_light);
update_house_code_states (guest_bathroom_flight);

update_house_code_states (guest_bathroom_fan);

// Guest Bedroom Descriptions
update_house_code_states (guest_bedroom_door_sensor);
update_house_code_states (guest_bedroom_window_sensor);
update_house_code_states (guest_main_light);
update_house_code_states (guest_bed_light);

// Steve's Room Descriptions
update_house_code_states (steve_bedroom_sensor);
update_house_code_states (steve_bedroom_wall_light);
update_house_code_states (steve_bedroom_window_light);
update_house_code_states (steve_bedroom_ceiling_light);

// Study Descriptions
update_house_code_states (study_sensor);
update_house_code_states (study_ceiling_light);

// Common Washroom Descriptions
update_house_code_states (common_washroom_sensor);
update_house_code_states (common_washroom_light);
update_house_code_states (common_washroom_flight);


// Common Bathroom Descriptions
update_house_code_states (common_bathroom_sensor);
update_house_code_states (common_bathroom_light);

// Master Bedroom Descriptions
update_house_code_states (master_bedroom_sensor);
update_house_code_states (master_bedroom_dad_light);
update_house_code_states (master_bedroom_mum_light);

update_house_code_states (master_bedroom_outside_light);
update_house_code_states (master_bedroom_closet_sensor);
```

```
update_house_code_states (master_bedroom_closet_light);
update_house_code_states (master_bathroom_sensor);
update_house_code_states (master_toilet_sensor);

// Garage Descriptions
update_house_code_states (garage_z71_sensor);
update_house_code_states (garage_bike_sensor);
update_house_code_states (garage_fridge_sensor);
update_house_code_states (garage_light);
update_house_code_states (garage_front_outside_light);
update_house_code_states (garage_back_outside_light);

// Season Icicle Descriptions
update_house_code_states (season_front_light);
update_house_code_states (season_back_light);

// Security Descriptions
update_house_code_states (security_alarm_siren);
update_house_code_states (barking_doggy);

}
```

```
//*************************************************************************
// Initialize System Control Database
//
// This funtion attempts to connect to the MySQL System running on the Linux
// machine.  If connection is established then a connection attempt is made to
// the system control database.  If the database does not exist then it is
// created.
//
// The MySQL database name is "system_control".
//
// This database contains the following three tables:
//
// 1. house_state (Home Mode or Security Mode)
// 2. house_code_events (acive inputs to be processed)
// 3. house_code_states (current house code states)
//
// If any error is detected, an error message is displayed and
// the program exits.
//*************************************************************************

void  initialize_system_control_database (void)
{
    char    message [255];


    // Access the MySQL system
    // ========================
    conn1 = mysql_init(NULL);

    if (conn1 == NULL)
    {
        // Cannot access the MySQL system - Error Exit
        sprintf (message, "Error_A %u: %s", mysql_errno(conn1),
mysql_error(conn1));
        print_log (message);
        exit(1);
    }


    // MySQL Active - Connect to MySQL Environment, "system_control" database
    // =====================================================================
    if (mysql_real_connect (conn1,
                            "192.168.1.176",
                            "steve",
                            "william",
                            "system_control",
                            0,
                            NULL,
                            0) == NULL)
    {
        // Can't connect to database - Perhaps database does not exist...
        sprintf (message, "Error_B %u: %s", mysql_errno(conn1),
mysql_error(conn1));
        print_log (message);
        print_log ("Creating 'system_control' database...");


        // If cannot connect to database then just log in to MySQL
```

```
        if (mysql_real_connect (conn1,
                                "192.168.1.176",
                                "steve",
                                "william",
                                NULL,
                                0,
                                NULL,
                                0) == NULL)
        {
            // Cannot log in - Error Exit
            sprintf (message, "Error_C %u: %s", mysql_errno(conn1),
mysql_error(conn1));
            print_log (message);
            exit(1);
        }

        // All is well, logged into MySQL
        print_log ("Logged into MySQL database system...");




        // Create the 'system_control' Data Base
        // =====================================
        if (mysql_query(conn1, "create database system_control"))
        {
            // Cannot create database - Error Exit
            sprintf (message, "Error_D %u: %s", mysql_errno(conn1),
mysql_error(conn1));
            print_log (message);
            exit(1);
        }

        // 'system_control' database successfully created
        print_log ("Created 'system_control' database...");


        // Now connect to the 'system_control' database
        // ===========================================
        conn2 = mysql_init(NULL);

        if (mysql_real_connect (conn2,
                                "192.168.1.176",
                                "steve",
                                "william",
                                "system_control",
                                0,
                                NULL,
                                0) == NULL)
        {
            // Cannot connect to the database - Error Exit
            sprintf (message, "Error_E %u: %s", mysql_errno(conn2),
mysql_error(conn2));
            print_log (message);
            exit(1);
        }

        print_log ("Logged into MySQL 'system_control' database...");
```

```
        // Create table 'house_state'
        // ==========================
        if (mysql_query(conn2, "CREATE TABLE house_state (security int,
security_delay int, sleep int, sleep_delay int, family_lights int, steve_lights
int, go_to_bed int, master_watch_tv int)"))
            {
                // Cannot create table - Error Exit
                sprintf (message, "Error_F %u: %s", mysql_errno(conn2),
mysql_error(conn2));
                print_log (message);
                exit(1);
            }
        else
            {
                print_log ("Created table 'system_control:house_state'...");

                // Initialize 'house_state' table if it has just been created.
                // Security not active (ie. home mode), sleep is inactive
                if (mysql_query(conn2, "INSERT INTO house_state
VALUES(0,0,0,0,0,0,0,0)"))
                    {
                        // Cannot initialize house state to 'HOME Mode' - Error Exit
                        sprintf (message, "Error_G %u: %s", mysql_errno(conn2),
mysql_error(conn2));
                        print_log (message);
                        exit(1);
                    }
                else
                    print_log ("Initialized table 'system_control:house_state'...");
            }


        // Create table 'house_code_events'
        // ================================
        if (mysql_query(conn2, "CREATE TABLE house_code_events (house int, unit
int, type int, state int, timestamp VARCHAR(20), timeout int, description
VARCHAR(50))"))
            {
                // Cannot create table - Error Exit
                sprintf (message, "Error_H %u: %s", mysql_errno(conn2),
mysql_error(conn2));
                print_log (message);
                exit(1);
            }
        else
            print_log ("Created table 'system_control:house_code_events'...");


        // Create table 'house_code_states'
        // ================================
        if (mysql_query(conn2, "CREATE TABLE house_code_states (house int, unit
int, type int, state int, timestamp VARCHAR(20), timeout int, presence int,
description VARCHAR(50))"))
            {
                // Cannot create table - Error Exit
                sprintf (message, "Error_I %u: %s", mysql_errno(conn2),
mysql_error(conn2));
```

```
            print_log (message);
            exit(1);
        }
        else
        {
            print_log ("Created table 'system_control:house_code_states'...");

            initialize_house_code_states_table();
            initialize_states_table_descriptions();
            print_log ("Initialized.. 'system_control:house_code_states'...");
        }

        // Now use conn1 to access database
        conn1 = conn2;
    }
    else
    {
        //  system_control database already exists!!!
        print_log ("system_control database already exists!!!");
    }

}
```

```
//****************************************************************************
// Convert RF Codes
//
// Convert RF Received Codes to House and Unit Codes
//
//****************************************************************************
void  convert_rf_codes (Uint8  house, Uint8  unit,  Uint8  offset)
{
    // Determine House Code - Convert to Range [1..16]
    house_code = house + 1;

    // Determine Unit ON/OFF Codes - Range [1..16]
    switch (unit)
    {
    // Unit Code '1' or '9'
    case 0x00: unit_code = 0x01 + offset; command = X10_ON;   return;
    case 0x20: unit_code = 0x01 + offset; command = X10_OFF;  return;

    // Unit Code '2' or '10'
    case 0x10: unit_code = 0x02 + offset; command = X10_ON;   return;
    case 0x30: unit_code = 0x02 + offset; command = X10_OFF;  return;

    // Unit Code '3' or '11'
    case 0x08: unit_code = 0x03 + offset; command = X10_ON;   return;
    case 0x28: unit_code = 0x03 + offset; command = X10_OFF;  return;

    // Unit Code '4' or '12'
    case 0x18: unit_code = 0x04 + offset; command = X10_ON;   return;
    case 0x38: unit_code = 0x04 + offset; command = X10_OFF;  return;

    // Unit Code '5' or '13'
    case 0x40: unit_code = 0x05 + offset; command = X10_ON;   return;
    case 0x60: unit_code = 0x05 + offset; command = X10_OFF;  return;

    // Unit Code '6' or '14'
    case 0x50: unit_code = 0x06 + offset; command = X10_ON;   return;
    case 0x70: unit_code = 0x06 + offset; command = X10_OFF;  return;

    // Unit Code '7' or '15'
    case 0x48: unit_code = 0x07 + offset; command = X10_ON;   return;
    case 0x68: unit_code = 0x07 + offset; command = X10_OFF;  return;

    // Unit Code '8' or '16'
    case 0x58: unit_code = 0x08 + offset; command = X10_ON;   return;
    case 0x78: unit_code = 0x08 + offset; command = X10_OFF;  return;

    // Error condition - Ignore message
    //      default:
    }

    // X10 RF Code Validity
    x10_rf_code = INVALID;

}
```

```
//****************************************************************************
// x10_convert_rf_codes
//
// This fucnction converts the X10 RF Codes to House and Unit codes.
//
//****************************************************************************
void  x10_convert_rf_codes (Uint8  byte_1, Uint8  byte_3)
{
    // X10 RF Code - Assume initially valid
    x10_rf_code = VALID;

    switch (byte_1)
    {
    // House Code 'A'
    case 0x60: convert_rf_codes (0x00, byte_3, 0x00); return;  // House A, Unit,
Offset
    case 0x64: convert_rf_codes (0x00, byte_3, 0x08); return;

    // House Code 'B'
    case 0x70: convert_rf_codes (0x01, byte_3, 0x00); return;  // House B, Unit,
Offset
    case 0x74: convert_rf_codes (0x01, byte_3, 0x08); return;

    // House Code 'C'
    case 0x40: convert_rf_codes (0x02, byte_3, 0x00); return;  // House C, Unit,
Offset
    case 0x44: convert_rf_codes (0x02, byte_3, 0x08); return;

    // House Code 'D'
    case 0x50: convert_rf_codes (0x03, byte_3, 0x00); return;  // House D, Unit,
Offset
    case 0x54: convert_rf_codes (0x03, byte_3, 0x08); return;

    // House Code 'E'
    case 0x80: convert_rf_codes (0x04, byte_3, 0x00); return;  // House E, Unit,
Offset
    case 0x84: convert_rf_codes (0x04, byte_3, 0x08); return;

    // House Code 'F'
    case 0x90: convert_rf_codes (0x05, byte_3, 0x00); return;  // House F, Unit,
Offset
    case 0x94: convert_rf_codes (0x05, byte_3, 0x08); return;

    // House Code 'G'
    case 0xA0: convert_rf_codes (0x06, byte_3, 0x00); return;  // House G, Unit,
Offset
    case 0xA4: convert_rf_codes (0x06, byte_3, 0x08); return;

    // House Code 'H'
    case 0xB0: convert_rf_codes (0x07, byte_3, 0x00); return;  // House H, Unit,
Offset
    case 0xB4: convert_rf_codes (0x07, byte_3, 0x08); return;

    // House Code 'I'
    case 0xE0: convert_rf_codes (0x08, byte_3, 0x00); return;  // House I, Unit,
Offset
    case 0xE4: convert_rf_codes (0x08, byte_3, 0x08); return;
```

```
    // House Code 'J'
    case 0xF0: convert_rf_codes (0x09, byte_3, 0x00); return;  // House J, Unit,
Offset
    case 0xF4: convert_rf_codes (0x09, byte_3, 0x08); return;

    // House Code 'K'
    case 0xC0: convert_rf_codes (0x0A, byte_3, 0x00); return;  // House K, Unit,
Offset
    case 0xC4: convert_rf_codes (0x0A, byte_3, 0x08); return;

    // House Code 'L'
    case 0xD0: convert_rf_codes (0x0B, byte_3, 0x00); return;  // House L, Unit,
Offset
    case 0xD4: convert_rf_codes (0x0B, byte_3, 0x08); return;

    // House Code 'M'
    case 0x00: convert_rf_codes (0x0C, byte_3, 0x00); return;  // House M, Unit,
Offset
    case 0x04: convert_rf_codes (0x0C, byte_3, 0x08); return;

    // House Code 'N'
    case 0x10: convert_rf_codes (0x0D, byte_3, 0x00); return;  // House N, Unit,
Offset
    case 0x14: convert_rf_codes (0x0D, byte_3, 0x08); return;

    // House Code 'O'
    case 0x20: convert_rf_codes (0x0E, byte_3, 0x00); return;  // House O, Unit,
Offset
    case 0x24: convert_rf_codes (0x0E, byte_3, 0x08); return;

    // House Code 'P'
    case 0x30: convert_rf_codes (0x0F, byte_3, 0x00); return;  // House P, Unit,
Offset
    case 0x34: convert_rf_codes (0x0F, byte_3, 0x08); return;

    // Error condition - Ignore message
    //      default:

    }

    // X10 RF Code - No code found - Code Invalid
    x10_rf_code = INVALID;

}
```

```
//*************************************************************************
// Device Code Set
//
// This function returns TRUE if the house and unit codes equals those of the
// X10 device parameter.
//
//*************************************************************************

Uint8  device_code_set (X10_DEVICE  device)
{

    // Is this device code set?
    return ((device.x10.house_code == house_code) &&
            (device.x10.unit_code  == unit_code));
}
```

```
//******************************************************************************
// Process Intruder Check
//
// This function determines if there was any activity within the home and if
// any such presence was detected then the alarm siren will be activated.
// A single email message (per location) is also broadcast.
//
//******************************************************************************

void  process_intruder_check (void)
{
    char         message[255];
    char         time_buffer[255];
    long int     current_time;


    // Compute current timestamp
    determine_system_timestamp (time_buffer);

    // Get current time in seconds
    current_time = get_raw_time();

    // Intruder at front door?
    if (device_code_set (front_porch_sensor))
    {
        // Yes - Has the timer expired?
        if (front_porch_sensor_security_timer == DELAY_EXPIRED)
        {
            // Yes - Send security alert email
            front_porch_sensor_security_timer = current_time + OFFSET_5MIN;
            sprintf (message, "%s - Someone is at the Front Door", time_buffer);
            send_security_email ("*** SECURITY ALERT ***", message);

            print_log ("A person is at the front door.");
            speak      ("A person is at the front door.");
        }
    }

    // Has the security timer expired
    if (current_time >= front_porch_sensor_security_timer)
    {
        // Yes - Reset the timer
        front_porch_sensor_security_timer = DELAY_EXPIRED;
    }


    // Intruder in Study?
    if (device_code_set (study_sensor) && (!study_sensor_security))
    {
        // Yes - Turn alarm siren on and send security alert email
        turn_alarm_siren_on();
        study_sensor_security = TRUE;

        print_log ("A person is in the study.");
        speak      ("A person is in the study.");

        snap_picture (STUDY_PICTURE_FILE);
        sprintf (message, "%s - Intruder in Study", time_buffer);
```

```
        send_security_email_with_attachment ("*** SECURITY ALERT ***", message,
STUDY_PICTURE_FILE);

        speak ("Your picture has been taken and sent to thee authorities.");  //
Spelling the as 'thee' sounds better
    }

    // Intruder in Steve's Bedroom?
    if (device_code_set (steve_bedroom_sensor) &&
(!steve_bedroom_sensor_security))
    {
        // Yes - Turn alarm siren on and send security alert email
        turn_alarm_siren_on();
        steve_bedroom_sensor_security = TRUE;

        print_log ("A person is in steve's bedroom.");
        speak      ("A person is in steve's bedroom.");

        sprintf (message, "%s - Intruder in Steve's Bedroom", time_buffer);
        send_security_email ("*** SECURITY ALERT ***", message);
    }

    // Intruder in Common Washroom?
    if (device_code_set (common_washroom_sensor) &&
(!common_washroom_sensor_security))
    {
        // Yes - Turn alarm siren on and send security alert email
        turn_alarm_siren_on();
        common_washroom_sensor_security = TRUE;

        print_log ("A person is in the common washroom.");
        speak      ("A person is in the common washroom.");

        sprintf (message, "%s - Intruder in Common Washroom", time_buffer);
        send_security_email ("*** SECURITY ALERT ***", message);
    }

    // Intruder in Common Bathroom?
    if (device_code_set (common_bathroom_sensor) &&
(!common_bathroom_sensor_security))
    {
        // Yes - Turn alarm siren on and send security alert email
        turn_alarm_siren_on();
        common_bathroom_sensor_security = TRUE;

        print_log ("A person is in the common bathroom.");
        speak      ("A person is in the common bathroom.");

        sprintf (message, "%s - Intruder in Common Bathroom", time_buffer);
        send_security_email ("*** SECURITY ALERT ***", message);
    }

    // Intruder in Mini-Hallway?
    if (device_code_set (mini_hallway_sensor) && (!mini_hallway_sensor_security))
    {
        // Yes - Turn alarm siren on and send security alert email
        turn_alarm_siren_on();
        mini_hallway_sensor_security = TRUE;
```

209

```
        print_log ("A person is in the mini hall way");
        speak      ("A person is in the mini hall way");

        sprintf (message, "%s - Intruder in Mini-Hallway", time_buffer);
        send_security_email ("*** SECURITY ALERT ***", message);
    }

    // Intruder in Familyroom?
    if (device_code_set (familyroom_sensor) && (!familyroom_sensor_security))
    {
        // Yes - Turn alarm siren on and send security alert email
        turn_alarm_siren_on();
        familyroom_sensor_security = TRUE;

        print_log ("A person is in the family room.");
        speak      ("A person is in the family room.");

        sprintf (message, "%s - Intruder in Familyroom", time_buffer);
        send_security_email ("*** SECURITY ALERT ***", message);
    }

    // Intruder at Inside Front Door?
    if (device_code_set (inside_front_door_sensor) &&
(!inside_front_door_sensor_security))
    {
        // Yes - Turn alarm siren on and send security alert email
        turn_alarm_siren_on();
        inside_front_door_sensor_security = TRUE;

        print_log ("A person is at the inside front door.");
        speak      ("A person is at the inside front door.");

        sprintf (message, "%s - Intruder at Inside Front Door", time_buffer);
        send_security_email ("*** SECURITY ALERT ***", message);
    }

    // Intruder in Main Hallway?
    if (device_code_set (main_hallway_sensor) && (!main_hallway_sensor_security))
    {
        // Yes - Turn alarm siren on and send security alert email
        turn_alarm_siren_on();
        main_hallway_sensor_security = TRUE;

        print_log ("A person is in the main hall way.");
        speak      ("A person is in the main hall way.");

        sprintf (message, "%s - Intruder in Main Hallway", time_buffer);
        send_security_email ("*** SECURITY ALERT ***", message);
    }

    // Intruder in Lounge Hallway?
    if (device_code_set (lounge_hallway_sensor) &&
(!lounge_hallway_sensor_security))
    {
        // Yes - Turn alarm siren on and send security alert email
        turn_alarm_siren_on();
        lounge_hallway_sensor_security = TRUE;
```

```
         print_log ("A person is in the lounge hall way.");
         speak     ("A person is in the lounge hall way.");

         sprintf (message, "%s - Intruder in Lounge Hallway", time_buffer);
         send_security_email ("*** SECURITY ALERT ***", message);
    }

    // Intruder in Master Hallway?
    if (device_code_set (master_hallway_sensor) &&
(!master_hallway_sensor_security))
    {
         // Yes - Turn alarm siren on and send security alert email
         turn_alarm_siren_on();
         master_hallway_sensor_security = TRUE;

         print_log ("A person is in the master hall way.");
         speak     ("A person is in the master hall way.");

         sprintf (message, "%s - Intruder in Master Hallway", time_buffer);
         send_security_email ("*** SECURITY ALERT ***", message);
    }

    // Intruder in Kitchen?
    if ((device_code_set (kitchen_sensor)                    ||
          device_code_set (counter_fridge_sensor)            ||
          device_code_set (counter_cooktop_left_sensor)      ||
          device_code_set (counter_cooktop_right_sensor)) &&
(!kitchen_sensor_security))
    {
         // Yes - Turn alarm siren on and send security alert email
         turn_alarm_siren_on();
         kitchen_sensor_security = TRUE;

         print_log ("A person is in the kitchen.");
         speak     ("A person is in the kitchen.");

         sprintf (message, "%s - Intruder in Kitchen", time_buffer);
         send_security_email ("*** SECURITY ALERT ***", message);
    }

    // Intruder in Kitchen Nook?
    if (device_code_set (kitchen_nook_sensor) && (!kitchen_nook_sensor_security))
    {
         // Yes - Turn alarm siren on and send security alert email
         turn_alarm_siren_on();
         kitchen_nook_sensor_security = TRUE;

         print_log ("A person is in the kitchen nook.");
         speak     ("A person is in the kitchen nook.");

         sprintf (message, "%s - Intruder in Kitchen Nook", time_buffer);
         send_security_email ("*** SECURITY ALERT ***", message);
    }


    // Intruder in Master Bedroom?
    if (device_code_set (master_bedroom_sensor) &&
(!master_bedroom_sensor_security))
```

211

```
    {
        // Yes - Turn alarm siren on and send security alert email
        turn_alarm_siren_on();
        master_bedroom_sensor_security = TRUE;

        print_log ("A person is in the master bedroom.");
        speak       ("A person is in the master bedroom.");

        sprintf (message, "%s - Intruder in Master Bedroom", time_buffer);
        send_security_email ("*** SECURITY ALERT ***", message);
    }

    // Intruder in Master Bathroom?
    if (device_code_set (master_bathroom_sensor) &&
(!master_bathroom_sensor_security))
    {
        // Yes - Turn alarm siren on and send security alert email
        turn_alarm_siren_on();
        master_bathroom_sensor_security = TRUE;

        print_log ("A person is in the master bathroom.");
        speak       ("A person is in the master bathroom.");

        sprintf (message, "%s - Intruder in Master Bathroom", time_buffer);
        send_security_email ("*** SECURITY ALERT ***", message);
    }

    // Intruder in Master Closet?
    if (device_code_set (master_bedroom_closet_sensor) &&
(!master_bedroom_closet_sensor_security))
    {
        // Yes - Turn alarm siren on and send security alert email
        turn_alarm_siren_on();
        master_bedroom_closet_sensor_security = TRUE;

        print_log ("A person is in the master closet.");
        speak       ("A person is in the master closet.");

        sprintf (message, "%s - Intruder in Master Bedroom Closet", time_buffer);
        send_security_email ("*** SECURITY ALERT ***", message);
    }

    // Intruder in Garage?
    if ((device_code_set (garage_fridge_sensor) ||
         device_code_set (garage_bike_sensor)    ||
         device_code_set (garage_z71_sensor))    && (!garage_sensor_security))
    {
        // Yes - Turn alarm siren on and send security alert email
        turn_alarm_siren_on();
        garage_sensor_security = TRUE;

        print_log ("A person is in the garage.");
        speak       ("A person is in the garage.");

        sprintf (message, "%s - Intruder in Garage", time_buffer);
        send_security_email ("*** SECURITY ALERT ***", message);
    }
```

```
    // Intruder in Pantry?
    if (device_code_set (pantry_sensor) && (!pantry_sensor_security))
    {
        // Yes - Turn alarm siren on and send security alert email
        turn_alarm_siren_on();
        pantry_sensor_security = TRUE;

        print_log ("A person is in the pantry.");
        speak     ("A person is in the pantry.");

        sprintf (message, "%s - Intruder in Pantry", time_buffer);
        send_security_email ("*** SECURITY ALERT ***", message);
    }

    // Intruder in Laundry?
    if (device_code_set (laundry_sensor) && (!laundry_sensor_security))
    {
        // Yes - Turn alarm siren on and send security alert email
        turn_alarm_siren_on();
        laundry_sensor_security = TRUE;

        print_log ("A person is in the laundry.");
        speak     ("A person is in the laundry.");

        sprintf (message, "%s - Intruder in Laundry", time_buffer);
        send_security_email ("*** SECURITY ALERT ***", message);
    }

    // Intruder in Guest Bathroom?
    if (device_code_set (guest_bathroom_sensor) &&
(!guest_bathroom_sensor_security))
    {
        // Yes - Turn alarm siren on and send security alert email
        turn_alarm_siren_on();
        guest_bathroom_sensor_security = TRUE;

        print_log ("A person is in the guest bathroom.");
        speak     ("A person is in the guest bathroom.");

        sprintf (message, "%s - Intruder in Guest Bathroom", time_buffer);
        send_security_email ("*** SECURITY ALERT ***", message);
    }

    // Intruder in Guest Bedroom?
    if (device_code_set (guest_bedroom_door_sensor) &&
(!guest_bedroom_door_sensor_security))
    {
        // Yes - Turn alarm siren on and send security alert email
        turn_alarm_siren_on();
        guest_bedroom_door_sensor_security = TRUE;

        print_log ("A person is in the guest bedroom.");
        speak     ("A person is in the guest bedroom.");

        sprintf (message, "%s - Intruder in Guest Bedroom", time_buffer);
        send_security_email ("*** SECURITY ALERT ***", message);
    }
}
```

```
//**************************************************************************
// Process Laundry Light
//
// This function places required laundry light on/off events into the
// house_code_events table.
//
//**************************************************************************

void  process_laundry_light (void)
{
    long int    turn_off_time;
    long int    current_time;


    // Laundry Sensor activated?
    if (device_code_set (laundry_sensor))
    {
        // Yes - Get current system time
        current_time = get_raw_time ();


        // Yes - Delete any existing laundry light OFF events
        delete_house_code_events (laundry_light);

        // Determine light timeout
        turn_off_time = current_time + OFFSET_1MIN;

        // Turn laundry light ON now
        activate_device (laundry_light, ON,  current_time);

        // Turn laundry light OFF after delay
        activate_device (laundry_light, OFF, turn_off_time);
        activate_device (laundry_light, OFF, turn_off_time + OFFSET_10SEC);
        activate_device (laundry_light, OFF, turn_off_time + OFFSET_20SEC);
    }
}
```

```
//****************************************************************************
// Process Pantry Light
//
// This function places required pantry light on/off events into the
// house_code_events table.
//
//****************************************************************************

void  process_pantry_light (void)
{
    long int    turn_off_time;
    long int    current_time;


    // Pantry Sensor activated?
    if (device_code_set (pantry_sensor))
    {
        // Get current system time
        current_time = get_raw_time ();


        // Yes - Delete any existing pantry light device OFF events
        delete_house_code_events (pantry_light);

        // Determine light timeout
        turn_off_time = current_time + OFFSET_1MIN;

        // Turn pantry light ON now
        activate_device (pantry_light,  ON, current_time);

        // Turn pantry light OFF after delay
        activate_device (pantry_light, OFF, turn_off_time);
        activate_device (pantry_light, OFF, turn_off_time + OFFSET_10SEC);
        activate_device (pantry_light, OFF, turn_off_time + OFFSET_20SEC);
    }
}
```

```
//*************************************************************************
// Process Front Porch Light
//
// This function places required front porch light on/off events into the
// house_code_events table.
//
//*************************************************************************

void  process_front_porch_light (void)
{
    long int    inside_entrance_turn_on_time;
    long int    inside_entrance_turn_off_time;
    long int    porch_turn_on_time;
    long int    porch_turn_off_time;
    long int    current_time;


    // Is it night time?
    if (nightime)
    {
        // Yes - Was the porch sensor activated?
        if (device_code_set (front_porch_sensor))
        {
            // Yes - Inform those at home
            speak ("Someone is at the front door.");

            // Delete any existing events
            delete_house_code_events (porch_outside_light);
            delete_house_code_events (inside_entrance_light);

            // Get current system time
            current_time = get_raw_time();

            // Determine light times
            inside_entrance_turn_on_time = current_time +
                    OFFSET_10SEC +
                    (rand() % OFFSET_7SEC);

            porch_turn_on_time = inside_entrance_turn_on_time +
                    OFFSET_3SEC                    +
                    (rand() % OFFSET_10SEC);

            inside_entrance_turn_off_time = porch_turn_on_time +
                    OFFSET_1MIN        +
                    (rand() % OFFSET_2MIN);

            porch_turn_off_time = porch_turn_on_time +
                    OFFSET_5MIN          +
                    (rand() % OFFSET_10MIN);


            // Turn lights ON
            activate_device (inside_entrance_light, ON,
inside_entrance_turn_on_time);
            activate_device (porch_outside_light,   ON, porch_turn_on_time);

            // Turn lights OFF
```

```
        activate_device (inside_entrance_light, OFF,
inside_entrance_turn_off_time);
        activate_device (porch_outside_light,   OFF, porch_turn_off_time);
    }
  }
}
```

```
//*************************************************************************
// Process Barking Doggy
//
// This function places required barking doggy on events into the
// house_code_events table.
//
// Note: The 'barking doggy' is an X10 device which when triggered will produce
//       approximately 25 seconds of digital barking over an amplified speaker.
//*************************************************************************

void  process_barking_doggy (void)
{
    long int    watchdog_trigger_time;
    long int    current_time;
    static int  retrigger_time = 0;


    // Is the house in SECURITY Mode
    if (security_mode)
    {
        // Yes - Was the porch sensor activated?
        if (device_code_set (front_porch_sensor))
        {
            // Yes - Kick the doggy
            // Get current system time
            current_time = get_raw_time();

            // Is it time to let the dog bark once more?
            if (current_time > retrigger_time)
            {
                // Yes - Reconfigure retrigger time
                retrigger_time = current_time + OFFSET_40SEC + (rand() %
OFFSET_30SEC);

                // Determine when to start barking
                watchdog_trigger_time = current_time + OFFSET_5SEC + (rand() %
OFFSET_10SEC);

                // Activate the watchdog
                activate_device (barking_doggy, ON, watchdog_trigger_time);
            }
        }
    }
}
```

```
//********************************************************************
// Process Main Hallway Light                        ONLY AT NIGHTTIME
//
// This function places required hallway lights on/off events into the
// house_code_events table.
//
//********************************************************************

void  process_main_hallway_light  (void)
{
    char        buffer[255];
    long int    turn_off_time;
    long int    current_time;


    // Is it between dusk and dawn?
    if (between_dusk_and_dawn)
    {
        // Yes - Is the house active mode engaged
        if (!sleep_mode) //(ACTIVE_MODE)
        {
            // Yes - Were the main hallway sensor activated?
            if (device_code_set (main_hallway_sensor)         ||
                device_code_set (lounge_hallway_sensor)       ||
                device_code_set (master_hallway_sensor))
            {
                // Yes - Delete any existing main hallway light device OFF events
                delete_house_code_events (main_hallway_light);


                // Get current system time
                current_time = get_raw_time();

                // Determine light timeout
                turn_off_time = current_time + OFFSET_1MIN;

                // Turn main hallway light ON now
                activate_device (main_hallway_light,  ON, current_time);

                // Turn main hallway light OFF after delay
                activate_device (main_hallway_light, OFF, turn_off_time);
            }
        }
    }
    else
    {
        // No - It is daytime - Was some movement detected in the hallway?
        if (device_code_set (main_hallway_sensor)         ||
            device_code_set (lounge_hallway_sensor)       ||
            device_code_set (master_hallway_sensor))
        {
            // Yes - We may have the condition in which the lights were manually
turned on.
            //        The system will automatically turn them off after a short
delay.

            // Delete any existing device OFF events
            delete_house_code_off_events_before_dusk (main_hallway_light);
```

```
            // Get current system time
            current_time = get_raw_time();

            // Determine light timeout
            turn_off_time = current_time + OFFSET_10MIN;

            // Ensure lights turned off just after dusk do not affect any existing
timers
            limit_turn_off_time_to_just_after_dusk (&turn_off_time);

            delete_house_code_off_events_at_timeout (main_hallway_light,
turn_off_time);

            // Turn light OFF after delay
            activate_device (main_hallway_light, OFF, turn_off_time);
        }
    }
}
```

```
//**************************************************************************
// Process Lounge Light                              EXTENDS LIGHTS UNTIL DAWN
//
// This function places required lounge light on/off events into the
// house_code_events table if there is movement in the hallways AFTER the sleep
// mode has been engaged.  The lounge light is used instead of the hallway
// lights since it is of a lower intensity.
//
//**************************************************************************

void  process_lounge_light (void)
{
    char        buffer[255];
    long int    turn_off_time;
    long int    current_time;


    // Get current system time
    current_time = get_raw_time();

    // Is it between dusk and dawn?
    if (between_dusk_and_dawn)
    {
        // Yes - Is the house sleep mode engaged
        if (sleep_mode)
        {
            // Yes - Were the main hallway sensors activated?
            if (device_code_set (main_hallway_sensor)      ||
                device_code_set (lounge_hallway_sensor)    ||
                device_code_set (master_hallway_sensor))
            {
                // Yes - Delete any existing lounge light events
                delete_house_code_events (lounge_wall_light);
                delete_house_code_events (lounge_window_light);

                // Determine turn off time
                turn_off_time = current_time + OFFSET_1MIN;

                // Turn only the lounge window light ON now
                activate_device (lounge_window_light,  ON, current_time);

                // Turn lounge lights OFF after delay
                activate_device (lounge_wall_light,    OFF, turn_off_time);
                activate_device (lounge_window_light, OFF, turn_off_time);
            }
        }
        else
        {
            // No - We are in active mode
            // Was the lounge hallway sensor activated?
            if (device_code_set (lounge_hallway_sensor))
            {
                // Yes - The lights are expected to still be on,
                //       so extend the lights turn off time until dawn.

                // Delete existing OFF events
                delete_house_code_off_events (lounge_wall_light);
                delete_house_code_off_events (lounge_window_light);
```

```
                // Is the time currently between midnight and sunrise?
                if (current_time < dawn_timeout)
                {
                    // Yes - Set the turn off time for dawn today
                    turn_off_time = dawn_timeout;
                }
                else
                {
                    // No - We are between dusk and midnight.
                    //      So set the turn off time for dawn tomorrow.
                    turn_off_time = dawn_timeout + OFFSET_24HRS;
                }


                // Turn lounge lights OFF after delay
                activate_device (lounge_wall_light,   OFF, turn_off_time);
                activate_device (lounge_window_light, OFF, turn_off_time);
            }
        }
    }
    else
    {
        // No - It is daytime - Was some movement detected in the lounge hallway?
        if (device_code_set (lounge_hallway_sensor))
        {
            // Yes - We may have the condition in which the lights were manually
turned on.
            //        The system will automatically turn them off after a short
delay.

            // Delete any existing device OFF events
            delete_house_code_off_events_before_dusk (lounge_wall_light);
            delete_house_code_off_events_before_dusk (lounge_window_light);

            // Get current system time
            current_time = get_raw_time();

            // Determine light timeout
            turn_off_time = current_time + OFFSET_20MIN;

            // Ensure lights turned off just after dusk do not affect any existing
timers
            limit_turn_off_time_to_just_after_dusk (&turn_off_time);

            delete_house_code_off_events_at_timeout (lounge_wall_light,
turn_off_time);
            delete_house_code_off_events_at_timeout (lounge_window_light,
turn_off_time);

            // Turn light OFF after delay
            activate_device (lounge_wall_light,   OFF, turn_off_time);
            activate_device (lounge_window_light, OFF, turn_off_time);
        }
    }
}
```

```
//***********************************************************************
// Process Familyroom Light                         EXTENDS LIGHTS UNTIL DAWN
//
// This function places required familyroom window light on/off events into the
// house_code_events table. If movement is detected then the lights turn off
// time is extended until dawn.
//
//***********************************************************************

void  process_familyroom_light (void)
{
    char        buffer[255];
    long int    turn_off_time;
    long int    current_time;


    // Get current system time
    current_time = get_raw_time ();

    // Is it between dusk and dawn?
    if (between_dusk_and_dawn)
    {
        // Yes - Was the familyroom sensor activated?
        if (device_code_set (familyroom_sensor))
        {
            // Yes - The lights are expected to still be on,
            //       so extend the lights turn off time until dawn.

            // Delete existing OFF events
            delete_house_code_off_events (familyroom_wall_light);
            delete_house_code_off_events (familyroom_window_light);
            delete_house_code_off_events (familyroom_track_tv_light);
            delete_house_code_off_events (familyroom_track_reading_light);
            delete_house_code_off_events (familyroom_wall_unit_light);
            delete_house_code_off_events (familyroom_wall_unit_spotlight);

            // Setup the OFF time for dawn
            // Is the time currently between midnight and sunrise?
            if (current_time < dawn_timeout)
            {
                // Yes - Set the turn off time for dawn today
                turn_off_time = dawn_timeout;
            }
            else
            {
                // No - We are between dusk and midnight.
                //      So set the turn off time for dawn tomorrow.
                turn_off_time = dawn_timeout + OFFSET_24HRS;
            }

            // Turn familyroom lights OFF after delay
            activate_device (familyroom_wall_light,          OFF, turn_off_time);
            activate_device (familyroom_window_light,        OFF, turn_off_time);
            activate_device (familyroom_track_tv_light,      OFF, turn_off_time);
            activate_device (familyroom_track_reading_light, OFF, turn_off_time);
            activate_device (familyroom_wall_unit_light,     OFF, turn_off_time);
            activate_device (familyroom_wall_unit_spotlight, OFF, turn_off_time);
        }
```

```
    }
    else
    {
        // No - It is daytime - Was some movement detected in the family room?
        if (device_code_set (familyroom_sensor))
        {
            // Yes - We may have the condition in which the lights were manually
turned on.
            //         The system will automatically turn them off after a short
delay.

            // Delete any existing device OFF events
            delete_house_code_off_events_before_dusk (familyroom_wall_light);
            delete_house_code_off_events_before_dusk (familyroom_window_light);
            delete_house_code_off_events_before_dusk (familyroom_track_tv_light);
            delete_house_code_off_events_before_dusk
(familyroom_track_reading_light);
            delete_house_code_off_events_before_dusk (familyroom_wall_unit_light);
            delete_house_code_off_events_before_dusk
(familyroom_wall_unit_spotlight);

            // Get current system time
            current_time = get_raw_time();

            // Determine light timeout
            turn_off_time = current_time + OFFSET_20MIN;

            // Ensure lights turned off just after dusk do not affect any existing
timers
            limit_turn_off_time_to_just_after_dusk (&turn_off_time);

            delete_house_code_off_events_at_timeout (familyroom_wall_light,
turn_off_time);
            delete_house_code_off_events_at_timeout (familyroom_window_light,
turn_off_time);
            delete_house_code_off_events_at_timeout (familyroom_track_tv_light,
turn_off_time);
            delete_house_code_off_events_at_timeout
(familyroom_track_reading_light, turn_off_time);
            delete_house_code_off_events_at_timeout (familyroom_wall_unit_light,
turn_off_time);
            delete_house_code_off_events_at_timeout
(familyroom_wall_unit_spotlight, turn_off_time);


            // Turn light OFF after delay
            activate_device (familyroom_wall_light,          OFF, turn_off_time);
            activate_device (familyroom_window_light,        OFF, turn_off_time);
            activate_device (familyroom_track_tv_light,      OFF, turn_off_time);
            activate_device (familyroom_track_reading_light, OFF, turn_off_time);
            activate_device (familyroom_wall_unit_light,     OFF, turn_off_time);
            activate_device (familyroom_wall_unit_spotlight, OFF, turn_off_time);
        }
    }
}
```

```
//*************************************************************************
// Process Master Bedroom Light                   EXTENDS LIGHTS UNTIL DAWN
//
// This function places required master bedroom light on/off events into the
// house_code_events table.  If movement is detected then the lights turn off
// time is extended until dawn.  In addition, the first time movement is
// detected, the bed side lamps for Mom and Dad will be turned on.
//
//*************************************************************************

void  process_master_bedroom_light (void)
{
    char       buffer[255];
    long int   turn_off_time;
    long int   current_time;
    static int repeated_night_access = TRUE; // Prevent lights turning on at night
if system restarted.
                                        // Mum and Dad will appreciate
this...

    // Get current system time
    current_time = get_raw_time ();

    // Is it between dusk and dawn?
    if (between_dusk_and_dawn)
    {
        // Yes - Was the master bedroom, bathroom or closet sensors activated?
        if ((device_code_set (master_bedroom_sensor))         ||
            (device_code_set (master_bathroom_sensor))        ||
            (device_code_set (master_bedroom_closet_sensor)))
        {
            // Yes - Extend the bedroom lights turn off time until dawn
            //       First delete existing events
            delete_house_code_events (master_bedroom_light);
            delete_house_code_events (master_bedroom_dad_light);
            delete_house_code_events (master_bedroom_mum_light);

            // Setup the OFF time for dawn
            // Is the time currently between midnight and dawn?
            if (current_time < dawn_timeout)
            {
                // Yes - Set the turn off time for dawn today
                turn_off_time = dawn_timeout;
            }
            else
            {
                // No - We are between dusk and midnight.
                //      So set the turn off time for dawn tomorrow.
                turn_off_time = dawn_timeout + OFFSET_24HRS;
            }

            // Turn all the master bedroom lights OFF after delay
            activate_device (master_bedroom_light,     OFF, turn_off_time);
            activate_device (master_bedroom_dad_light, OFF, turn_off_time);
            activate_device (master_bedroom_mum_light, OFF, turn_off_time);

            // Have we been in the Master Bedroom previously this night?
            if (repeated_night_access)
```

```
        {
            // Yes - Don't do anything
            return;
        }

        // No - Remember we have been in the master bedroom
        repeated_night_access = TRUE;

        // Turn all the master bedroom lights ON
        activate_device (master_bedroom_light,      ON, current_time);
        activate_device (master_bedroom_dad_light,  ON, current_time);
        activate_device (master_bedroom_mum_light,  ON, current_time);
    }
}
else
{
    // No - It is daytime - Was some movement detected in the master bedroom?
    if ((device_code_set (master_bedroom_sensor))        ||
        (device_code_set (master_bathroom_sensor))       ||
        (device_code_set (master_bedroom_closet_sensor)))
    {
    // Yes - We may have the condition in which the lights were manually
turned on.
        //      The system will automatically turn them off after a short
delay.

        // Delete any existing device OFF events
        delete_house_code_off_events_before_dusk (master_bedroom_light);
        delete_house_code_off_events_before_dusk (master_bedroom_dad_light);
        delete_house_code_off_events_before_dusk (master_bedroom_mum_light);

        // Get current system time
        current_time = get_raw_time();

        // Determine light timeout
        turn_off_time = current_time + OFFSET_20MIN;

        // Ensure lights turned off just after dusk do not affect any existing
timers
        limit_turn_off_time_to_just_after_dusk (&turn_off_time);

        delete_house_code_off_events_at_timeout (master_bedroom_light,
turn_off_time);
        delete_house_code_off_events_at_timeout (master_bedroom_dad_light,
turn_off_time);
        delete_house_code_off_events_at_timeout (master_bedroom_mum_light,
turn_off_time);

        // Turn light OFF after delay
        activate_device (master_bedroom_light,      OFF, turn_off_time);
        activate_device (master_bedroom_dad_light, OFF, turn_off_time);
        activate_device (master_bedroom_mum_light, OFF, turn_off_time);
    }

    // Reset access
    repeated_night_access = FALSE;
    }
}
```

```
//***************************************************************************
// Process Master Bedroom Closet Light
//
// This function places required master bedroom closet light on/off events into
// the house_code_events table.
//
//***************************************************************************

void  process_master_bedroom_closet_light (void)
{
    long int    turn_off_time;
    long int    current_time;


    // Master closet Sensor activated?
    if (device_code_set (master_bedroom_closet_sensor))
    {
        // Get current system time
        current_time = get_raw_time ();


        // Yes - Delete any existing master closet light device OFF events
        delete_house_code_events (master_bedroom_closet_light);

        // Determine light timeout
        turn_off_time = current_time + OFFSET_5MIN;

        // Turn master closet light ON now
        activate_device (master_bedroom_closet_light,  ON, current_time);

        // Turn master closet light OFF after delay
        activate_device (master_bedroom_closet_light, OFF, turn_off_time);
    }
}
```

```
//****************************************************************************
// Process Inside Entrance Light
//
// This function places required inside entrance lights on/off events into the
// house_code_events table.
//
//****************************************************************************
void  process_inside_entrance_light (void)
{
    char        buffer[255];
    long int    turn_off_time;
    long int    current_time;


    // Is it between dusk and dawn?
    if (between_dusk_and_dawn)
    {
        // Yes - Have we gone to sleep?
        if (sleep_mode)
        {
            // Yes - Do nothing
            return;
        }

        // Was the inside entrance sensor activated?
        if (device_code_set (inside_front_door_sensor))
        {
            // Yes - Delete any existing pantry light device events
            delete_house_code_events (inside_entrance_light);


            // Get current system time
            current_time = get_raw_time ();

            // Determine light timeout
            turn_off_time = current_time + OFFSET_1MIN;

            // Turn inside entrance light ON now
            activate_device (inside_entrance_light,  ON, current_time);

            // Turn inside entrance light OFF after delay
            activate_device (inside_entrance_light, OFF, turn_off_time);
        }
    }
    else
    {
        // No - It is daytime - Was some movement detected in the inside entrance?
        if (device_code_set (inside_front_door_sensor))
        {
            // Yes - We may have the condition in which the lights were manually
turned on.
            //        The system will automatically turn them off after a short
delay.

            // Delete any existing device OFF events
            delete_house_code_off_events_before_dusk (inside_entrance_light);
```

```
            // Get current system time
            current_time = get_raw_time();

            // Determine light timeout
            turn_off_time = current_time + OFFSET_5MIN;

            // Ensure lights turned off just after dusk do not affect any existing
timers
            limit_turn_off_time_to_just_after_dusk (&turn_off_time);

            delete_house_code_off_events_at_timeout (inside_entrance_light,
turn_off_time);

            // Turn light OFF after delay
            activate_device (inside_entrance_light, OFF, turn_off_time);
        }
    }
}
```

```
//****************************************************************************
// Process Kitchen Light
//
// This function places required kitchen lights on/off events into the
// house_code_events table.
//
//****************************************************************************

void  process_kitchen_light (void)
{
    char       buffer[255];
    long int   turn_off_time;
    long int   current_time;


    // Is it between dusk and dawn?
    if (between_dusk_and_dawn)
    {
        // Yes - Were any Kitchen Nook / Kitchen sensors activated?
        if (device_code_set (kitchen_nook_sensor)             ||
            device_code_set (kitchen_sensor)                  ||
            device_code_set (counter_fridge_sensor)           ||
            device_code_set (counter_cooktop_left_sensor)     ||
            device_code_set (counter_cooktop_right_sensor))
        {
            // Yes - Delete any existing kitchen light device OFF events
            delete_house_code_events (kitchen_light);


            // Get current system time
            current_time = get_raw_time();

            // Determine light timeout
            turn_off_time = current_time + OFFSET_10MIN;

            // Turn kitchen light ON now
            activate_device (kitchen_light,  ON, current_time);

            // Turn kitchen light OFF after delay
            activate_device (kitchen_light, OFF, turn_off_time);
        }
    }
    else
    {
        // No - It is daytime - Was some movement detected in the kitchen?
        if (device_code_set (kitchen_nook_sensor)             ||
            device_code_set (kitchen_sensor)                  ||
            device_code_set (counter_fridge_sensor)           ||
            device_code_set (counter_cooktop_left_sensor)     ||
            device_code_set (counter_cooktop_right_sensor))
        {
            // Yes - We may have the condition in which the lights were manually
turned on.
            //        The system will automatically turn them off after a short
delay.

            // Delete any existing device OFF events
            delete_house_code_off_events_before_dusk (kitchen_light);
```

```
            delete_house_code_off_events_before_dusk (kitchen_nook_light);

            // Get current system time
            current_time = get_raw_time();

            // Determine light timeout
            turn_off_time = current_time + OFFSET_15MIN;

            // Ensure lights turned off just after dusk do not affect any existing
timers

            limit_turn_off_time_to_just_after_dusk (&turn_off_time);

            delete_house_code_off_events_at_timeout (kitchen_light,
turn_off_time);
            delete_house_code_off_events_at_timeout (kitchen_nook_light,
turn_off_time);

            // Turn light OFF after delay
            activate_device (kitchen_light,      OFF, turn_off_time);
            activate_device (kitchen_nook_light, OFF, turn_off_time);
        }
    }
}
```

```
//****************************************************************************
// Process Kitchen Nook Light
//
// This function places required kitchen nook light on/off events into the
// house_code_events table.
//
//****************************************************************************
void  process_kitchen_nook_light (void)
{
    char        buffer[255];
    long int    turn_off_time;
    long int    current_time;


    // Is it between dusk and dawn?
    if (between_dusk_and_dawn)
    {
        // Yes - Was the kitchen nook sensor activated?
        if (device_code_set (kitchen_nook_sensor))
        {
            // Yes - Delete any existing kitchen nook light device events
            delete_house_code_events (kitchen_nook_light);


            // Get current system time
            current_time = get_raw_time();

            // Determine light timeout
            turn_off_time = current_time + OFFSET_10MIN;

            // Turn kitchen nook light ON now
            activate_device (kitchen_nook_light,  ON, current_time);

            // Turn kitchen nook light OFF after delay
            activate_device (kitchen_nook_light, OFF, turn_off_time);
        }
    }
    else
    {
        // No - It is daytime - Was some movement detected in the kitchen nook?
        if (device_code_set (kitchen_nook_sensor))
        {
        // Yes - We may have the condition in which the lights were manually
turned on.
        //         The system will automatically turn them off after a short
delay.

            // Delete any existing device OFF events
            delete_house_code_off_events_before_dusk (kitchen_light);
            delete_house_code_off_events_before_dusk (kitchen_nook_light);

            // Get current system time
            current_time = get_raw_time();

            // Determine light timeout
            turn_off_time = current_time + OFFSET_15MIN;
```

```
        // Ensure lights turned off just after dusk do not affect any existing
timers
        limit_turn_off_time_to_just_after_dusk (&turn_off_time);

        delete_house_code_off_events_at_timeout (kitchen_light,
turn_off_time);
        delete_house_code_off_events_at_timeout (kitchen_nook_light,
turn_off_time);

        // Turn light OFF after delay
        activate_device (kitchen_light,      OFF, turn_off_time);
        activate_device (kitchen_nook_light, OFF, turn_off_time);
    }
  }
}
```

```
//*************************************************************************
// Process Common Bathroom Light
//
// This function places required common bathroom light on/off events into the
// house_code_events table.
//
//*************************************************************************
void  process_common_bathroom_light (void)
{
    char        buffer[255];
    long int    turn_off_time;
    long int    current_time;


    // Is it between dusk and dawn?
    if (between_dusk_and_dawn)
    {
        // Yes - Was the common bathroom sensor activated?
        if (device_code_set (common_bathroom_sensor))
        {
            // Yes - Get current system time
            current_time = get_raw_time();

            // Get high resolution timer
            common_bathroom_event = get_high_resolution_timer();

            // Delete any existing common bathroom device OFF events
            delete_house_code_events (common_bathroom_light);

            // Determine light timeout
            turn_off_time = current_time + OFFSET_3MIN;

            // Turn common bathroom light ON now
            activate_device (common_bathroom_light,  ON, current_time);

            // Turn common bathroom light OFF after delay
            activate_device (common_bathroom_light, OFF, turn_off_time);
        }
    }
    else
    {
        // No - It is daytime - Was some movement detected in the common bathroom?
        if (device_code_set (common_bathroom_sensor))
        {
        // Yes - We may have the condition in which the lights were manually
turned on.
        //        The system will automatically turn them off after a short
delay.

            // Delete any existing device OFF events
            delete_house_code_off_events_before_dusk (common_bathroom_light);

            // Get current system time
            current_time = get_raw_time();

            // Determine light timeout
            turn_off_time = current_time + OFFSET_5MIN;
```

```
        // Ensure lights turned off just after dusk do not affect any existing
timers
        limit_turn_off_time_to_just_after_dusk (&turn_off_time);

        delete_house_code_off_events_at_timeout (common_bathroom_light,
turn_off_time);

        // Turn light OFF after delay
        activate_device (common_bathroom_light, OFF, turn_off_time);
    }
  }
}
```

How to build a LAMP project

```
//**************************************************************************
// Process Common Washroom Light
//
// This function places required common washroom light on/off events into the
// house_code_events table.
//
//**************************************************************************
void  process_common_washroom_light (void)
{
    char        buffer[255];
    long int    turn_off_time;
    long int    current_time;


    // Is it between dusk and dawn?
    if (between_dusk_and_dawn)
    {
        // Yes - Was the common washroom sensor activated?
        if (device_code_set (common_washroom_sensor))
        {
            // Yes - Get current system time
            current_time = get_raw_time ();

            // Get high resolution timer
            common_washroom_event = get_high_resolution_timer ();

            // Delete any existing common washroom device OFF events
            delete_house_code_events (common_washroom_light);
            delete_house_code_events (common_washroom_flight);
            delete_house_code_events (common_bathroom_light);

            // Determine light timeout
            turn_off_time = current_time + OFFSET_3MIN;

            // Turn common washroom light ON
            activate_device (common_washroom_light,  ON, current_time);

            // Since we are in the washroom, turn off the common bathroom light
            activate_device (common_bathroom_light,  OFF, current_time+10);

            // Turn common washroom light OFF after delay
            activate_device (common_washroom_light,  OFF, turn_off_time);
            activate_device (common_washroom_flight, OFF, turn_off_time);
        }
    }
    else
    {
        // No - It is daytime - Was some movement detected in the common washroom?
        if (device_code_set (common_washroom_sensor))
        {
            // Yes - We may have the condition in which the lights were manually
turned on.
            //          The system will automatically turn them off after a short
delay.

            // Delete any existing device OFF events
            delete_house_code_off_events_before_dusk (common_washroom_light);
```

236

```
            delete_house_code_off_events_before_dusk (common_washroom_flight);

            // Get current system time
            current_time = get_raw_time();

            // Determine light timeout
            turn_off_time = current_time + OFFSET_5MIN;

            // Ensure lights turned off just after dusk do not affect any existing
timers

            limit_turn_off_time_to_just_after_dusk (&turn_off_time);

            delete_house_code_off_events_at_timeout (common_washroom_light,
turn_off_time);
            delete_house_code_off_events_at_timeout (common_washroom_flight,
turn_off_time);

            // Turn light OFF after delay
            activate_device (common_washroom_light,  OFF, turn_off_time);
            activate_device (common_washroom_flight, OFF, turn_off_time);
        }
    }
}
```

```
//*************************************************************************
// Process Steve Bedroom Wall Light
//
// This function places required Steve bedroom wall light on/off events into the
// house_code_events table.
//
//*************************************************************************
void  process_steve_bedroom_wall_light (void)
{
    int        parameter;
    char       buffer[255];
    long int   turn_off_time;
    long int   current_time;


    // Have we turned in for the night?
    if (sleep_mode)
    {
        // Yes - Do not activate any wall lights in Steve's bedroom
        return;
    }


    // Is it between dusk and dawn?
    if (between_dusk_and_dawn)
    {
        // Yes - Was Steve's bedroom sensor activated?
        if (device_code_set (steve_bedroom_sensor))
        {
            // Yes - Get current system time
            current_time = get_raw_time();

            // Get high resolution timer
            steve_bedroom_event = get_high_resolution_timer();

            // Get Steve's lights control parameter
            if (get_house_state_parameter (HS_STEVE_LIGHTS, &parameter) == SUCCESS)
            {
                // Are we watching TV?
                if (parameter == HS_TV_MODE)
                {
                    // Yes - Do not switch on Steve's room lights
                    return;
                }
            }

            // Delete any existing Steve's bedroom light device events
            delete_house_code_events (steve_bedroom_ceiling_light);
            delete_house_code_events (steve_bedroom_window_light);
            delete_house_code_events (steve_bedroom_wall_light);
            delete_house_code_events (steve_bedroom_reading_light);

            // Get current system time
            current_time = get_raw_time();

            // Determine light timeout
            turn_off_time = current_time + OFFSET_10MIN;
```

238

```
                // Turn Steve's bedroom light ON now
                activate_device (steve_bedroom_wall_light,   ON, current_time);
                activate_device (steve_bedroom_window_light, ON, current_time);

                // Turn Steve's bedroom light OFF after delay
                activate_device (steve_bedroom_ceiling_light, OFF, turn_off_time);
                activate_device (steve_bedroom_wall_light,    OFF, turn_off_time);
                activate_device (steve_bedroom_window_light,  OFF, turn_off_time);
                activate_device (steve_bedroom_reading_light, OFF, turn_off_time);
            }
        }
    else
        {
        // No - It is daytime - Was some movement detected in the common bathroom?
        if (device_code_set (steve_bedroom_sensor))
            {
            // Yes - We may have the condition in which the lights were manually
turned on.
            //          The system will automatically turn them off after a short
delay.

                // Delete any existing device OFF events
                delete_house_code_off_events_before_dusk (steve_bedroom_ceiling_light);
                delete_house_code_off_events_before_dusk (steve_bedroom_window_light);
                delete_house_code_off_events_before_dusk (steve_bedroom_wall_light);
                delete_house_code_off_events_before_dusk (steve_bedroom_reading_light);

                // Get current system time
                current_time = get_raw_time();

                // Determine light timeout
                turn_off_time = current_time + OFFSET_10MIN;

                // Ensure lights turned off just after dusk do not affect any existing
timers
                limit_turn_off_time_to_just_after_dusk (&turn_off_time);

                delete_house_code_off_events_at_timeout (steve_bedroom_ceiling_light,
turn_off_time);
                delete_house_code_off_events_at_timeout (steve_bedroom_wall_light,
turn_off_time);
                delete_house_code_off_events_at_timeout (steve_bedroom_window_light,
turn_off_time);
                delete_house_code_off_events_at_timeout (steve_bedroom_reading_light,
turn_off_time);

                // Turn light OFF after delay
                activate_device (steve_bedroom_ceiling_light, OFF, turn_off_time);
                activate_device (steve_bedroom_wall_light,    OFF, turn_off_time);
                activate_device (steve_bedroom_window_light,  OFF, turn_off_time);
                activate_device (steve_bedroom_reading_light, OFF, turn_off_time);
            }
        }
    }
```

```
//*************************************************************************
// Process Study Ceiling Light
//
// This function places required study ceiling light on/off events into the
// house_code_events table.
//
//*************************************************************************

void  process_study_ceiling_light (void)
{
    char                buffer[255];
    long int            turn_off_time;
    long int            current_time;


    // Is it between dusk and dawn?
    if (between_dusk_and_dawn)
    {
        // Yes - Was the study sensor activated?
        if (device_code_set (study_sensor))
        {
            // Yes - Get current system time
            current_time = get_raw_time();

            // Get high resolution timer
            study_event = get_high_resolution_timer();

            // Delete any existing study ceiling light device OFF events
            delete_house_code_events (study_ceiling_light);

            // Determine light timeout
            turn_off_time = current_time + OFFSET_15MIN;

            // Turn Study ceiling light ON now
            activate_device (study_ceiling_light,  ON, current_time);

            // Turn Study ceiling light OFF after delay
            activate_device (study_ceiling_light, OFF, turn_off_time);
        }
    }
    else
    {
        // No - It is daytime - Was some movement detected in the common bathroom?
        if (device_code_set (study_sensor))
        {
            // Yes - We may have the condition in which the lights were manually
turned on.
            //       The system will automatically turn them off after a short
delay.

            // Delete any existing device OFF events
            delete_house_code_off_events_before_dusk (study_ceiling_light);

            // Get current system time
            current_time = get_raw_time();

            // Determine light timeout
```

```
        turn_off_time = current_time + OFFSET_10MIN;

        // Ensure lights turned off just after dusk do not affect any existing
timers
        limit_turn_off_time_to_just_after_dusk (&turn_off_time);

        delete_house_code_off_events_at_timeout (study_ceiling_light,
turn_off_time);

        // Turn light OFF after delay
        activate_device (study_ceiling_light, OFF, turn_off_time);
      }
    }
}
```

```
//**********************************************************************
// Fast Transition
//
// This function determines if the first event occurred prior to the second
// event.  Remember that these event counts are in milliseconds.
//
//**********************************************************************

Uint8  fast_transition (long int  event1,  long int  event2)
{

    // Did the two events take place within fifteen seconds of each other?
    if (abs(event1 - event2) < 15000)
    {
        // Yes - Determine the order of the events
        return (event1 < event2);
    }
    else
    {
        // No - Ignore the transition
        return (FALSE);
    }

}
```

```
//****************************************************************************
// Determine Fast Transition Events
//
// This function attempts to switch lights off determined upon the user's
// movement from one room to another.
//
//****************************************************************************

void   determine_fast_transition_events (void)
{
    long int    current_time;
    long int    turn_off_time;
    char        message[255];

    static Uint8    study_to_steve_bedroom    = FALSE;
    static Uint8    steve_bedroom_to_study    = FALSE;
    static Uint8    study_to_common_bathroom = FALSE;
    static Uint8    steve_bedroom_to_common_bathroom = FALSE;
    static Uint8    common_bathroom_to_study_or_steve_bedroom = FALSE;


    // Yes - Get current system time
    current_time = get_raw_time ();

    // Determine light timeout
    turn_off_time = current_time + OFFSET_30SEC;


    // Person leaving study and entering Steve's bedroom
    if (fast_transition (study_event, common_washroom_event) &&
        fast_transition (common_washroom_event, steve_bedroom_event))
    {
        if (!study_to_steve_bedroom)
        {
            // Print log message
            print_log ("Fast Transition: Study -> Steve's Bedroom");

            // Delete any existing device ON/OFF events
            delete_house_code_events (study_ceiling_light);
            delete_house_code_events (common_washroom_light);
            delete_house_code_events (common_washroom_flight);

            // Turn lights OFF after delay
            activate_device (study_ceiling_light,    OFF, turn_off_time);
            activate_device (common_washroom_light,  OFF, turn_off_time+3);
            activate_device (common_washroom_flight, OFF, turn_off_time+3);

            // Prevent repeated operation
            study_to_steve_bedroom = TRUE;
        }
    }
    else
    {
        study_to_steve_bedroom = FALSE;
    }


    // Person leaving Steve's bedroom and entering Study
```

243

```
if (fast_transition (steve_bedroom_event, common_washroom_event) &&
    fast_transition (common_washroom_event, study_event))
{
    if (!steve_bedroom_to_study)
    {
        // Print log message
        print_log ("Fast Transition: Steve's Bedroom -> Study");

        // Delete any existing device ON/OFF events
        delete_house_code_events (steve_bedroom_ceiling_light);
        delete_house_code_events (steve_bedroom_window_light);
        delete_house_code_events (steve_bedroom_wall_light);
        delete_house_code_events (steve_bedroom_reading_light);
        delete_house_code_events (common_washroom_flight);
        delete_house_code_events (common_washroom_light);
        delete_house_code_events (common_bathroom_light);

        // Turn lights OFF after delay
        activate_device (steve_bedroom_ceiling_light, OFF, turn_off_time);
        activate_device (steve_bedroom_window_light, OFF, turn_off_time);
        activate_device (steve_bedroom_wall_light,   OFF, turn_off_time);
        activate_device (steve_bedroom_reading_light, OFF, turn_off_time);
        activate_device (common_washroom_flight,     OFF, turn_off_time+3);
        activate_device (common_washroom_light,      OFF, turn_off_time+3);
        activate_device (common_bathroom_light,      OFF, turn_off_time+3);

        // Prevent repeated operation
        steve_bedroom_to_study = TRUE;
    }
}
else
{
    steve_bedroom_to_study = FALSE;
}


// Person leaving Steve's bedroom to enter the Common Bathroom
if (fast_transition (steve_bedroom_event, common_washroom_event) &&
    fast_transition (common_washroom_event, common_bathroom_event))
{
    if (!steve_bedroom_to_common_bathroom)
    {
        // Print log message
        print_log ("Fast Transition: Steve's Bedroom -> Common Bathroom");

        // Delete any existing device ON/OFF events
        delete_house_code_events (steve_bedroom_ceiling_light);
        delete_house_code_events (steve_bedroom_window_light);
        delete_house_code_events (steve_bedroom_wall_light);
        delete_house_code_events (steve_bedroom_reading_light);
        delete_house_code_events (common_washroom_light);
        delete_house_code_events (common_washroom_flight);

        // Turn lights OFF after delay
        activate_device (steve_bedroom_ceiling_light, OFF, turn_off_time);
        activate_device (steve_bedroom_window_light, OFF, turn_off_time);
        activate_device (steve_bedroom_wall_light,   OFF, turn_off_time);
        activate_device (steve_bedroom_reading_light, OFF, turn_off_time);
```

```
                activate_device (common_washroom_light,        OFF, turn_off_time+3);
                activate_device (common_washroom_flight,       OFF, turn_off_time+3);

                // Prevent repeated operation
                steve_bedroom_to_common_bathroom = TRUE;
            }
        }
        else
        {
            steve_bedroom_to_common_bathroom = FALSE;
        }


        // Person leaving Study to enter the Common Bathroom
        if (fast_transition (study_event, common_washroom_event) &&
            fast_transition (common_washroom_event, common_bathroom_event))
        {
            if (!study_to_common_bathroom)
            {
                // Print log message
                print_log ("Fast Transition: Study -> Common Bathroom");

                // Delete any existing device ON/OFF events
                delete_house_code_events (study_ceiling_light);
                delete_house_code_events (common_washroom_light);
                delete_house_code_events (common_washroom_flight);

                // Turn lights OFF after delay
                activate_device (study_ceiling_light,    OFF, turn_off_time);
                activate_device (common_washroom_light,  OFF, turn_off_time+3);
                activate_device (common_washroom_flight, OFF, turn_off_time+3);

                // Prevent repeated operation
                study_to_common_bathroom = TRUE;
            }
        }
        else
        {
            study_to_common_bathroom = FALSE;
        }


        // Person leaving Common Bathroom to enter Study or Steve's Bedroom
        if (fast_transition (common_bathroom_event, common_washroom_event) &&
            (fast_transition (common_washroom_event, study_event) ||
            fast_transition (common_washroom_event, steve_bedroom_event)))
        {
            if (!common_bathroom_to_study_or_steve_bedroom)
            {
                // Print log message
                print_log ("Fast Transition: Common Bathroom -> Study or Steve's
Bedroom");

                // Delete any existing device ON/OFF events
                delete_house_code_events (common_bathroom_light);
                delete_house_code_events (common_washroom_light);
                delete_house_code_events (common_washroom_flight);
```

```
            // Turn lights OFF after delay
            activate_device (common_bathroom_light,  OFF, turn_off_time);
            activate_device (common_washroom_light,  OFF, turn_off_time+3);
            activate_device (common_washroom_flight, OFF, turn_off_time+3);

            // Prevent repeated operation
            common_bathroom_to_study_or_steve_bedroom = TRUE;
        }
    }
    else
    {
        common_bathroom_to_study_or_steve_bedroom = FALSE;
    }

}
```

```
//***************************************************************************
// Process ON Events
//
// This function places required events into the house_code_events table
//
//***************************************************************************

void  process_on_events (void)
{
    int  house_state_security;
    int  house_state_sleep;


    // Determine home security state
    if (get_house_state_security (&house_state_security) == SUCCESS)
    {
        // Has the house security mode been engaged?
        if (house_state_security == SECURITY_MODE_ACTIVE)
        {
            // Yes - Security mode status engaged
            security_mode = TRUE;
        }
        else
        {
            // No - Home mode status engaged
            security_mode = FALSE;

            // Reset the security detection flags
            reset_security_detection_flags();
        }
    }


    // Determine sleep state
    if (get_house_state_sleep (&house_state_sleep) == SUCCESS)
    {
        // Has the house active mode been engaged?
        if (house_state_sleep == SLEEP_MODE_INACTIVE)
        {
            // Yes - Active mode status engaged
            sleep_mode = FALSE;
        }

        // Has the house sleep mode been activated?
        else if (house_state_sleep == SLEEP_MODE_INITIATED)
        {
            // Yes - Sleep mode status pending

        }
        else if (house_state_sleep == SLEEP_MODE_DELAY)
        {
            // Yes - Sleep mode status pending

        }
        else if (house_state_sleep == SLEEP_MODE_ACTIVE)
        {
            // Sleep mode status fully engaged
            sleep_mode  = TRUE;
```

```
    }
}


// Is the HOME SECURITY mode engaged?
if (security_mode)
{
    // Yes - Keep a watchfull eye on things...
    process_front_porch_light();
    process_barking_doggy();

    // Check to see if there is an intruder
    process_intruder_check();
}
else
{
    // No - Home Security is deactivated
    // Let the user control the house lights
    process_laundry_light();
    process_pantry_light();
    process_main_hallway_light();
    process_front_porch_light();
    process_inside_entrance_light();
    process_kitchen_light();
    process_kitchen_nook_light();
    process_steve_bedroom_wall_light();
    process_common_bathroom_light();
    process_common_washroom_light();
    process_study_ceiling_light();
    process_familyroom_light();
    process_lounge_light();
    process_master_bedroom_light();
    process_master_bedroom_closet_light();

    // Determine if fast transition occured which might
    // allow the system to turn off lights quicker.
    determine_fast_transition_events();
}

}
```

```
//****************************************************************************
// Process WF800 State Changes
//
// This function reads data from the serial port attached to the WF800 device.
// The received data provides X10 house and unit codes of the infra-red sensor
// device that detected someone's presence.
//
//****************************************************************************

void  process_wf800_state_changes (void)
{
    int         hu_state;
    int         num_bytes_read;
    char        buffer[255];
    char        input_buffer[255];
    char        time_buffer[255];
    char        message [255];
    long int    current_time;

    static int       last_hu_state  = 0;
    static int       last_house_code = 0;
    static int       last_unit_code = 0;
    static long int  last_time = 0;



    // Blocking read characters from the Serial Port.
    // Wait until 4 chars read or a 100ms inter-character timeout occurs.
    // This does NOT wait for 100ms if no characters are received!!!
    num_bytes_read = read(fd, input_buffer, 255);


    // Convert First and Third RF Message Bytes into House / Unit Codes
    x10_convert_rf_codes (input_buffer[0], input_buffer[2]);

    // Was a valid RF code received?
    if (x10_rf_code == VALID)
    {
        // Get current system time
        current_time = get_raw_time();

        // Indicate if ON or OFF operation
        if (command == X10_ON)
        {
            hu_state = 1;
        }
        else
        {
            hu_state = 0;
        }

        // Was this a repeat message?
        if ((hu_state  == last_hu_state)       &&
                (house_code == last_house_code)       &&
                (unit_code  == last_unit_code))
        {
            // Yes - Was it within the last 5 seconds?
            if ((current_time - last_time) < 5)
```

249

```
            {
                // Yes - Ignore this command
                return;
            }
        }
        else
        {
            // No - This is a new message
            //      Remember this message parameters
            last_hu_state   = hu_state;
            last_house_code = house_code;
            last_unit_code  = unit_code;
        }


        // Remember last time the same message was processed
        last_time = current_time;

        // Compute current timestamp
        determine_system_timestamp (time_buffer);


        // House Code States DATABASE
        // ==========================
        // Create the MySQL command to update the 'house_code_states' table
        // with an entry for the RF house/unit code data received

        if (hu_state == 1)
        {
            // Configure state ON
            sprintf (buffer,
                    "UPDATE house_code_states SET state=%d, timestamp='%s',
timeout=%ld, presence=%ld WHERE house=%d AND unit=%d",
                    hu_state,
                    time_buffer,
                    current_time + OFFSET_2MIN,
                    ZERO_PRESENCE_TIMEOUT,
                    //                     current_time +
presence_timeout[house_code][unit_code],
                    house_code,
                    unit_code);

            // Yes - Display House and Unit Codes
            // printf ("House = %c, Unit = %d, ON\n", (0x40 + house_code),
unit_code);

            // We now have received a valid X10 Infra-Red code
            // Process the command for this event time
            process_on_events();
        }
        else
        {
            // Configure state OFF
            sprintf (buffer,
                    "UPDATE house_code_states SET state=%d, timestamp='%s'  WHERE
house=%d AND unit=%d",
                    hu_state,
```

```
                    time_buffer,
                    house_code,
                    unit_code);

        // Yes - Display House and Unit Codes
        // printf ("House = %c, Unit = %d, OFF\n", (0x40 + house_code),
unit_code);
        }

    // Display the MySQL Command on the terminal (or log file)
    // printf ("%s\n", buffer);

    // Issue the update command to the MySQL Database
    if (mysql_query(conn1, buffer))
    {
        // Error Detected - Print error message but still continue...
        sprintf (message, "Error_E1 %u: %s", mysql_errno(conn1),
mysql_error(conn1));
        print_log (message);
    }
}
else
{
    // An invalid RF Code was received
    // printf ("Invalid House and Unit Codes!!!\n");
}
}
```

How to build a LAMP project

```
//****************************************************************************
// main()
//
// The RF control codes are converted from their
// internal representation into standard X10 House/Unit codes.
//
// These codes are subsequently placed into the MySQL database.
//
//****************************************************************************

main()
{
    char    message[255];
    char    time_buffer[255];


    // Identify program
    print_log ("");
    print_log ("Program 'hc_main' Started...\n");

    // Install the termination interrupt handler
    install_signal_interrupt_handler();

    // Sleep a few seconds [May require more if initializing all the databases!!!]
    // This allows the Mysql system to startup
    msleep (5000);      // Five seconds

    // Compute current timestamp
    determine_system_timestamp (time_buffer);

    // Send email stating Security Mode Activation
    sprintf (message, "%s - Home Control Program Started [HC_MAIN]...",
time_buffer);
//  send_security_email ("*** SECURITY INFO ***", message);

    // Verify System Startup snap picture and email operation
    print_log ("Program 'hc_main' has taken a test picture...\n");
    snap_picture (STUDY_PICTURE_FILE);
    msleep (1000);

    snap_picture (STUDY_PICTURE_FILE);
    sprintf (message, "%s - System Startup [HC_MAIN] - Study Test Image",
time_buffer);
//  send_security_email_with_attachment ("*** SECURITY INFO ***", message,
STUDY_PICTURE_FILE);
    speak ("A test picture has been taken.");

    // Initialize serial port for WF800 RF32A Receiver
    initialize_serial_port_for_wf800();

    // Initialize the 'system_control' database
    initialize_system_control_database();

    // Prepare to start the main loop
    print_log ("*");
    print_log ("* Initialization completed *");
    print_log ("*");
```

```
    // Do Forever
    while (!exit_flag)
    {
        // Determine Day/Night Transition Times
        determine_periodic_transition_times();

        // Process events that occur at start of solar periods
        process_events_that_occur_at_midnight();
        process_events_that_occur_at_sunrise();
        process_events_that_occur_at_sunset();

        // Process any IR-RF X-10 state changes (Blocking)
        process_wf800_state_changes();
    }


    // Program is being terminated...
    // Restore the Serial Port to its previous configuration
    tcsetattr(fd, TCSANOW, &old_options);

    // Program terminated
    speak ("The program has been terminated.");
    print_log ("");
    print_log ("Program 'hc_main' has been terminated.");
}
```

File: hc_ti103.c

```
//****************************************************************************
//  Author: Stephen W. McClure
//    Date: March 2014
// Project: Designing Embedded Systems [Book]
//
//****************************************************************************
// Purpose:
//
// This program interfaces with the TI103 X-10 Line Interface Unit.
//
// The TI103 Interface is a device that can transmit and receive X10 commands
// over the household 110VAC mains wiring.  The TI103 program interface is
// controlled by sending commands over the computer system RS232 Serial Port.
//
// Commands may be sent to this unit and status replies received.
// Currently the TI103 is configured only for transmitted commands.
//
//****************************************************************************
//
// File Name: hc_ti103.c
//
// Build command
// gcc hc_ti103.c -o hc_ti103 `mysql_config --cflags --libs`
//
// Execution Command
// ./hc_ti103 > hc_ti103.log &
//
//
// But first don't forget to sign in as SU and give the appropriate serial
// ports the access right permissions (eg.: chmod a+rw /dev/ttyS1) and to
// also use the static ip address: 192.168.1.176 (set by using wired network
// connection icon in the bottom right of the Mint 13 GUI)
//
// For example:
// $ su
// Password: enter super user password
// # chmod a+rw   /dev/ttyS0
// # chmod a+rw   /dev/ttyS1
// # exit
//
// chmod a+r   /dev/ttyS0  Set ttyS0 for Input Only [ORION-ITX TOP    Port]
// chmod a+rw  /dev/ttyS1  Set ttyS1 for I/O        [ORION-ITX BOTTOM Port]
//
// ttyS0  -  Top Port    = RF X10 Commands
// ttyS1  -  Bottom Port = TI-103
//
// Or make the user 'orion' part of the "dialout" group
// which will give it RW permission to the ttys0 and ttys1 serial ports
// by issuing the following instruction: sudo adduser orion dialout
// (will need to provide the su password).
//
// When using autostart a delay is required at the start of this program's
// execution in order to allow the MySQL system to be initialized prior to it
// being accessed.
//****************************************************************************
```

254

```
// Include System Files
#include <sys/types.h>
#include <sys/stat.h>
#include <fcntl.h>
#include <unistd.h>
#include <stdio.h>
#include <stdlib.h>
#include <my_global.h>
#include <mysql.h>
#include <sys/time.h>
#include <string.h>
#include <termios.h>
#include <signal.h>
#include <time.h>


// Include local header Files
#include "hc_literals.h"
#include "hc_typedefs.h"
#include "hc_publics.h"

// Include local modules
#include "hc_common.c"
```

```
//**********************************************************************
// initialize_serial_port_for_ti103_control
//
// Initialize the serial port for X-10 TI103 control.
//
//**********************************************************************

void  initialize_serial_port_for_ti103_control (void)
{
    // Open Com1 for Read/Write Operations
    fd = open(SERIAL_PORT_1, O_RDWR | O_NOCTTY | O_NDELAY);

    // Was the serial port opened successfully?
    if (fd == -1)
    {
        // No - Display error message and exit
        perror("open_port: Unable to open /dev/ttyS1");
        exit(1);
    }
    else
    {
        // Yes -
        fcntl(fd, F_SETFL, FNDELAY);   // Return immediately
//  fcntl(fd, F_SETFL, 0);             // Block if no characters are available
    }


    // Save the current options for the port...
    tcgetattr(fd, &old_options);

    // Get the current options for the port...
    tcgetattr(fd, &new_options);

    // Set the baud rates to 9600...
    cfsetispeed(&new_options, B9600);
    cfsetospeed(&new_options, B9600);

    // Enable the receiver and set local mode...
    new_options.c_cflag |= (CLOCAL | CREAD);

    // Set No Parity, 8-N-1
    new_options.c_cflag &= ~PARENB;
    new_options.c_cflag &= ~CSTOPB;
    new_options.c_cflag &= ~CSIZE;
    new_options.c_cflag |= CS8;

    // Set the new options for the port...
    tcsetattr(fd, TCSANOW, &new_options);
}
```

```
//*************************************************************************
// Setup Outside Light OFF Events
//
// This function performs the following operations:
//
// 1. Remove all existing light events from event database table
// 2. Create new light events
// 3. Lights activate at sunset + delta
//
// Note: Included retries in case of electrical noise affecting lamp turn off.
//*************************************************************************

void  setup_outside_light_OFF_events (void)
{
    long int    timeout1, timeout2, timeout3;
    long int    timeout4, timeout5, timeout6;
    long int    override_off_timeout;
    long int    current_time;


    // Log operation
    print_log ("Processed Outside Light OFF events");

    // Get current time in seconds
    current_time = get_raw_time();


    // Setup Sunrise lamp off events
    timeout1 = sunrise_timeout + OFFSET_30MIN + (rand() % OFFSET_30MIN);
    timeout2 = sunrise_timeout + OFFSET_30MIN + (rand() % OFFSET_30MIN);
    timeout3 = sunrise_timeout + OFFSET_30MIN + (rand() % OFFSET_30MIN);
    timeout4 = sunrise_timeout + OFFSET_30MIN + (rand() % OFFSET_30MIN);
    timeout5 = sunrise_timeout + OFFSET_30MIN + (rand() % OFFSET_30MIN);
    timeout6 = sunrise_timeout + OFFSET_30MIN + (rand() % OFFSET_30MIN);


    // Program the lamp OFF events (Only if it is between midnight and dusk)
    if (current_time <= dusk_timeout)
    {
        // Delete existing outside light events
        delete_house_code_off_events (garage_back_outside_light);
        delete_house_code_off_events (familyroom_outside_light);
        delete_house_code_off_events (diningroom_outside_light);
        delete_house_code_off_events (master_bedroom_outside_light);
        delete_house_code_off_events (garage_front_outside_light);
        delete_house_code_off_events (porch_outside_light);


        activate_device (garage_back_outside_light,    OFF, timeout1);
        activate_device (garage_back_outside_light,    OFF, timeout1+OFFSET_5MIN);
        activate_device (garage_back_outside_light,    OFF,
timeout1+OFFSET_10MIN);

        activate_device (familyroom_outside_light,     OFF, timeout2);
        activate_device (familyroom_outside_light,     OFF, timeout2+OFFSET_5MIN);
        activate_device (familyroom_outside_light,     OFF,
timeout2+OFFSET_10MIN);
```

```
        activate_device (diningroom_outside_light,       OFF, timeout3);
        activate_device (diningroom_outside_light,       OFF, timeout3+OFFSET_5MIN);
        activate_device (diningroom_outside_light,       OFF,
timeout3+OFFSET_10MIN);

        activate_device (master_bedroom_outside_light, OFF, timeout4);
        activate_device (master_bedroom_outside_light, OFF, timeout4+OFFSET_5MIN);
        activate_device (master_bedroom_outside_light, OFF,
timeout4+OFFSET_10MIN);

        activate_device (garage_front_outside_light,   OFF, timeout5);
        activate_device (garage_front_outside_light,   OFF, timeout5+OFFSET_5MIN);
        activate_device (garage_front_outside_light,   OFF,
timeout5+OFFSET_10MIN);

        activate_device (porch_outside_light,           OFF, timeout6);
        activate_device (porch_outside_light,           OFF, timeout6+OFFSET_5MIN);
        activate_device (porch_outside_light,           OFF,
timeout6+OFFSET_10MIN);
    }

}
```

```
//****************************************************************************
// Setup Outside Light ON Events
//
// This function performs the following operations:
//
// 1. Remove all existing light events from event database table
// 2. Create new light events
// 3. Lights activate at sunset + delta
//
// Note: Included retries in case of electrical noise affecting lamp turn on.
//****************************************************************************

void  setup_outside_light_ON_events (void)
{
    long int    timeout1, timeout2, timeout3;
    long int    timeout4, timeout5, timeout6;
    long int    override_off_timeout;
    long int    current_time;


    // Log operation
    print_log ("Processed Outside Light ON events");

    // Get current time in seconds
    current_time = get_raw_time();

    // Setup Sunset lamp on events
    timeout1 = sunset_timeout + OFFSET_10MIN + (rand() % OFFSET_15MIN);
    timeout2 = sunset_timeout + OFFSET_10MIN + (rand() % OFFSET_15MIN);
    timeout3 = sunset_timeout + OFFSET_10MIN + (rand() % OFFSET_15MIN);
    timeout4 = sunset_timeout + OFFSET_10MIN + (rand() % OFFSET_15MIN);
    timeout5 = sunset_timeout + OFFSET_10MIN + (rand() % OFFSET_15MIN);
    timeout6 = sunset_timeout + OFFSET_10MIN + (rand() % OFFSET_15MIN);


    // Delete existing outside light ON events
    delete_house_code_on_events (garage_back_outside_light);
    delete_house_code_on_events (familyroom_outside_light);
    delete_house_code_on_events (diningroom_outside_light);
    delete_house_code_on_events (garage_front_outside_light);


    // Program the lamp ON events
    activate_device (garage_back_outside_light,    ON, timeout1);
    activate_device (familyroom_outside_light,     ON, timeout2);
    activate_device (diningroom_outside_light,     ON, timeout3);
    activate_device (garage_front_outside_light,   ON, timeout4);

    activate_device (garage_back_outside_light,    ON, timeout1+OFFSET_5MIN);
    activate_device (familyroom_outside_light,     ON, timeout2+OFFSET_5MIN);
    activate_device (diningroom_outside_light,     ON, timeout3+OFFSET_5MIN);
    activate_device (garage_front_outside_light,   ON, timeout4+OFFSET_5MIN);

    activate_device (garage_back_outside_light,    ON, timeout1+OFFSET_10MIN);
    activate_device (familyroom_outside_light,     ON, timeout2+OFFSET_10MIN);
    activate_device (diningroom_outside_light,     ON, timeout3+OFFSET_10MIN);
    activate_device (garage_front_outside_light,   ON, timeout4+OFFSET_10MIN);
```

How to build a LAMP project

```
    // Master bedroom outside light override OFF [between 10pm and 10:30pm]
    // Dad does not like the light shining in through the bedroom window
    override_off_timeout = midnight_timeout + OFFSET_22HRS + (rand() %
OFFSET_30MIN);

    // Only install ON/OFF events if master bedroom outside lamp is not about to
be turned off
    if (current_time < (override_off_timeout - OFFSET_2MIN))
    {
        delete_house_code_events (master_bedroom_outside_light);

        activate_device (master_bedroom_outside_light, ON, timeout5);
        activate_device (master_bedroom_outside_light, ON, timeout5+OFFSET_5MIN);
        activate_device (master_bedroom_outside_light, ON, timeout5+OFFSET_10MIN);

        activate_device (master_bedroom_outside_light, OFF, override_off_timeout);
        activate_device (master_bedroom_outside_light, OFF,
override_off_timeout+OFFSET_5MIN);
        activate_device (master_bedroom_outside_light, OFF,
override_off_timeout+OFFSET_10MIN);
    }
    else
    {
        // Otherwise just switch the lamp off
        delete_house_code_off_events (master_bedroom_outside_light);

        activate_device (master_bedroom_outside_light, OFF, current_time);
        activate_device (master_bedroom_outside_light, OFF,
current_time+OFFSET_5MIN);
        activate_device (master_bedroom_outside_light, OFF,
current_time+OFFSET_10MIN);
    }


    // Front porch outside light override OFF [between 9pm and 9:40pm]
    override_off_timeout = midnight_timeout + OFFSET_21HRS + (rand() %
OFFSET_40MIN);

    // Only install ON/OFF events if porch lamp is not about to be turned off
    if (current_time < (override_off_timeout - OFFSET_2MIN))
    {
        delete_house_code_events (porch_outside_light);

        activate_device (porch_outside_light,  ON, timeout6);
        activate_device (porch_outside_light,  ON, timeout6+OFFSET_5MIN);
        activate_device (porch_outside_light,  ON, timeout6+OFFSET_10MIN);

        activate_device (porch_outside_light, OFF, override_off_timeout);
        activate_device (porch_outside_light, OFF,
override_off_timeout+OFFSET_5MIN);
        activate_device (porch_outside_light, OFF,
override_off_timeout+OFFSET_10MIN);
    }
    else
    {
        // Otherwise just switch the lamp off
        delete_house_code_off_events (porch_outside_light);
```

260

```
        activate_device (porch_outside_light, OFF, current_time);
        activate_device (porch_outside_light, OFF, current_time+OFFSET_5MIN);
        activate_device (porch_outside_light, OFF, current_time+OFFSET_10MIN);
    }

}
```

```
//****************************************************************************
// Setup Seasonal Light Events   (Hanging Icicles)
//
// This function performs the following operations:
//
// 1. Remove all existing light events from event database table
// 2. Create new light events
// 3. Lights activate at sunset + delta offset
//
//****************************************************************************

void  setup_seasonal_light_events (void)
{
    long int    front_turn_on_time, front_turn_off_time;
    long int    back_turn_on_time,  back_turn_off_time;
    long int    current_time;
    Uint16      month;


    // Get current month
    determine_current_month (&month);

    // Does the month fall in [DECEMBER..JANUARY] range?
    if ((month != JANUARY) && (month != DECEMBER))
    {
        // No - Delete any existing icicle time events
        print_log ("Processed Non-Seasonal Light events");

        delete_house_code_events (season_front_light);
        delete_house_code_events (season_back_light);

        // Ensure icicle Lights are turned OFF
        activate_device (season_front_light, OFF, current_time);
        activate_device (season_back_light,  OFF, current_time);
        return;
    }


    // Log operation
    print_log ("Processed Seasonal Light events");

    // Get current time in seconds
    current_time = get_raw_time ();

    // We are in month range [DECEMBER..JANUARY]
    // Setup front icicle turn on/off timeout events
    front_turn_on_time  = sunset_timeout      + OFFSET_10MIN + (rand() %
OFFSET_15MIN);   // On  [10min..25min] after sunset
    front_turn_off_time = front_turn_on_time + OFFSET_3HRS  + (rand() %
OFFSET_15MIN);   // Off [3HRS..3HRS15min] later

    // Is current time before the 'turn off' time?
    if (current_time < (front_turn_off_time - OFFSET_2MIN))
    {
        // Yes - Delete existing front seasonal light events
        delete_house_code_events (season_front_light);

        // Install seasonal lights turn on/off events
```

```
        activate_device (season_front_light, ON,  front_turn_on_time);
        activate_device (season_front_light, OFF, front_turn_off_time);
    }


    // We are in month range [DECEMBER..JANUARY]
    // Setup back icicle turn on/off timeout events
    back_turn_on_time  = sunset_timeout      + OFFSET_10MIN + (rand() %
OFFSET_15MIN);  // On  [10min..25min] after sunset
    back_turn_off_time = back_turn_on_time  + OFFSET_3HRS  + (rand() %
OFFSET_15MIN);  // Off [3HRS..3HRS15min] later

    // Is current time before the 'turn off' time?
    if (current_time < (back_turn_off_time  - OFFSET_2MIN))
    {
        // Yes - Delete existing back seasonal light events
        delete_house_code_events (season_back_light);

        // Install seasonal lights turn on/off events
        activate_device (season_back_light,  ON,  back_turn_on_time);
        activate_device (season_back_light,  OFF, back_turn_off_time);
    }

}
```

```
//*************************************************************************
// Setup Fishtank Light Events
//
// This function performs the following operations:
//
// 1. Remove all existing fishtank light events from event database table
// 2. Create new light events
//
// Note: The command is repeated a number of times since the fishtank
//       lights use flourescent tubes which are inherently noisy and sometimes
//       cause the X10 controlling switch to turn on and immediately turn off.
//*************************************************************************

void  setup_fishtank_light_events (void)
{
    long int    turn_on_time;
    long int    turn_off_time;
    long int    current_time;


    // Log operation
    print_log ("Processed Fishtank light events");

    // Get current time in seconds
    current_time = get_raw_time ();

    // Setup Fishtank Light turn on/off timeout events
    turn_on_time  = midnight_timeout + OFFSET_9HRS;     //  9am
    turn_off_time = midnight_timeout + OFFSET_23HRS;    // 11pm


    // Is current time before the 'turn off' time?
    if (current_time < (turn_off_time - OFFSET_2MIN))
    {
        // Delete existing fishtank light events
        delete_house_code_events (fishtank_light);

        // Install the Fishtank Lights turn on events
        activate_device (fishtank_light, ON,  turn_on_time);
        activate_device (fishtank_light, ON,  turn_on_time+OFFSET_15SEC);
        activate_device (fishtank_light, ON,  turn_on_time+OFFSET_30SEC);

        // Install the Fishtank Lights turn off events
        activate_device (fishtank_light, OFF, turn_off_time);
        activate_device (fishtank_light, OFF, turn_off_time+OFFSET_15SEC);
        activate_device (fishtank_light, OFF, turn_off_time+OFFSET_30SEC);
    }


}
```

```
//****************************************************************************
// Setup Family Room Light Events
//
// This function performs the following operations during HOME mode:
//
// 1. Remove all existing family room light events from event database table
// 2. Create new light events
// 3. The general case has the family room lights being turned off at night,
//    however, if movement is detected during that time the turn off time
//    is extended to dawn the following day as a convenience to the user for
//    they just might be staying up all night and we don't want the lights
//    turning off prematurely.
//
//****************************************************************************

void  setup_family_room_light_events (void)
{
    long int    turn_on_time;
    long int    turn_off_time;
    long int    current_time;


    // Log operation
    print_log ("Processed Family Room lights events");

    // Get current time in seconds
    current_time = get_raw_time();

    // Setup family room light turn on/off timeout events
    turn_on_time  = dusk_timeout + OFFSET_2MIN + (rand() % OFFSET_2MIN);
// Dusk-ish
    turn_off_time = midnight_timeout + OFFSET_23HRS + (rand() % OFFSET_20MIN);
// 11pm..11:20pm


    // Is current time before the 'turn off' time?
    if (current_time < (turn_off_time - OFFSET_2MIN))
    {
        // Delete existing family room light events
        delete_house_code_events_after_sunset (familyroom_window_light);
        delete_house_code_events_after_sunset (familyroom_wall_light);

        // Family room light turn on events
        activate_device (familyroom_wall_light,   ON, turn_on_time);
        activate_device (familyroom_window_light, ON, turn_on_time);

        // Family room light turn off events
        activate_device (familyroom_wall_light,   OFF, turn_off_time);
        activate_device (familyroom_window_light, OFF, turn_off_time);
    }

}
```

```
//****************************************************************************
// Setup Master Bedroom Light Events
//
// This function performs the following operations during HOME mode:
//
// 1. Remove all existing master bedroom light events from event database table
// 2. Create new light events
//
//****************************************************************************

void  setup_master_bedroom_light_events (void)
{
    long int    turn_on_time;
    long int    turn_off_time;
    long int    current_time;


    // Log operation
    print_log ("Processed Master Bedroom light events");

    // Get current time in seconds
    current_time = get_raw_time();

    // Setup master bedroom Light turn on/off timeout events
    turn_on_time  = dusk_timeout + OFFSET_2MIN + (rand() % OFFSET_3MIN);
// Dusk-ish;
    turn_off_time = midnight_timeout + OFFSET_23HRS_40MIN + (rand() %
OFFSET_20MIN);    // 11:40pm..11:59pm

    // Is current time before the 'turn off' time?
    if (current_time < (turn_off_time - OFFSET_2MIN))
    {
        // Delete existing master bedroom light events
        delete_house_code_events_after_sunset (master_bedroom_light);
        delete_house_code_events_after_sunset (master_bedroom_dad_light);
        delete_house_code_events_after_sunset (master_bedroom_mum_light);

        // Master bedroom Lights turn on events
        activate_device (master_bedroom_light,  ON, turn_on_time);

        // Master bedroom Lights turn off events
        activate_device (master_bedroom_light,         OFF, turn_off_time);
        activate_device (master_bedroom_dad_light,     OFF, turn_off_time);
        activate_device (master_bedroom_mum_light,     OFF, turn_off_time);
        activate_device (master_bedroom_closet_light, OFF, turn_off_time);
    }

}
```

266

```
//***************************************************************************
// Setup Lounge Light Events
//
// This function performs the following operations during HOME mode:
//
// 1. Remove all existing lounge light events from event database table
// 2. Create new light events
//
//***************************************************************************

void  setup_lounge_light_events (void)
{
    long int    turn_on_time;
    long int    turn_off_time;
    long int    current_time;


    // Log report
    print_log ("Processed Lounge Light events()");

    // Get current time in seconds
    current_time = get_raw_time();

    // Setup lounge light turn on/off timeout events
    turn_on_time  = dusk_timeout + OFFSET_2MIN + (rand() % OFFSET_3MIN);
// Dusk-ish
    turn_off_time = midnight_timeout + OFFSET_23HRS_20MIN + (rand() %
OFFSET_20MIN);    // 11:20pm..11:39pm

    // Is current time before the 'turn off' time?
    if (current_time < (turn_off_time - OFFSET_2MIN))
    {
        // Delete existing lounge light events
        delete_house_code_events_after_sunset (lounge_wall_light);
        delete_house_code_events_after_sunset (lounge_window_light);

        // Lounge light turn on events
        activate_device (lounge_wall_light,   ON,  turn_on_time);
        activate_device (lounge_window_light, ON,  turn_on_time);

        // Lounge light turn off events
        activate_device (lounge_wall_light,   OFF, turn_off_time);
        activate_device (lounge_window_light, OFF, turn_off_time);
    }
}
```

```
//****************************************************************************
// SECURITY Setup Master Bedroom Light Events
//
// This function performs the following operations during SECURITY mode:
//
// 1. Remove all existing master bedroom light events from event database table
// 2. Create new light events
//
//****************************************************************************

void  SECURITY_setup_master_bedroom_light_events (void)
{
    long int    turn_on_time;
    long int    turn_off_time;
    long int    current_time;
    char        time_on  [255];
    char        time_off [255];
    char        message [255];


    // Log file
    print_log ("\n");
    print_log ("SECURITY - Setup Master Bedroom Light Events");

    // Get current time in seconds
    current_time = get_raw_time ();

    // Setup master bedroom Light turn on/off timeout events
    turn_on_time = sunset_timeout   + OFFSET_10MIN + (rand() % OFFSET_60MIN);   //
After Sunset
    turn_off_time = midnight_timeout + OFFSET_23HRS + (rand() % OFFSET_59MIN);   //
11pm..11:59pm

    // Is current time past the 'turn off' time?
    if (current_time > (turn_off_time - OFFSET_5MIN))
    {
        // Yes - Do not install these events
        print_log ("SECURITY - Events ignored since activation time already
expired...");
        return;
    }

    // Delete existing master bedroom light events
    delete_house_code_events_after_sunset (master_bedroom_light);
    delete_house_code_events_after_sunset (master_bedroom_mum_light);
    delete_house_code_events_after_sunset (master_bedroom_dad_light);
    delete_house_code_events_after_sunset (master_bedroom_closet_light);

    // Master bedroom Lights turn on events
    activate_device (master_bedroom_light, ON, turn_on_time);

    // Master bedroom Lights turn off events
    activate_device (master_bedroom_light,         OFF, turn_off_time);
    activate_device (master_bedroom_mum_light,     OFF, turn_off_time);
    activate_device (master_bedroom_dad_light,     OFF, turn_off_time);
    activate_device (master_bedroom_closet_light,  OFF, turn_off_time);

    // Display security times
```

```
    determine_standard_time (turn_on_time,  time_on);
    determine_standard_time (turn_off_time, time_off);
    sprintf (message, "SECURITY - [ON=%s,  OFF=%s]", time_on, time_off);
    print_log (message);

}
```

```
//***************************************************************************
// SECURITY Setup Lounge Light Events
//
// This function performs the following operations during SECURITY mode:
//
// 1. Remove all existing lounge light events from event database table
// 2. Create new light events
*/**************************************************************************

void  SECURITY_setup_lounge_light_events (void)
{
    long int    turn_on_time;
    long int    turn_off_time;
    long int    current_time;
    char        time_on  [255];
    char        time_off [255];
    char        message [255];

    // Log file
    print_log ("");
    print_log ("SECURITY - Setup Lounge Light Events");

    // Get current time in seconds
    current_time = get_raw_time();

    // Setup lounge light turn on/off timeout events
    turn_on_time  = sunset_timeout   + OFFSET_10MIN + (rand() % OFFSET_20MIN);  //
Sunset..+30min
    turn_off_time = midnight_timeout + OFFSET_22HRS + (rand() % OFFSET_59MIN);  //
10pm..10:59pm

    // Is current time past the 'turn off' time?
    if (current_time > (turn_off_time - OFFSET_5MIN))
    {
        // Yes - Do not install these events
        print_log ("SECURITY - Events ignored since activation time already
expired...");
        return;
    }

    // Delete existing lounge light events
    delete_house_code_events_after_sunset (lounge_wall_light);
    delete_house_code_events_after_sunset (lounge_window_light);

    // Lounge light turn on events
    activate_device (lounge_wall_light,   ON,  turn_on_time);
    activate_device (lounge_window_light, ON,  turn_on_time);

    // Lounge light turn off events
    activate_device (lounge_wall_light,   OFF, turn_off_time);
    activate_device (lounge_window_light, OFF, turn_off_time);

    // Display security times
    determine_standard_time (turn_on_time,  time_on);
    determine_standard_time (turn_off_time, time_off);
    sprintf (message, "SECURITY - [ON=%s,  OFF=%s]", time_on, time_off);
    print_log (message);
}
```

```
//*************************************************************************
// SECURITY Setup Family Room Light Events
//
// This function performs the following operations during SECURITY mode:
//
// 1. Remove all existing family room light events from event database table
// 2. Create new light events
//
//*************************************************************************

void  SECURITY_setup_family_room_light_events (void)
{
    long int    turn_on_time;
    long int    turn_off_time;
    long int    current_time;
    char        time_on  [255];
    char        time_off [255];
    char        message  [255];


    // Log file
    print_log ("");
    print_log ("SECURITY - Setup Family Room Light Events");

    // Get current time in seconds
    current_time = get_raw_time();

    // Setup family room light turn on/off timeout events
    turn_on_time  = sunset_timeout + OFFSET_2MIN + (rand() % OFFSET_5MIN);      //
Sunset-ish;
    turn_off_time = midnight_timeout + OFFSET_23HRS + (rand() % OFFSET_55MIN);  //
11pm..11:55pm

    // Is current time past the 'turn off' time?
    if (current_time > (turn_off_time - OFFSET_5MIN))
    {
        // Yes - Do not install these events
        print_log ("SECURITY - Events ignored since activation time already
expired...");
        return;
    }

    // Delete existing family room light events
    delete_house_code_events_after_sunset (familyroom_window_light);
    delete_house_code_events_after_sunset (familyroom_wall_light);

    // Family room light turn on events
    activate_device (familyroom_wall_light,   ON, turn_on_time);
    activate_device (familyroom_window_light, ON, turn_on_time);

    // Family room light turn off events
    activate_device (familyroom_wall_light,            OFF, turn_off_time);
    activate_device (familyroom_window_light,          OFF, turn_off_time);
    activate_device (familyroom_track_tv_light,        OFF, turn_off_time);
    activate_device (familyroom_track_reading_light,   OFF, turn_off_time);
    activate_device (familyroom_wall_unit_light,       OFF, turn_off_time);
    activate_device (familyroom_wall_unit_spotlight,   OFF, turn_off_time);
```

271

```
    // Display security times
    determine_standard_time (turn_on_time,  time_on);
    determine_standard_time (turn_off_time, time_off);
    sprintf (message, "SECURITY - [ON=%s,  OFF=%s]", time_on, time_off);
    print_log (message);
}
```

```
//****************************************************************************
// SECURITY Setup Guest Bedroom Light Events
//
// This function performs the following operations during SECURITY mode:
//
// 1. Remove all existing guest room light events from event database table
// 2. Create new light events
//
//****************************************************************************

void  SECURITY_setup_guest_bedroom_light_events (void)
{
    Uint8       index;
    Uint8       event_count;
    Uint8       existing_light_events_deleted = FALSE;
    long int    max_on_time;
    long int    turn_on_time;
    long int    turn_off_time;
    long int    current_time;
    char        time_on  [255];
    char        time_off [255];
    char        message [255];


    // Determine number of random events
    event_count = (rand() % 3) + 1;         // Range [1..3]

    // Log file
    print_log ("");
    sprintf (message, "SECURITY - Setup Guest Bedroom [%d events]", event_count);
    print_log (message);

    // Get current time in seconds
    current_time = get_raw_time();

    // Determine maximum on time based upon the number of events for the evening
    max_on_time = OFFSET_3HRS / event_count;

    // Initialize first turn on time
    turn_on_time  = sunset_timeout + OFFSET_2MIN + (rand() % OFFSET_30MIN);

    // Setup random time events
    for (index = 0; index < event_count; index++)
    {
        // Determine the turn off time
        turn_off_time = turn_on_time + (max_on_time - OFFSET_45MIN) + (rand() %
OFFSET_35MIN);

        // Is current time past the 'turn off' time?
        if (current_time > (turn_off_time - OFFSET_5MIN))
        {
            // Yes - Do not install these events
            sprintf (message, "SECURITY - Event %d ignored since activation time
already expired...", (index + 1));
            print_log (message);
            continue;
        }
```

```
        // Have we deleted the existing events?
        if (!existing_light_events_deleted)
        {
            // No - Go ahead and delete these events
            existing_light_events_deleted = TRUE;

            // Delete existing guest bedroom light events
            delete_house_code_events_after_sunset (guest_main_light);
        }

        // Does the last event finish before 11:58pm?
        if (turn_off_time > (midnight_timeout + OFFSET_23HRS_58MIN))
        {
            // No - Force last even to finish at 11:58pm
            turn_off_time = midnight_timeout + OFFSET_23HRS_58MIN - (rand() %
OFFSET_10MIN);
        }

        // Program the guest light on/off events
        activate_device (guest_main_light,  ON, turn_on_time);
        activate_device (guest_main_light, OFF, turn_off_time);

        // Display security times
        determine_standard_time (turn_on_time,  time_on);
        determine_standard_time (turn_off_time, time_off);
        sprintf (message, "SECURITY#%d - [ON=%s,  OFF=%s]", index+1, time_on,
time_off);
        print_log (message);

        // Determine next turn on time
        turn_on_time = turn_off_time + OFFSET_15MIN + (rand() % OFFSET_15MIN);

        // Does the last event start before 11:30pm?
        if (turn_on_time > (midnight_timeout + OFFSET_23HRS_30MIN))
        {
            // No - Cancel any additional events
            break;
        }
    }

}
```

```
//****************************************************************************
// SECURITY Setup Steve Bedroom Light Events
//
// This function performs the following operations during SECURITY mode:
//
// 1. Remove all existing room light events from event database table
// 2. Create new light events
//
//****************************************************************************

void  SECURITY_setup_steve_bedroom_light_events (void)
{
    Uint8       index;
    Uint8       event_count;
    Uint8       existing_light_events_deleted = FALSE;
    long int    max_on_time;
    long int    turn_on_time;
    long int    turn_off_time;
    long int    current_time;
    char        time_on  [255];
    char        time_off [255];
    char        message [255];


    // Determine number of random events
    event_count = (rand() % 3) + 2;          // Range [2..4]

    // Log file
    print_log ("");
    sprintf (message, "SECURITY - Setup Steve's Bedroom [%d events]",
event_count);
    print_log (message);

    // Get current time in seconds
    current_time = get_raw_time();


    // Determine maximum on time based upon the number of events for the evening
    max_on_time = OFFSET_4HRS / event_count;

    // Initialize first turn on time
    turn_on_time  = sunset_timeout + OFFSET_2MIN + (rand() % OFFSET_30MIN);

    // Setup random time events
    for (index = 0; index < event_count; index++)
    {
        // Determine the turn off time
        turn_off_time = turn_on_time + (max_on_time - OFFSET_45MIN) + (rand() %
OFFSET_35MIN);

        // Does the last event finish before 11:58pm?
        if (turn_off_time > (midnight_timeout + OFFSET_23HRS_58MIN))
        {
            // No - Force last even to finish at 11:58pm
            turn_off_time = midnight_timeout + OFFSET_23HRS_58MIN - (rand() %
OFFSET_10MIN);
        }
```

```
        // Is current time past the 'turn off' time?
        if (current_time > (turn_off_time - OFFSET_5MIN))
        {
            // Yes - Do not install these events
            sprintf (message, "SECURITY - Event %d ignored since activation time
already expired...", (index + 1));
            print_log (message);
            continue;
        }

        // Have we deleted the existing events?
        if (!existing_light_events_deleted)
        {
            // No - Go ahead and delete these events
            existing_light_events_deleted = TRUE;

            // Delete existing Steve's bedroom light events
            delete_house_code_events_after_sunset (steve_bedroom_ceiling_light);
            delete_house_code_events_after_sunset (steve_bedroom_wall_light);
            delete_house_code_events_after_sunset (steve_bedroom_window_light);
            delete_house_code_events_after_sunset (steve_bedroom_reading_light);
        }


        // Program Steve's bedroom light on/off events
        activate_device (steve_bedroom_window_light,  ON, turn_on_time);
        activate_device (steve_bedroom_window_light, OFF, turn_off_time);

        // Display security times
        determine_standard_time (turn_on_time,  time_on);
        determine_standard_time (turn_off_time, time_off);
        sprintf (message, "SECURITY#%d - [ON=%s,  OFF=%s]", index+1, time_on,
time_off);
        print_log (message);

        // Determine next turn on time
        turn_on_time  = turn_off_time + OFFSET_15MIN + (rand() % OFFSET_15MIN);

        // Does the last event start before 11:30pm?
        if (turn_on_time > (midnight_timeout + OFFSET_23HRS_30MIN))
        {
            // No - Cancel any additional events
            break;
        }
    }

}
```

```
//*************************************************************************
// SECURITY Setup Common Bathroom Light Events
//
// This function performs the following operations during SECURITY mode:
//
// 1. Remove all existing room light events from event database table
// 2. Create new light events
//
//*************************************************************************

void  SECURITY_setup_common_bathroom_light_events (void)
{
    Uint8       index;
    Uint8       event_count;
    Uint8       existing_light_events_deleted = FALSE;
    long int    max_on_time;
    long int    turn_on_time;
    long int    turn_off_time;
    long int    current_time;
    char        time_on  [255];
    char        time_off [255];
    char        message [255];


    // Determine number of random evening events
    event_count = (rand() % 3) + 3;        // Range [3..5]

    // Log file
    print_log ("");
    sprintf (message, "SECURITY - Setup Common Bathroom Room [%d evening events]",
event_count);
    print_log (message);

    // Get current time in seconds
    current_time = get_raw_time();

    // Initialize first turn on time
    turn_on_time  = sunset_timeout + OFFSET_2MIN + (rand() % OFFSET_30MIN);

    // Setup random time events
    for (index = 0; index < event_count; index++)
    {
        // Determine the turn off time
        turn_off_time = turn_on_time + (OFFSET_3MIN + (rand() % OFFSET_15MIN));

        // Does the last event finish after 11:58pm?
        if (turn_off_time > (midnight_timeout + OFFSET_23HRS_58MIN))
        {
            // Yes - Force last event to finish at 11:58pm
            turn_off_time = midnight_timeout + OFFSET_23HRS_58MIN - (rand() %
OFFSET_10MIN);
        }

        // Is current time past the 'turn off' time?
        if (current_time > (turn_off_time - OFFSET_5MIN))
        {
            // Yes - Do not install these events
```

```
            sprintf (message, "SECURITY - Event %d ignored since activation time
already expired...", (index + 1));
            print_log (message);
            continue;
        }

        // Have we deleted the existing events?
        if (!existing_light_events_deleted)
        {
            // No - Go ahead and delete these events
            existing_light_events_deleted = TRUE;

            // Delete existing common bathroom light events
            delete_house_code_events_after_sunset (common_bathroom_light);
        }


        // Program light on/off events
        activate_device (common_bathroom_light,  ON, turn_on_time);
        activate_device (common_bathroom_light, OFF, turn_off_time);

        // Display security times
        determine_standard_time (turn_on_time,  time_on);
        determine_standard_time (turn_off_time, time_off);
        sprintf (message, "SECURITY#%d - [ON=%s,  OFF=%s]", index+1, time_on,
time_off);
        print_log (message);

        // Determine next turn on time
        turn_on_time  = turn_off_time + OFFSET_35MIN + (rand() % OFFSET_20MIN);

        // Does the last event start after 11:30pm?
        if (turn_on_time > (midnight_timeout + OFFSET_23HRS_30MIN))
        {
            // Yes - Cancel any additional events
            break;
        }
    }


    // Determine number of random early hour events (after midnight but before the
dawn)
    event_count = (rand() % 3) + 1;         // Range [1..3]

    // Log file
    print_log ("");
    sprintf (message, "SECURITY - Setup Common Bathroom Room [%d early hour
events]", event_count);
    print_log (message);

    // Initialize first turn on time
    turn_on_time  = midnight_timeout + OFFSET_1HR + (rand() % OFFSET_1HR);

    // Setup random time events
    for (index = 0; index < event_count; index++)
    {
        // Determine the turn off time
```

```
        turn_off_time = turn_on_time + (OFFSET_1MIN + (rand() % OFFSET_3MIN));

        // Does the last event finish less than 30 minutes before dawn?
        if (turn_off_time > (dawn_timeout - OFFSET_30MIN))
        {
            // Yes - Force last event to finish 30 minutes before dawn
            turn_off_time = dawn_timeout - OFFSET_30MIN - (rand() % OFFSET_20MIN);
        }

        // Is current time past the 'turn off' time?
        if (current_time > (turn_off_time - OFFSET_5MIN))
        {
            // Yes - Do not install these events
            sprintf (message, "SECURITY - Event %d ignored since activation time
already expired...", (index + 1));
            print_log (message);
            continue;
        }

        // Have we deleted the existing events?
        if (!existing_light_events_deleted)
        {
            // No - Go ahead and delete these events
            existing_light_events_deleted = TRUE;

            // Delete existing common bathroom light events
            delete_house_code_events (common_bathroom_light);
        }

        // Program light on/off events
        activate_device (common_bathroom_light,  ON, turn_on_time);
        activate_device (common_bathroom_light, OFF, turn_off_time);

        // Display security times
        determine_standard_time (turn_on_time,  time_on);
        determine_standard_time (turn_off_time, time_off);
        sprintf (message, "SECURITY#%d - [ON=%s,  OFF=%s]", index+1, time_on,
time_off);
        print_log (message);

        // Determine next turn on time
        turn_on_time  = turn_off_time + OFFSET_45MIN + (rand() % OFFSET_45MIN);

        // Does the last event start less than 1 hour before dawn?
        if (turn_on_time > (dawn_timeout - OFFSET_1HR))
        {
            // Yes - Cancel any additional events
            break;
        }
    }

}
```

279

```
//****************************************************************************
// SECURITY Setup Study Light Events
//
// This function performs the following operations during SECURITY mode:
//
// 1. Remove all existing room light events from event database table
// 2. Create new light events
//
//****************************************************************************

void  SECURITY_setup_study_light_events (void)
{
    Uint8       index;
    Uint8       event_count;
    Uint8       existing_light_events_deleted = FALSE;
    long int    max_on_time;
    long int    turn_on_time;
    long int    turn_off_time;
    long int    current_time;
    char        time_on  [255];
    char        time_off [255];
    char        message [255];


    // Determine number of random events
    event_count = (rand() % 4) + 1;        // Range [1..4]

    // Log file
    print_log ("");

    sprintf (message, "SECURITY - Setup Study [%d events]", event_count);
    print_log (message);

    // Get current time in seconds
    current_time = get_raw_time();

    // Determine maximum on time based upon the number of events for the evening
    max_on_time = OFFSET_4HRS / event_count;


    // Initialize first turn on time
    turn_on_time = sunset_timeout + OFFSET_2MIN + (rand() % OFFSET_30MIN);

    // Setup random time events
    for (index = 0; index < event_count; index++)
    {
        // Determine the turn off time
        turn_off_time = turn_on_time + (max_on_time - OFFSET_45MIN) + (rand() %
OFFSET_35MIN);

        // Does the last event finish before 11:58pm?
        if (turn_off_time > (midnight_timeout + OFFSET_23HRS_58MIN))
        {
            // No - Force last even to finish at 11:58pm
            turn_off_time = midnight_timeout + (OFFSET_23HRS_58MIN - (rand() %
OFFSET_10MIN));
        }
```

```
        // Is current time past the 'turn off' time?
        if (current_time > (turn_off_time - OFFSET_5MIN))
        {
            // Yes - Do not install these events
            sprintf (message, "SECURITY - Event %d ignored since activation time
already expired...", (index + 1));
            print_log (message);
            continue;
        }

        // Have we deleted the existing events?
        if (!existing_light_events_deleted)
        {
            // No - Go ahead and delete these events
            existing_light_events_deleted = TRUE;

            // Delete existing study light events
            delete_house_code_events_after_sunset (study_ceiling_light);
        }


        // Program light on/off events
        activate_device (study_ceiling_light,  ON, turn_on_time);
        activate_device (study_ceiling_light, OFF, turn_off_time);

        // Display security times
        determine_standard_time (turn_on_time,  time_on);
        determine_standard_time (turn_off_time, time_off);
        sprintf (message, "SECURITY#%d - [ON=%s,  OFF=%s]", index+1, time_on,
time_off);
        print_log (message);

        // Determine next turn on time
        turn_on_time  = turn_off_time + OFFSET_15MIN + (rand() % OFFSET_15MIN);

        // Does the last event start before 11:30pm?
        if (turn_on_time > (midnight_timeout + OFFSET_23HRS_30MIN))
        {
            // No - Cancel any additional events
            break;
        }
    }

}
```

```
//***********************************************************************
// SECURITY Setup Kitchen Light Events
//
// This function performs the following operations during SECURITY mode:
//
// 1. Remove all existing room light events from event database table
// 2. Create new light events
//
//***********************************************************************

void  SECURITY_setup_kitchen_light_events (void)
{
    Uint8       index;
    Uint8       event_count;
    Uint8       existing_light_events_deleted = FALSE;
    long int    max_on_time;
    long int    turn_on_time;
    long int    turn_off_time;
    long int    current_time;
    char        time_on  [255];
    char        time_off [255];
    char        message [255];


    // Determine number of random events
    event_count = (rand() % 4) + 4;          // Range [4..7]

    // Log File
    print_log ("");
    sprintf (message, "SECURITY - Setup Kitchen [%d events]", event_count);
    print_log (message);

    // Get current time in seconds
    current_time = get_raw_time();

    // Determine maximum on time based upon the number of events for the evening
    max_on_time = OFFSET_4HRS / event_count;

    // Initialize first turn on time
    turn_on_time  = sunset_timeout + OFFSET_2MIN + (rand() % OFFSET_30MIN);

    // Setup random time events
    for (index = 0; index < event_count; index++)
    {
        // Determine the turn off time
        turn_off_time = turn_on_time + (max_on_time - OFFSET_20MIN) + (rand() %
OFFSET_15MIN);

        // Does the last event finish before 11:58pm?
        if (turn_off_time > (midnight_timeout + OFFSET_23HRS_58MIN))
        {
            // No - Force last even to finish at 11:58pm
            turn_off_time = midnight_timeout + OFFSET_23HRS_58MIN - (rand() %
OFFSET_10MIN);
        }

        // Is current time past the 'turn off' time?
        if (current_time > (turn_off_time - OFFSET_5MIN))
```

282

```
        {
            // Yes - Do not install these events
            sprintf (message, "SECURITY - Event %d ignored since activation time
already expired...", (index + 1));
            print_log (message);
            continue;
        }

        // Have we deleted the existing events?
        if (!existing_light_events_deleted)
        {
            // No - Go ahead and delete these events
            existing_light_events_deleted = TRUE;

            // Delete existing kitchen light events
            delete_house_code_events_after_sunset (kitchen_light);
        }


        // Program light on/off events
        activate_device (kitchen_light,  ON, turn_on_time);
        activate_device (kitchen_light, OFF, turn_off_time);

        // Display security times
        determine_standard_time (turn_on_time,  time_on);
        determine_standard_time (turn_off_time, time_off);
        sprintf (message, "SECURITY#%d - [ON=%s,  OFF=%s]", index+1, time_on,
time_off);
        print_log (message);

        // Determine next turn on time
        turn_on_time  = turn_off_time + OFFSET_15MIN + (rand() % OFFSET_15MIN);

        // Does the last event start before 11:30pm?
        if (turn_on_time > (midnight_timeout + OFFSET_23HRS_30MIN))
        {
            // No - Cancel any additional events
            break;
        }
    }

}
```

```
//*************************************************************************
// SECURITY Setup Kitchen Nook Light Events
//
// This function performs the following operations during SECURITY mode:
//
// 1. Remove all existing room light events from event database table
// 2. Create new light events
//
//*************************************************************************

void  SECURITY_setup_kitchen_nook_light_events (void)
{
    Uint8      index;
    Uint8      event_count;
    Uint8      existing_light_events_deleted = FALSE;
    long int   max_on_time;
    long int   turn_on_time;
    long int   turn_off_time;
    long int   current_time;
    char       time_on  [255];
    char       time_off [255];
    char       message [255];


    // Determine number of random events
    event_count = (rand() % 3) + 1;        // Range [1..3]

    // Log File
    print_log ("");
    sprintf (message, "SECURITY - Setup Kitchen Nook [%d events]", event_count);
    print_log (message);

    // Get current time in seconds
    current_time = get_raw_time();

    // Determine maximum on time based upon the number of events for the evening
    max_on_time = OFFSET_45MIN;

    // Initialize first turn on time
    turn_on_time  = sunset_timeout + OFFSET_2MIN + (rand() % OFFSET_30MIN);

    // Setup random time events
    for (index = 0; index < event_count; index++)
    {
        // Determine the turn off time
        turn_off_time = turn_on_time + (max_on_time - OFFSET_20MIN) + (rand() %
OFFSET_20MIN);

        // Does the last event finish before 11:58pm?
        if (turn_off_time > (midnight_timeout + OFFSET_23HRS_58MIN))
        {
            // No - Force last even to finish at 11:58pm
            turn_off_time = midnight_timeout + OFFSET_23HRS_58MIN;
        }

        // Is current time past the 'turn off' time?
        if (current_time > (turn_off_time - OFFSET_5MIN))
        {
```

```
            // Yes - Do not install these events
            sprintf (message, "SECURITY - Event %d ignored since activation time
already expired...", (index + 1));
            print_log (message);
            continue;
        }

        // Have we deleted the existing events?
        if (!existing_light_events_deleted)
        {
            // No - Go ahead and delete these events
            existing_light_events_deleted = TRUE;

            // Delete existing kitchen nook light events
            delete_house_code_events_after_sunset (kitchen_nook_light);
        }


        // Program light on/off events
        activate_device (kitchen_nook_light,  ON, turn_on_time);
        activate_device (kitchen_nook_light, OFF, turn_off_time);

        // Display security times
        determine_standard_time (turn_on_time,  time_on);
        determine_standard_time (turn_off_time, time_off);
        sprintf (message, "SECURITY#%d - [ON=%s,  OFF=%s]", index+1, time_on,
time_off);
        print_log (message);

        // Determine next turn on time
        turn_on_time  = turn_off_time + OFFSET_30MIN + (rand() % OFFSET_15MIN);

        // Does the last event start before 11:30pm?
        if (turn_on_time > (midnight_timeout + OFFSET_23HRS_30MIN))
        {
            // No - Cancel any additional events
            break;
        }
    }

}
```

```
//****************************************************************************
// Access Home Control Database
//
// house_state (Home Mode or Security Mode)
// house_code_inputs (acive inputs to be processed)
// house_code_states (current house code states)
//
//****************************************************************************
void  access_home_control_database (void)
{
    char    message [255];


    // Connect to MySQL system
    conn1 = mysql_init(NULL);

    // Was the connection successfull?
    if (conn1 == NULL)
    {
        // No - Display error message and exit.
        sprintf (message, "Error_A %u: %s", mysql_errno(conn1),
mysql_error(conn1));
        print_log (message);
        exit(1);
    }

    // Successfully connected to the MySQL System.
    // Now connect to the MySQL "system_control" database.
    if (mysql_real_connect(conn1, "192.168.1.176", "steve", "william",
"system_control", 0, NULL, 0) == NULL)
    {
        // Connection not established - Display error message.
        sprintf(message, "Error_B %u: %s", mysql_errno(conn1),
mysql_error(conn1));
        print_log (message);
        print_log("Exiting...");
        exit (1);
    }
    else
    {
        // Now connected to    system_control database.
        print_log ("*** Connected to 'system_control' database.");
    }

}
```

```
//****************************************************************************
// Hex to ASCII
//
// This function converts a hex digit to an ASCII character.
//
//****************************************************************************

char  hex_to_ascii (char hex_digit)
{
    // Is the hex digit in the numeric range of [0..9]'?
    if (hex_digit < 10)
    {
        // Yes - Convert the numeric digit into an ASCII character
        return (0x30 + hex_digit);         // Handle '0' .. '9'
    }
    else
    {
        // No - Cater for a hex digit in the numeric range [10..15]
        return (0x41 + (hex_digit - 10));   // Handle 'A' .. 'F'
    }
}
```

```
//****************************************************************************
// TI103 Add Checksum
//
// This function appends the checksum to the message string.
//
//****************************************************************************

void  ti103_add_checksum (char * buffer)
{
    int   index;
    int   msg_size;
    unsigned char checksum;


    // Initialization
    checksum = 0;

    msg_size = strlen (buffer);
    //  printf("msg_size = %d\n", msg_size);


    // Compute checksum
    for (index = 0; index < msg_size; index++)
    {
        checksum += buffer[index];
    }

    // Add checksum to message buffer
    buffer[msg_size++] = hex_to_ascii ((checksum & 0xF0) >> 4);
    buffer[msg_size++] = hex_to_ascii  (checksum & 0x0F);
    buffer[msg_size++] = 0x00;

}
```

```
//***************************************************************************
// TI103 Build Get Status String
//
// This function builds the 'Get Status' string and appends the checksum.
//
//***************************************************************************

void  ti103_build_get_status_string (char * buffer)
{

    // Build the Get Status command
    sprintf (buffer, "$>280000");

    // Append the checksum
    ti103_add_checksum (buffer);

    // Finalize with the '#' symbol
    strcat (buffer, "#");

}
```

```
//****************************************************************************
// TI103 Build Command String
//
// This function builds the TI103 command string and appends the checksum.
//
//****************************************************************************
void  ti103_build_command_string (char   * buffer,
         int     house_code,
         int     unit_code,
         char   * command)
{
    int  msg_size;


    // Build start of command message
    strcpy (buffer, "$>28001");
    msg_size = strlen (buffer);


    // Bring in the device address
    buffer[msg_size++] = 0x40 + house_code;          // Handle  'A' .. 'P'
    buffer[msg_size++] = 0x30 + (unit_code / 10);    // Handle '01' .. '16'
    buffer[msg_size++] = 0x30 + (unit_code % 10);

    // Add in the device address (one more time)
    buffer[msg_size++] = 0x40 + house_code;          // Handle  'A' .. 'P'
    buffer[msg_size++] = 0x30 + (unit_code / 10);    // Handle '01' .. '16'
    buffer[msg_size++] = 0x30 + (unit_code % 10);

    // Bring in the command
    buffer[msg_size++] = 0x40 + house_code;          // Handle  'A' .. 'P'
    buffer[msg_size++] = 0x00;

    strcat (buffer, command);                        // Add in the command string
    msg_size = strlen (buffer);

    // Bring in the command (one more time)
    buffer[msg_size++] = 0x40 + house_code;          // Handle  'A' .. 'P'
    buffer[msg_size++] = 0x00;

    strcat (buffer, command);                        // Add in the command string
    msg_size = strlen (buffer);


    // Add in the checksum
    ti103_add_checksum (buffer);

    // Finalize with the '#' symbol
    strcat (buffer, "#");
}
```

```c
//**************************************************************************
// Process Events
//
// The House Code Events table is used to contain the devices that are to be
// turned ON or OFF.
//
// This function accesses the MySQL database and obtains the device's house
// and unit codes along with its state code.  It then builds an X-10 control
// message and sends it to the device via the TI-103.
//
//**************************************************************************

void  process_events (void)
{
    Uint8           status = FALSE;
    MYSQL_RES       *mysqlResult;
    MYSQL_ROW        mysqlRow;
    MYSQL_FIELD     *mysqlFields;
    my_ulonglong     numRows;
    unsigned int     numFields;
    long int         current_time;
    unsigned long    timeout;

    int      house, unit, state;
    int      num_bytes_written;
    char     buffer[255];
    char     timestamp[255];
    char     message [255];


    // Get current time in seconds
    current_time = get_raw_time ();


    // EVENTS DATABASE
    // ===============

    // Determine if there are any event entries in the database
    // These are User Operations requested from the web pages
    sprintf (buffer, "SELECT * FROM house_code_events WHERE timeout<=%ld ORDER BY
timeout",
            (long int) current_time);

    if (mysql_query(conn1, buffer))
    {
        // Error detected - Print error message
        sprintf (message, "Error_G1 %u: %s", mysql_errno(conn1),
mysql_error(conn1));
        print_log (message);
        return;
    }


    // Determine the number of event entries
    mysqlResult = mysql_store_result (conn1);

    // Are there any entries?
    if (mysqlResult)
```

```c
    {
        // Yes - Get the number of database table rows and fields
        numRows = mysql_num_rows(mysqlResult);

        numFields = mysql_num_fields (mysqlResult);

        // Print these out when testing
        // printf ("Number of Rows = %lld,  Number of Fields = %d \n", numRows,
numFields);


        // Get the first row in the table
        while (mysqlRow = mysql_fetch_row(mysqlResult))
        {
            // Get the house, unit, etc. parameters from the MySQL table
            house   = (int) (atoi (mysqlRow[HCE_HOUSE]));
            unit    = (int) (atoi (mysqlRow[HCE_UNIT]));
            state   = (int) (atoi (mysqlRow[HCE_STATE]));
            timeout = (int) (atoi (mysqlRow[HCE_TIMEOUT]));

            // Does the timestamp string exist?
            if (mysqlRow[HCE_TIMESTAMP] != NULL)
            {
                // Yes - Use it
                strncpy (timestamp, mysqlRow[HCE_TIMESTAMP], 60);

                // Is the timestamp length valid?
                if (strlen(timestamp) != 19)
                {
                    // No - Use a default time
                    strcpy (timestamp, "----/--/-- --:--:--");
                }
            }
            else
            {
                // No - Use a default time
                strcpy (timestamp, "----/--/-- --:--:--");
            }


            // Build the TI103 Command String
            if (state == 1)
            {
                // Turn the required device identified by (House,Unit) ON
                ti103_build_command_string (buffer, house, unit, "ON");
            }
            else
            {
                // Turn the required device identified by (House, Unit) OFF
                ti103_build_command_string (buffer, house, unit, "OFF");
            }

            // Output this command string to the serial port assigned to the TI103
            num_bytes_written = write(fd, buffer, strlen(buffer));

            if (num_bytes_written != strlen(buffer))
            {
```

```
            sprintf (message, "TI103 CMD ERROR - Bytes written %d/%d",
num_bytes_written, strlen(buffer));
            print_log (message);
        }

        // Display the command information on the terminal screen
        // for user verification.
        // printf ("Command = %s\n", buffer);
        // printf ("Number Bytes Written = %d/%d\n", num_bytes_written,
strlen(buffer));


        // EVENTS DATABASE
        // ===============

        // Now that the specific event has been processed,
        // proceed to build a MySQL command to delete the
        // house/unit code entry for this device from the EVENTS database
        sprintf (buffer, "DELETE FROM house_code_events WHERE house=%d AND
unit=%d AND state=%d AND timeout=%ld",
                house, unit, state, timeout);

        // Disply this command for user verification
        // printf ("%s\n", buffer);

        // Issue the command to the MySQL database
        if (mysql_query(conn1, buffer))
        {
            // Error - Print error message
            sprintf (message, "Error_E1 %u: %s", mysql_errno(conn1),
mysql_error(conn1));
            print_log (message);
        }


        // Build command to update device info in house_code_states database
table
        // This will identify the current state of the device and also provide
the
        // timestamp as to when the device state was effected.
        sprintf (buffer,
                "UPDATE house_code_states SET state=%d, timestamp='%s',
timeout=%ld, presence=%ld WHERE house=%d AND unit=%d",
                state,
                timestamp,
                timeout,
                ZERO_PRESENCE_TIMEOUT,
                house,
                unit);

        // Issue the update command to the MySQL Database
        if (mysql_query(conn1, buffer))
        {
            // Error Detected - Print error message but still continue...
            sprintf (message, "Error_E2 %u: %s", mysql_errno(conn1),
mysql_error(conn1));
            print_log (message);
        }
```

```
            // Sleep between successive commands...
            msleep (EXECUTION_SLEEP_MS);
        }


        // Was a MySQL result pointer returned?
        if (mysqlResult)
        {
            // Yes - Free the pointer
            mysql_free_result(mysqlResult);
            mysqlResult = NULL;
        }
    }
}
```

```
//***************************************************************************
// Determine Initial Security Mode
//
// This function accesses the security parameter in the House_State database.
//
// If the system is powering up and the Security mode is already engaged then
// the Security events are configured.  Otherwise, if the system is in Home
// mode then the Home events are configured.
//
//***************************************************************************

void  determine_initial_security_mode (void)
{
    int     house_state_security;
    char    time_buffer[255];
    char    message[255];
    char    buffer[255];


    // Get the security mode
    if (get_house_state_security (&house_state_security) == SUCCESS)
    {
        // Is the security mode active?
        if (house_state_security == SECURITY_MODE_ACTIVE)
        {
            // Yes - System is powering up in SECURITY mode
            print_log ("*** System is powering up [SECURITY ON]");

            // Activate SECURITY mode flags
            security_mode         = TRUE;
            security_mode_started = TRUE;
            security_mode_stopped = FALSE;

            // Compute current timestamp
            determine_system_timestamp (time_buffer);

            // Send email stating Security Mode Reactivated
            sprintf (message, "%s - System is powering up [SECURITY ON]",
time_buffer);
            send_security_email ("*** SECURITY INFO ***", message);
            speak ("System startup.  Security mode activated.");
        }
        else
        {
            // No - System is powering up in HOME mode
            //       This is the case even if we had a restart during transition to
SECURITY mode
            print_log ("*** System is powering up [SECURITY OFF]");

            // All transition security modes forced to INACTIVE state
            sprintf (buffer, "UPDATE house_state SET security=%d",
SECURITY_MODE_INACTIVE);
            mysql_query(conn1, buffer);

            // Deactivate SECURITY mode flags
            security_mode         = FALSE;
            security_mode_started = FALSE;
            security_mode_stopped = TRUE;
```

295

```
            // Compute current timestamp
            determine_system_timestamp (time_buffer);

            // Send email stating Security Mode Reactivated
            sprintf (message, "%s - System is powering up [Security OFF]",
time_buffer);
            send_security_email ("*** SECURITY INFO ***", message);
            speak ("System startup.  Security mode is off.");

            // Test the alarm system
            print_log ("*** Alarm siren test.");
            speak ("Alarm siren test.");
            turn_alarm_siren_on();
            process_events();
            sleep (3);

            // Switch the alarm off
            turn_alarm_siren_off();
            process_events();
            print_log ("*** Alarm siren reset.");
            speak ("Alarm siren reset.");

            // Test the watchdog
            print_log ("*** Watchdog test.");
            speak ("Watchdog test.");
            kick_the_dog();
            process_events();
            sleep (3);

            // Switch the doggy off
            tell_the_dog_to_be_quiet();
            process_events();
            print_log ("*** Watchdog reset.");
            speak ("Watchdog reset.");
        }
    }
}
```

```
//*************************************************************************
// Monitor Security Mode Transition
//
// This function monitors the MySQL house_state security parameters.
//
// This value can take on the following four different states:
//
// SECURITY_MODE_INACTIVE  = Security mode is deactive.
// SECURITY_MODE_INITIATED = User pressed the SECURITY button on web page.
// SECURITY_MODE_DELAY     = Security delay is counting.
// SECURITY_MODE_ACTIVE    = Delay expired and security mode is now active.
//
// This gives the web page user the facility to initiate the change to security
// mode and provides them with a timed delay during which they can exit the
// building prior to the security mode being fully engaged.
//
//*************************************************************************

void  monitor_security_mode_transition (void)
{
    int  house_state_security;
    char buffer[255];
    char message[255];
    char time_buffer[255];
    long   int  delay_count;
    long   int  current_time;
    static int  last_current_time = 0;
    static int  security_delay_timeout;


    // Get the house code security parameter
    if (get_house_state_security (&house_state_security) == SUCCESS)
    {
        // Has the web page user pressed the [SECURITY OFF] button?
        if (house_state_security == SECURITY_MODE_INACTIVE)
        {
            // Yes - Was the security mode previously active?
            if (security_mode)
            {
                // Yes - Deactivate security mode and install normal HOME events
                security_mode         = FALSE;
                security_mode_started = FALSE;
                security_mode_stopped = TRUE;

                // Compute current timestamp
                determine_system_timestamp (time_buffer);

                // Send email stating Security Mode Deactivated
                sprintf (message, "%s - SECURITY Mode DEACTIVATED [Operator
action]", time_buffer);
                send_security_email ("*** SECURITY INFO ***", message);
                speak ("Security mode is off.");

                // Switch the alarm off
                turn_alarm_siren_off ();
            }
        }
```

```
        // Has the web page user pressed the [SECURITY ON] button?
        else if (house_state_security == SECURITY_MODE_INITIATED)
        {
            // Yes - Initiate the security delay
            sprintf ( buffer, "UPDATE house_state SET security=%d",
SECURITY_MODE_DELAY);
            mysql_query(conn1, buffer);

            // Get current time in seconds
            current_time = get_raw_time();

            // Setup the security delay
            security_delay_timeout = current_time + OFFSET_5MIN;  // Time to exit
the home
            speak ("Security mode has been initiated.");
        }

        // Is the security delay active?
        else if (house_state_security == SECURITY_MODE_DELAY)
        {
            // Yes - Get current time in seconds
            current_time = get_raw_time();

            // Determine the delay count value
            delay_count = security_delay_timeout - current_time;

            // Has the delay count expired?
            if (delay_count < 0)
            {
                // Yes - Force the delay count to zero
                delay_count = DELAY_EXPIRED;
            }

            // Has the second count changed?
            if (last_current_time != current_time)
            {
                // Yes - Remember this current time
                last_current_time = current_time;

                // Update MySQL house_state table security_delay parameter
                // to provide the web page with the decrementing delay count.
                sprintf (buffer,
                    "UPDATE house_state SET security_delay=%ld",
                    delay_count);

                mysql_query(conn1, buffer);
            }

            // Has the security transition delay expired?
            if (delay_count == DELAY_EXPIRED)
            {
                // Yes - SECURITY MODE is now ACTIVE
                //       Reflect this status in the MySQL house_state table
                sprintf (buffer,
                    "UPDATE house_state SET security=%d, security_delay=0",
                    SECURITY_MODE_ACTIVE);

                mysql_query(conn1, buffer);
```

```
              // Activate security mode and install security events
              security_mode        = TRUE;
              security_mode_started = TRUE;
              security_mode_stopped = FALSE;

              // Prepare for security presence detection
              reset_security_detection_flags ();

              // Compute current timestamp
              determine_system_timestamp (time_buffer);

              // Send email stating Security Mode Activation
              sprintf (message, "%s - Security Mode Activated [Operator action]",
time_buffer);
              send_security_email ("*** SECURITY INFO ***", message);
              speak ("Security mode is now active.");
          }
        }
      }

    }
```

```
//****************************************************************************
// Monitor Sleep Mode Transition
//
// This function monitors the MySQL house_state sleep parameters.
//
// This value can take on the following four different states:
//
// SLEEP_MODE_INACTIVE  = Sleep mode is deactive.
// SLEEP_MODE_INITIATED = User pressed the SLEEP button on web page.
// SLEEP_MODE_DELAY     = Sleep delay is counting.
// SLEEP_MODE_ACTIVE    = Delay expired and sleep mode is now active.
//
// This gives the web page user the facility to initiate the change to sleep
// mode and provides them with a timed delay during which they can get into bed
// prior to the sleep mode being fully engaged.
//
//****************************************************************************

void  monitor_sleep_mode_transition (void)
{
    int   house_state_sleep;
    char buffer[255];
    long   int  delay_count;
    long   int  current_time;
    static int  last_current_time = 0;
    static int  sleep_delay_timeout;


    // Get the house code sleep parameter
    if (get_house_state_sleep (&house_state_sleep) == SUCCESS)
    {
        // Has the web page user pressed the [SLEEP OFF] button?
        if (house_state_sleep == SLEEP_MODE_INACTIVE)
        {
            // Was the sleep mode previously active?
            if (sleep_mode)
            {
                // Yes - Deactivate security mode and install normal user events
                sleep_mode       = FALSE;
                sleep_mode_start = FALSE;
                //          active_mode_start = TRUE;

                // Yes - Inform the user
//              speak ("Sleep mode cancelled.");
            }
        }

        // Has the web page user pressed the [SLEEP ON] button?
        else if (house_state_sleep == SLEEP_MODE_INITIATED)
        {
            // Yes - Initiate the sleep delay
            speak ("Sleep mode initiated.");
            sprintf ( buffer, "UPDATE house_state SET sleep=%d", SLEEP_MODE_DELAY);
            mysql_query(conn1, buffer);

            // Get current time in seconds
            current_time = get_raw_time ();
```

```
        // Setup the sleep delay
        sleep_delay_timeout = current_time + OFFSET_20SEC;  // Twenty seconds
    }

    // Is the sleep delay active?
    else if (house_state_sleep == SLEEP_MODE_DELAY)
    {
        // Yes - Get current time in seconds
        current_time = get_raw_time();

        // Determine the delay count value
        delay_count = sleep_delay_timeout - current_time;

        // Has the delay count expired?
        if (delay_count < 0)
        {
            // Yes - Force the delay count to zero
            delay_count = 0;
        }

        // Has the second count changed?
        if (last_current_time != current_time)
        {
            // Yes - Remember this current time
            last_current_time = current_time;

            // Update MySQL house_state table sleep_delay parameter
            // to provide the web page with the decrementing delay count.
            sprintf (buffer,
                    "UPDATE house_state SET sleep_delay=%ld",
                    delay_count);

            mysql_query(conn1, buffer);
        }

        // Has the sleep transition delay expired?
        if (delay_count == DELAY_EXPIRED)
        {
            // Yes - SLEEP MODE is now ACTIVE
            //       Reflect this status in the MySQL house_state table
            speak_time_and_date();
            speak ("Sleep mode active. Good night Steve.");

            sprintf (buffer,
                    "UPDATE house_state SET sleep=%d, sleep_delay=0",
                    SLEEP_MODE_ACTIVE);

            mysql_query(conn1, buffer);

            // Activate security mode and install security events
            sleep_mode       = TRUE;
            sleep_mode_start = TRUE;
        }
    }
}
}
```

```
//****************************************************************************
// Setup Events For Retiring To Bedroom
//
// The House State 'go_to_bed' parameter is used to indicate that the user is
// going to the bedroom.  This implies that all the house lounge, family,
// kitchen, etc. lights are to be turned off so that the house can be darkened.
//
//****************************************************************************

void  setup_events_for_retiring_to_bedroom (void)
{
    int house_state_go_to_bed;
    long int    current_time;


    // Get current time in seconds
    current_time = get_raw_time();


    if (get_house_state_go_to_bed (&house_state_go_to_bed) == SUCCESS)
    {
        // Was the 'Go To Bed' button pressed?
        if (house_state_go_to_bed == 1)
        {
            // Set MySQL house_state go_to_bed back to '0'
            mysql_query(conn1, "UPDATE house_state SET go_to_bed=0");


            // Switch on various lamps for going to bed
            // =====================================
            activate_device (master_bedroom_light,              ON, current_time);
            activate_device (master_bedroom_dad_light,          ON, current_time);
            activate_device (master_bedroom_mum_light,          ON, current_time);


            // Switch off various lamps for going to bed
            // =====================================
            activate_device (main_hallway_light,                OFF, current_time);
            activate_device (fishtank_light,                    OFF, current_time);
            activate_device (lounge_wall_light,                 OFF, current_time);
            activate_device (lounge_window_light,               OFF, current_time);
            activate_device (inside_entrance_light,             OFF, current_time);
            activate_device (diningroom_table_light,            OFF, current_time);
            activate_device (kitchen_light,                     OFF, current_time);
            activate_device (kitchen_nook_light,                OFF, current_time);
            activate_device (familyroom_window_light,           OFF, current_time);
            activate_device (familyroom_wall_light,             OFF, current_time);
            activate_device (familyroom_track_tv_light,         OFF, current_time);
            activate_device (familyroom_track_reading_light,    OFF, current_time);
            activate_device (familyroom_wall_unit_light,        OFF, current_time);
            activate_device (familyroom_wall_unit_spotlight,    OFF, current_time);
            activate_device (familyroom_radio,                  OFF, current_time);
            activate_device (pantry_light,                      OFF, current_time);
            activate_device (laundry_light,                     OFF, current_time);
        }
    }

}
```

```
//*********************************************************************
// Setup Events For Master Watching TV
//
// The House State 'go_to_bed' parameter is used to indicate that the user is
// going to the bedroom.  This implies that all the house lounge, family,
// kitchen, etc. lights are to be turned off so that the house can be darkened.
//
//*********************************************************************

void   setup_events_for_master_watching_tv (void)
{
    int          house_state_master_watch_tv;
    long int     current_time;


    // Get current time in seconds
    current_time = get_raw_time();


    if (get_house_state_parameter (HS_MASTER_WATCH_TV,
&house_state_master_watch_tv) == SUCCESS)
    {
        // Was the 'Go To Bed' button pressed?
        if (house_state_master_watch_tv == 1)
        {
            // Set MySQL house_state go_to_bed back to '0'
            mysql_query(conn1, "UPDATE house_state SET master_watch_tv=0");


            // Switch on various lamps for watching TV
            // =====================================
            activate_device (master_bedroom_light, ON, current_time);


            // Switch off various lamps for going to bed
            // =====================================
            activate_device (master_bedroom_dad_light, OFF, current_time);
            activate_device (master_bedroom_mum_light, OFF, current_time);
        }
    }


}
```

```
//***********************************************************************
// Cancel Locked Device States
//
// Sometimes there are times when an RF sensor OFF command is not received.
// This can occur during simultaneous transmissions from two devices.
// If also affects RF devices that have no OFF command transmission (in this
// home configuration this applies to the front porch sensor).
//
// To overcome this, a timeout number is stored in the house_code_states
// MySQL database table.  This value is the current event time in seconds plus
// 120 seconds.  The function below checks for all devices that are in a set
// state and if the current event time in seconds has exceeded this timeout
// value the sensor state is reset.
//***********************************************************************

void  cancel_locked_device_states (void)
{

    MYSQL_RES       *mysqlResult;
    MYSQL_ROW        mysqlRow;
    MYSQL_FIELD     *mysqlFields;
    my_ulonglong     numRows;
    unsigned int     numFields;


    int         house, unit, state;
    int         num_bytes_written;
    long int    current_time;
    char        buffer[255];
    char        message [255];


    // Get the current time in seconds
    current_time = get_raw_time ();


    // STATES DATABASE
    // ===============
    // Determine if there are any event SET entries
    // in the database which have timed out...
    sprintf (buffer, "SELECT * FROM house_code_states WHERE state=1 AND
timeout>=999 AND timeout<%ld",
            (long int) current_time);

    if (mysql_query(conn1, buffer))
    {
        // Error detected - Print error message
        sprintf (message, "Error_G1 %u: %s", mysql_errno(conn1),
mysql_error(conn1));
        print_log (message);
    }
    else
    {
        // Determine the number of event entries
        mysqlResult = mysql_store_result (conn1);

        // Are there any entries?
        if (mysqlResult)
        {
```

```
    // Yes - Get the number of database table rows and fields
    numRows = mysql_num_rows (mysqlResult);

    //          numFields = mysql_field_count (conn1);

    numFields = mysql_num_fields (mysqlResult);
}


// Get the first row in the table (if it exists)
mysqlRow = mysql_fetch_row (mysqlResult);

while (mysqlRow)
{
    // Yes - Get the parameters from the MySQL table
    house = (int) (atoi (mysqlRow[0]));
    unit  = (int) (atoi (mysqlRow[1]));

    // Sensor timed out, reset device state to inactive
    sprintf (buffer, "UPDATE house_code_states SET state=0 WHERE house=%d
AND unit=%d", house, unit);

    // Display this command for user verification
    //          printf ("%s\n", buffer);

    // Issue the command to the MySQL database
    if (mysql_query(conn1, buffer))
    {
        // Error - Print error message
        sprintf (message, "Error_E1 %u: %s", mysql_errno(conn1),
mysql_error(conn1));
        print_log (message);
    }


    // Get the next row in the table (if it exists)
    mysqlRow = mysql_fetch_row(mysqlResult);
}

// Was a MySQL result pointer returned?
if (mysqlResult)
{
    // Yes - Free the pointer
    mysql_free_result(mysqlResult);
    mysqlResult = NULL;
}
    }
}
```

```
//********************************************************************
// Switch Off All Controlled Devices
//
// This function switches off every device in the house.
//
//********************************************************************

void  switch_off_all_controlled_devices (void)
{
    long int   current_time;


    // Set the current time to midnight this morning
    current_time = midnight_timeout;


    // Delete all house code events
    print_log ("*** Switch off ALL controlled devices... ");

    activate_device (study_ceiling_light,            OFF, current_time++);

    activate_device (steve_bedroom_ceiling_light,    OFF, current_time++);

    activate_device (diningroom_table_light,         OFF, current_time++);

    activate_device (steve_bedroom_wall_light,       OFF, current_time++);
    activate_device (steve_bedroom_window_light,     OFF, current_time++);
    activate_device (steve_bedroom_reading_light,    OFF, current_time++);
    activate_device (common_washroom_light,          OFF, current_time++);
    activate_device (common_washroom_flight,         OFF, current_time++);
    activate_device (common_bathroom_light,          OFF, current_time++);

    activate_device (kitchen_light,                  OFF, current_time++);
    activate_device (kitchen_nook_light,             OFF, current_time++);
    activate_device (kitchen_counter_light,          OFF, current_time++);
    activate_device (kitchen_sink_light,             OFF, current_time++);

    activate_device (garage_light,                   OFF, current_time++);

    activate_device (security_alarm_siren,           OFF, current_time++);

    activate_device (pantry_light,                   OFF, current_time++);
    activate_device (laundry_light,                  OFF, current_time++);

    activate_device (mini_hallway_light,             OFF, current_time++);
    activate_device (main_hallway_light,             OFF, current_time++);
    activate_device (inside_entrance_light,          OFF, current_time++);

    if (daytime)
    {
        activate_device (garage_back_outside_light,    OFF, current_time++);
        activate_device (familyroom_outside_light,     OFF, current_time++);
        activate_device (diningroom_outside_light,     OFF, current_time++);
        activate_device (master_bedroom_outside_light, OFF, current_time++);
        activate_device (garage_front_outside_light,   OFF, current_time++);
        activate_device (porch_outside_light,          OFF, current_time++);
    }
```

```
        activate_device (guest_main_light,                OFF, current_time++);
        activate_device (guest_bed_light,                 OFF, current_time++);
        activate_device (lounge_wall_light,               OFF, current_time++);
        activate_device (lounge_window_light,             OFF, current_time++);

        activate_device (fishtank_light,                  OFF, current_time++);

        activate_device (familyroom_window_light,         OFF, current_time++);
        activate_device (familyroom_wall_light,           OFF, current_time++);
        activate_device (familyroom_track_tv_light,       OFF, current_time++);
        activate_device (familyroom_track_reading_light,  OFF, current_time++);
        activate_device (familyroom_wall_unit_light,      OFF, current_time++);
        activate_device (familyroom_wall_unit_spotlight,  OFF, current_time++);
        activate_device (familyroom_radio,                OFF, current_time++);

        activate_device (master_bedroom_light,            OFF, current_time++);
        activate_device (master_bedroom_mum_light,        OFF, current_time++);
        activate_device (master_bedroom_dad_light,        OFF, current_time++);
        activate_device (master_bedroom_closet_light,     OFF, current_time++);

        activate_device (season_front_light,              OFF, current_time++);
        activate_device (season_back_light,               OFF, current_time++);

}
```

```
//****************************************************************************
// Setup Events For System Startup                     UNIQUE TO HC_TI103
//
// This function creates the initial startup events.
//
//****************************************************************************
void  setup_events_for_system_startup (void)
{
    long int    current_time;


    // Determine the current time conditions
    determine_periodic_transition_times ();

    // Get current time in seconds
    current_time = get_raw_time ();

    // Determine if we have triggered any start flags
    if (current_time > midnight_timeout) midnight_start   = TRUE;
    if (current_time > sunrise_timeout)         day_start  = TRUE;
    if (current_time > dawn_timeout)    dawn_start         = TRUE;
    if (current_time > midday_timeout)        midday_start = TRUE;
    if (current_time > dusk_timeout)    dusk_start         = TRUE;
    if (current_time > sunset_timeout)        night_start  = TRUE;

    // Delete all existing events in the database
    delete_all_house_code_events ();

    // Is a full device reset in order?
    if (device_reset)
    {
        // Yes - Switch everything off (except the outside lights)
        print_log ("*** Device Reset ***");
        switch_off_all_controlled_devices ();
    }

    // Determine if we are coming up in Security or Home mode
    determine_initial_security_mode ();

}
```

```
//***************************************************************************
// Setup Events For Midnight                              UNIQUE TO HC_TI103
//
// This function handles events that occur at midnight.
//
//***************************************************************************

void  setup_events_for_midnight (void)
{

    // Has midnight just started?
    if (midnight_start == TRUE)
    {
        // Yes - Process outside light on/off events
        // This is called only once each day at midnight (or at startup)
        print_log ("...Setup events for midnight");

        // Setup common events (which should occur before daybreak)
        setup_outside_light_OFF_events();
        setup_fishtank_light_events();

        // This will setup random activations of the common bathroom lights
        SECURITY_setup_common_bathroom_light_events();

        // Reset event flag
        midnight_start = FALSE;
    }

}
```

```
//**************************************************************************
// Setup Events For Sunrise                              UNIQUE TO HC_TI103
//
// This function handles events that occur as night transitions into day.
//
//**************************************************************************

void  setup_events_for_sunrise (void)
{

    // Has the day just started?
    if (day_start == TRUE)
    {
        // Place all day start events here...
        // ================================
        print_log ("...Setup events for sunrise");


        // Reset event flag
        day_start = FALSE;
    }


}
```

```
//**********************************************************************
// Setup Events For Dawn                               UNIQUE TO HC_TI103
//
// This function handles events that occur at dawn.
// Dawn starts some time AFTER sunrise.
//
//**********************************************************************

void  setup_events_for_dawn (void)
{

    // Has the dawn just started?
    if (dawn_start == TRUE)
    {
        // Place all dawn start events here...
        // ==================================
        print_log ("...Setup events for dawn");

        // Reset SLEEP mode back to ACTIVE,
        // Reset family room and steve's bedroom lights for 'Normal Mode'
        mysql_query(conn1, "UPDATE house_state SET sleep=0, sleep_delay=0,
family_lights=0, steve_lights=0");


        // Reset event flag
        dawn_start = FALSE;
    }

}
```

311

```
//*************************************************************************
// Setup Events For Midday                              UNIQUE TO HC_TI103
//
// This function handles events that occur at midday.
//
//*************************************************************************

void  setup_events_for_midday (void)
{

    // Has the midday just started?
    if (midday_start == TRUE)
    {
        // Place all midday start events here...
        // ===================================
        print_log ("...Setup events for midday");

        // Are we operating in SECURITY mode?
        if (security_mode)
        {
            // Yes - Install the SECURITY mode events for today
            //       as per function: setup_events_when_security_activated()
            security_mode_started = TRUE;
        }
        else
        {
            // No  - Install the HOME mode events for today
            //       as per function: setup_events_when_security_deactivated()
            security_mode_stopped = TRUE;
        }


        // Reset event flag
        midday_start = FALSE;
    }


}
```

```
//*************************************************************************
// Setup Events For Dusk                                    UNIQUE TO HC_TI103
//
// This function handles events that occur at dusk.
// Dusk starts some time BEFORE sunset.
//
//*************************************************************************

void  setup_events_for_dusk (void)
{

    // Has the dusk just started?
    if (dusk_start == TRUE)
    {
        // Place all dusk start events here...
        // ===================================
        print_log ("...Setup events for dusk");


        // Reset event flag
        dusk_start = FALSE;
    }


}
```

```
//**************************************************************************
// Setup Events For Sunset                                 UNIQUE TO HC_TI103
//
// This function handles events that occur as day transitions into night.
//
//**************************************************************************

void  setup_events_for_sunset (void)
{

    // Has the night just started?
    if (night_start == TRUE)
    {
        // Place all night start events here...
        // =================================
        print_log ("...Setup events for sunset");

        // Reset event flag
        night_start = FALSE;
    }


}
```

```
//*************************************************************************
// Setup Events For Sleeping                          UNIQUE TO HC_TI103
//
// This function handles events that occur as sleep timeout expires.
//*************************************************************************

void  setup_events_for_sleeping (void)
{
    long int    current_time;

    // Place all sleep events here...
    // ==============================

    // Get current time in seconds
    current_time = get_raw_time();

    // Ensure that the following actions are only performed once
    if (sleep_mode_start == TRUE)
    {
        print_log ("...Setup events for sleeping");

        // Going to sleep, put off all nearby lights
        activate_device (study_ceiling_light,          OFF, current_time);
        activate_device (steve_bedroom_ceiling_light, OFF, current_time+1);
        activate_device (common_bathroom_light,        OFF, current_time+2);
        activate_device (common_washroom_light,        OFF, current_time+3);
        activate_device (steve_bedroom_wall_light,     OFF, current_time+4);
        activate_device (steve_bedroom_window_light,   OFF, current_time+4);
        activate_device (steve_bedroom_reading_light,  OFF, current_time+4);
        activate_device (mini_hallway_light,           OFF, current_time+5);
        activate_device (inside_entrance_light,        OFF, current_time+6);
        activate_device (lounge_wall_light,            OFF, current_time+7);

        activate_device (study_ceiling_light,          OFF, current_time+11);
        activate_device (steve_bedroom_ceiling_light, OFF, current_time+12);
        activate_device (common_bathroom_light,        OFF, current_time+13);
        activate_device (common_washroom_light,        OFF, current_time+14);
        activate_device (steve_bedroom_wall_light,     OFF, current_time+15);
        activate_device (steve_bedroom_window_light,   OFF, current_time+15);
        activate_device (steve_bedroom_reading_light,  OFF, current_time+15);
        activate_device (mini_hallway_light,           OFF, current_time+16);
        activate_device (inside_entrance_light,        OFF, current_time+17);
        activate_device (lounge_wall_light,            OFF, current_time+18);

        // Reset event flag
        sleep_mode_start = FALSE;
    }
}
```

```
//****************************************************************************
// Setup Events When Security Activated                    UNIQUE TO HC_TI103
//
// This function handles events that occur when security is activated.
// This occurs when the user presses the SECURITY ON button.
// It is also re-triggered on a daily basis to setup the various security events.
//****************************************************************************

void  setup_events_when_security_activated (void)
{
    int  house_state_security;


    if (security_mode_started)
    {
        // Log action
        print_log ("");
        print_log ("...Setup events for SECURITY mode...");
        print_log ("");
        print_log ("SECURITY\n");
        print_log ("SECURITY - Configure ON/OFF Events...");
        print_log ("SECURITY - ===========================");
        print_log ("SECURITY");


        // Setup the standard events
        setup_outside_light_ON_events();
        setup_outside_light_OFF_events();
        setup_seasonal_light_events();
        setup_fishtank_light_events();

        // Setup the security mode events
        SECURITY_setup_lounge_light_events();
        SECURITY_setup_family_room_light_events();
        SECURITY_setup_master_bedroom_light_events();
        SECURITY_setup_guest_bedroom_light_events();
        SECURITY_setup_steve_bedroom_light_events();
        SECURITY_setup_common_bathroom_light_events();
        SECURITY_setup_study_light_events();
        SECURITY_setup_kitchen_light_events();
        SECURITY_setup_kitchen_nook_light_events();


        // Reset event flag
        security_mode_started = FALSE;
    }
}
```

```
//****************************************************************************
// Setup Events When Security Deactivated                  UNIQUE TO HC_TI103
//
// This function handles events that occur when security is deactivated.
// This occurs when the user presses the SECURITY OFF button.
// It is also re-triggered on a daily basis to setup the various home events.
//****************************************************************************

void  setup_events_when_security_deactivated (void)
{

    if (security_mode_stopped)
    {
        // Log action
        print_log ("");
        print_log ("...Setup events for SECURITY DEACTIVATED.");
        print_log ("");
        print_log ("SECURITY");
        print_log ("SECURITY - Configure ON/OFF Events...");
        print_log ("SECURITY - ===========================");
        print_log ("SECURITY");

        // Setup the standard events
        setup_outside_light_ON_events();
        setup_outside_light_OFF_events();
        setup_seasonal_light_events();
        setup_fishtank_light_events();

        // Setup the home mode events
        setup_lounge_light_events();
        setup_family_room_light_events();
        setup_master_bedroom_light_events();

        // The following events are initialized but will be
        // replaced when room presence is detected
        SECURITY_setup_study_light_events();
        SECURITY_setup_steve_bedroom_light_events();
        SECURITY_setup_common_bathroom_light_events();


        // Reset event flag
        security_mode_stopped = FALSE;
    }
}
```

```
//****************************************************************************
// main()
//
// This is the main loop.  It first initializes the serial port for TI103
// control then it loops monitoring / processing any X10 control events and
// performing the transition to security mode when required.
//
//****************************************************************************

int main (int argc, char * const argv[], char * const envp[])
{
    char        message[255];
    char        time_buffer[255];
    long int    time_in_seconds;


    // Identify program
    print_log ("");
    print_log ("Program 'hc_ti103' Started...");

//  printf ("%d %s %s\n", argc, argv[0], argv[1]);

    // Determine if device reset is to occur
    if ((argc == 2) && (strcmp(argv[1], "RESET") == 0))
    {
        print_log ("RESET Parameter detected...");
        device_reset = TRUE;
    }

    speak_time_and_date ();

    // Install the termination interrupt handler
    install_signal_interrupt_handler ();

    // Compute current timestamp
    determine_system_timestamp (time_buffer);

    // Send email stating Security Mode Activation
    sprintf (message, "%s - Home Control Program Started [HC_TI103]...",
time_buffer);
//  send_security_email ("*** SECURITY INFO ***", message);

    // Initialize serial port for x-10 TI103 control
    initialize_serial_port_for_ti103_control ();

    // Sleep for a little bit...
    // This allows the Mysql system to startup during AUTOSTART
    // [May require more if 'hc_main()' is initializing all the databases!!!]
    msleep (7000);   // Sleep for  7 seconds (increase if we need to sleep
longer...)

    // Initialize random number generator with time seed
    time_in_seconds = get_raw_time ();
    srand ((unsigned int) time_in_seconds);

    // Access/Initialize 'home_control' database
    access_home_control_database ();
```

318

```
    // Setup specific system startup events
    setup_events_for_system_startup();

    // Initialization completed...
    print_log ("*");
    print_log ("* Initialization completed... *");
    print_log ("*");

    // Do Forever
    while (!exit_flag)
    {
        // Process all existing events for this time
        process_events();

        // Determine Day/Night Transition Times
        determine_periodic_transition_times();

        // Setup specific day/night events
        setup_events_for_midnight();
        setup_events_for_sunrise();
        setup_events_for_dawn();
        setup_events_for_midday();
        setup_events_for_dusk();
        setup_events_for_sunset();

        // Setup specific user selected modes
        setup_events_for_retiring_to_bedroom();
        setup_events_for_master_watching_tv();
        setup_events_for_sleeping();

        // Monitor home security
        monitor_security_mode_transition();

        // Control home security events as per the security status
        setup_events_when_security_activated();
        setup_events_when_security_deactivated();

        // Monitor sleep transitions
        monitor_sleep_mode_transition();

        // Cancel any locked states (ie. devices with only set command)
        cancel_locked_device_states();
    }

    // Program is being terminated...
    // Restore the Serial Port to its previous configuration
    tcsetattr(fd, TCSANOW, &old_options);

    // Program terminated
    speak ("The program has been terminated.");
    print_log ("");
    print_log ("Program 'hc_ti103' has been terminated.");

}
```

Project Options

Apache Web Server

The Apache Web server on the Linux machine uses default directory: /var/www

The Home control / Security application is placed in directory: /var/www/HomeControl/

The HomeControl directory was then 'shared' and identified as a 'Windows Network (SMB)' directory with the shared name of 'HomeControl'. (The Linux root password will be required to share this drive. Leave the '[ ] Read Only' box unchecked to permit read/write access by Microsoft Expression Web 4).

When Microsoft Expression Web 4 is used to publish the home control web application it will use the following directories on the Linux system:

```
/var/www/HomeControl/css
/var/www/HomeControl/download
/var/www/HomeControl/images
/var/www/HomeControl/js
/var/www/HomeControl/php
```

Microsoft Expression Web 4

The Web design package Microsoft Expression Web 4 should be configured to access the '/var/www/HomeControl/' directory for publishing. This is achieved by first accessing the top menu 'Site' label and then 'Publishing Settings'. Under the 'General' tab enter the directory local to your PC in which the web application is being developed.

For example: c:\Projects\HomeControl\

Then, under the Publishing tab press [Add] and select Connection Type 'File System'.

Next use the [Browse] button to search your network to find the shared Linux network drive 'HomeControl' as identified previously. Once this directory has been selected your web files will be published (ie. transferred) to your Linux system each time you select the 'Publishing' menu item.

Note: The CSS, JavaScript, Images and PHP web directories should be used to contain the home control example files identified in the Handbook + LAMP Project book. The CSS files are placed in the css directory, JS files in the js directory, PHP files in the php directory.

Linux System

Static IP Address

During installation of the LAMP features (the Linux, Apache, MySQL and PHP) a specific IP address was selected. This same IP address must be associated with each of the LAMP features. That implies we do not want the Linux system to use a dynamically allocated IP address since such an address may change. The Linux IP address must be static (ie. fixed to a specific value - the same IP address value that was selected when the LAMP features were installed).

The Linux system (Mint version) displays the Ethernet connection as a symbol consisting of two cables with separated connectors (this symbol is located in the bottom right-hand corner of the Linux monitor screen, just left of the date and time). Place the mouse above the Ethernet connection symbol and right-click. Select 'Edit Connections' and access your IPv4 settings. Set the IP address to be the same address that you entered for the other LAMP features (eg. '192.168.1.176' - be sure that no other devices on your network (other than those associated with LAMP) are using this IP address). The Net Mask can be set to '255.255.255.0' and the Gateway set to '192.168.1.1'. Save these settings and then reboot the Linux system. The Linux system will now be using this static IP address every time your system powers up.

Auto Start

The 'hc_main.c' and 'hc_ti103.c' modules (along with the other header files, etc) may be placed in any suitable development directory. When compiled and you are satisfied that they are functional, the 'hc_main' and 'hc_ti103' executables are then copied across to a separate directory. These two files are to be executed on system startup. This is achieved by first using the mouse to access the Linux Menu (bottom left screen icon). Under 'Applications' select 'Preferences' and in the right-hand column select 'Startup Applications'. Press the [Add] button and then use the [Browse] button to find the appropriate directory where the 'hc_main' executable file is located. Enter a suitable 'Name' for this executable. Press [Add] and the file is now in the startup list. Repeat the process for the 'hc_ti103' executable. The next time the Linux system is started these two home control executables will be automatically started.

Note that if additional development work is performed on the home control system and the system files are executed, you will have multiple copies of the executables executing simultaneously (with surprising effect). To perform any testing the startup executables should first be terminated. This is achieved by once more selecting the Linux 'Menu'. Under 'Applications' select 'System Tools' and in the right-hand column select 'System Monitor'. Using the mouse select your process from the Process Name list and with the right-hand mouse button select 'Kill Process'. Do this for both 'hc_main' and "hc_ti103'.

Linux applications downloaded.

Use the Linux Menu (bottom left screen icon) and select 'Software Manager'.
Use the search feature to select and then download the following utilities:

sendemail
festival
fswebcam

Project Review

This book provides a LAMP (Linux Apache MySQL PHP) design for a Web-Based Home Control / Security Application. Source code has been provided (as is, no implied suitability is inferred).

This book is applicable to both the seasoned Embedded Software Engineer and to the Hobbyist who just wants to learn a little bit about writing code.

But what of the novice?

What of the person wanting to gain some understanding in the field of embedded software engineering?

Where do they start?

Do they need a Computer Science or Electrical Engineering degree before they can even begin to learn how to program an embedded system?

All too many books discuss programming from an advanced level.

Well, this book is not like that at all.

The idea is to get anyone that is interested in programming up and running in a short period of time.

The language of choice today is C or C++.

For an easy entrance into the world of programming the C language was chosen for the code examples presented within this book. The embedded application is a program that continually executes on a computer system and as it does so, it interacts with its environment.

For this, the home control lighting security system is the ideal application.

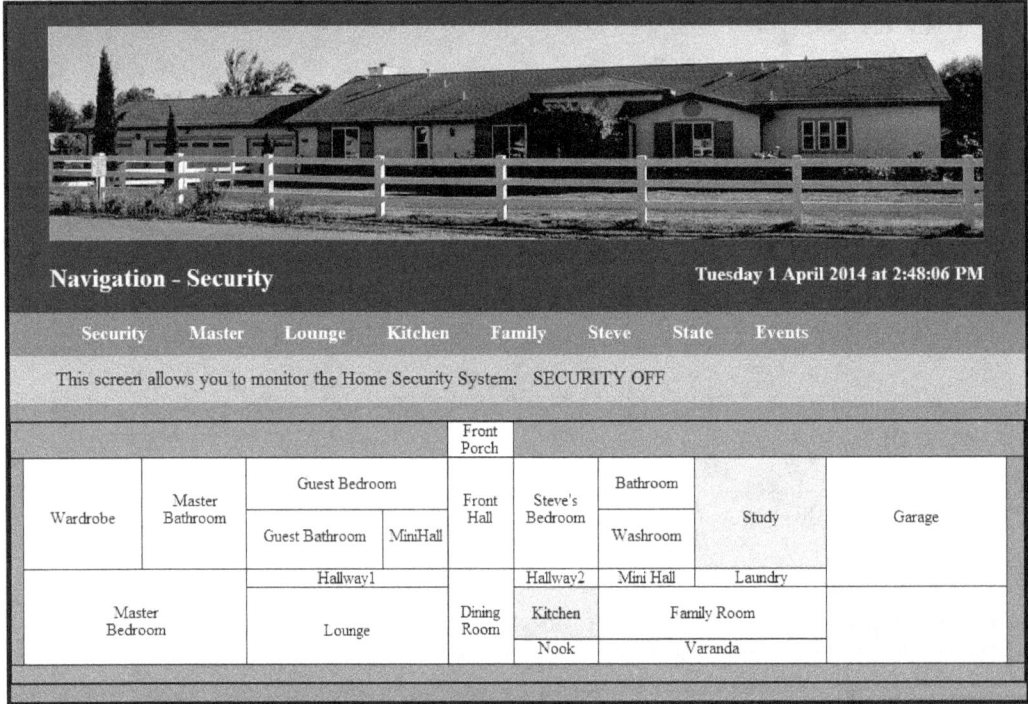

By the time you have finished reading this book you would know how:

- To install LAMP (Linux, Apache (Web Server), MySQL and PHP) on your PC computer
- To backup/restore your Linux hard drive
- To automatically execute your application at system startup
- To apply Java Script to your own Web page
- To apply MySQL to your own Web page
- To apply PHP to your own Web page
- To build a C application that communicates over a serial port.
- To build a C application that use MySQL
- To write a Home Control / Security application
- To have your Home Control / Security application send email messages with webcam picture attachments
- To have your Home Control / Security application speak
- To compute sunrise and sunset times for each day of the year

... more to follow...

Oh! And there's one added bonus. With this system you do not require any monthly monitoring fee. Since your Home Control / Security application simply sends you an email when it detects an intruder, you can immediately go home or call a friend or neighbor to check on the house. No need to fork out $25 or more per month for some 'service' charge.

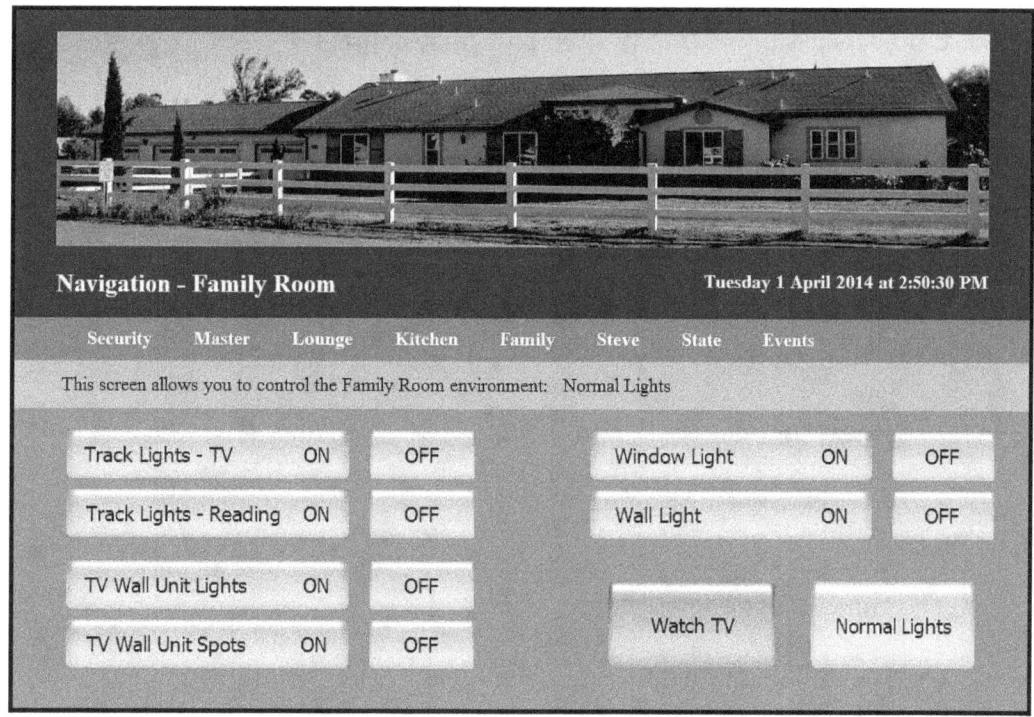

They say that knowledge is power. That may be true, but to sit at home using your iPAD or iPHONE (or some other Tablet, or even a web page on one of your computers) and to bring up your Home Control web page and click on a button to turn on a light or to initiate a sequence of events for evening television viewing, well, that is really neat and this book presents all this information to you in an easy to read form.

The application software was designed to use the following components:
WF800RF32A RF Receiver (www.wgldesigns.com, www.homeseer.com)
ACT TI103 Interface to transmit X10 signals over household mains wiring
       (Obtainable from www.act-remote.com, www.smarthomeusa.com)
MS13A X10 HawkEye Motion Detector (by X10 Active Home)
MS16A ActiveEye Motion Sensor (Outdoor sensor)
X10 Pro Universal Module (Alarm siren plus relay contacts)
X10 On Guard Barking Dog Alarm (SD20a) www.x10.com
X10 Appliance and X10 Lamp Modules

The application software may be modified to suit any interface of your choice.

Additional Useful Web Sites for X10 products:

www.smarthome.com

www.x10.com

www.thehomeautomationstore.com

www.smarthomeusa.com

www.homeseer.com

www.amazon.com

Author Titles

The author is self-published and the following titles are available from Amazon both in e-book and paperback formats.

Technical Books

Designing Embedded Systems - Guidebook
By Steve McClure

This Guidebook reviews the Software Development and Engineering Principles involved in the Design of Embedded Computer Systems. It provides a standard procedure which may be used by the Systems, Software, Embedded, Firmware and Hardware departments. Various design and development documents are produced at specific points in the project and are passed out for review prior to being used by other team members. By having this consistency the entire team now know which design elements will be produced and the need for implementing any reverse-engineering will be eliminated. Product costs for maintenance will be greatly reduced. Manufacturing and Test departments will now have the necessary details with which to complete their work.
ISBN-13: 978-1499117592
ISBN-10: 1499117590

Designing Embedded Systems - Handbook
By Steve McClure

This book expands upon the detail presented in The Guidebook and provides additional detail gleaned by the author during his 30+ years of experience in the field of Embedded Systems Engineering.
ISBN-13: 978-1497592339
ISBN-10: 149759233X

Designing Embedded Systems - LAMP (Linux Apache MySQL PHP)
By Steve McClure

This book expands upon the Handbook and provides an embedded Linux project to implement a Web-based Home Control / Security System (source code listing provided).
ISBN-13: 978-1483916231
ISBN-10: 1483916235

Sci/Fi - Fantasy Novels

Like many in the engineering industry the author has enjoyed both films and books of the Science Fiction and Fantasy genre. After much persuasion he decided to write a novel. This attempt turned out quite successful and encouraging and has expanded itself into the following series of books.

Stryders Odyssey
A fantastic tale of epic proportion
The truth was out there somewhere and it was waiting to be discovered. Travel with Sam and Cody as they jump through Portals to other Worlds, ride Space Ships controlled by Computers with Artificial Intelligence and befriend Strange Creatures that can Shape Shift into anything they or you can imagine. But watch out for 'the Order'. For they have their own plan regarding the dominion of worlds. For readers of all ages.

Stryders Odyssey - 1
New Beginnings
By Steve McClure
ISBN-13: 978-1490442525
ISBN-10: 1490442529

Stryders Odyssey - 2
First Contact
By Steve McClure
ISBN-13: 978-1492855477
ISBN-10: 1492855472

Stryders Odyssey - 3
Shangri Prime
By Steve McClure
ISBN-13: 978-1493695379
ISBN-10: 1493695371

Author Contact E-Mail

steve_mcclure@cox.net